Original Sin and Time

Original Sin and Time

ANDRÉ BARBERA

WIPF & STOCK · Eugene, Oregon

ORIGINAL SIN AND TIME

Copyright © 2024 André Barbera. All rights reserved. Except for brief quotations in critical publications or reviews, no part of this book may be reproduced in any manner without prior written permission from the publisher. Write: Permissions, Wipf and Stock Publishers, 199 W. 8th Ave., Suite 3, Eugene, OR 97401.

Wipf & Stock
An Imprint of Wipf and Stock Publishers
199 W. 8th Ave., Suite 3
Eugene, OR 97401

www.wipfandstock.com

PAPERBACK ISBN: 979-8-3852-2911-6
HARDCOVER ISBN: 979-8-3852-2912-3
EBOOK ISBN: 979-8-3852-2913-0

VERSION NUMBER 12/06/24

Scripture quotations are from the Revised Standard Version of the Bible, Copyright © 1946, 1952, AND 1971 the Division of Christian Education of the National Council of the Churches of Christ in the United States of America. Used by permission. All rights reserved.

Contents

Preface | vii

1. Original Sin and Time: The Problem | 1
2. The Eternal and the Temporal | 25
3. Sin and Culpability | 51
4. Concupiscence and Original Justice | 73
5. Perseverance | 99
6. The Fall (The Choice or The Event) | 119
    A. The Temporal Garden | 121
    B. Orientation to the Task at Hand | 125
    C. The Prohibition | 130
    D. Original Sin and the Bible | 136
    E. The Meaning of the Myth | 142
    F. The Fallen Angels | 153
7. Time as Sin | 166
    A. Evidence: Desire and Waiting | 172
    B. One: Soul (I) and Disruption | 176
    C. Time | 182
    D. Suffering | 186
    E. No Reconciliation | 190
    F. Summary of the Deduction | 195
8. Foreknowledge, Predestination, and Freedom | 196
9. Universalism | 220
10. Integrity | 237

Bibliography | 255

Subject Index | 263

Scripture Index | 269

Preface

THIS BOOK BEGAN IN another on faith and works, *On Faith, Works, Eternity and the Creatures We Are*, in which appears a dispassionate God who loves his creation. What can we know about eternity? To give the question eschatological color, what do we mean when we speak of eternal salvation and eternal damnation? Departing from that book with some pious although contradictory claims about God, I inquired about time, then sin, and finally original sin: the order of discovery. This book, however, proceeds from the landing point, original sin.

We don't like to talk about sin—that is why we have so many euphemisms for it—and we especially don't like to talk about *original* sin, a sin for which we deny responsibility. If we are not responsible, i.e., blameworthy, how can it be sin? Sin implies culpability, and so we seem to be suffering the consequences, indeed the punishment for something that we didn't do.

The vast majority of biblical exegesis, commentary, and preaching on original sin attempts to temper the apparent harshness of this notion. We rush to contextualize the condemnation, historically, psychologically, and spiritually. Things aren't *that* bad.

What if they are? This book explores the possibility that each and every one of us is guilty for all misery and woe, for our willful transgressions, for the cruelty of others as well as our own, and for so-called natural disasters such as earthquakes. We commit the sin of self-reference, we say "I," and thereby we temporalize ourselves. Original sin and time are the same thing. Two entirely common experiences provide clues for the argument. The first is waiting, pure and simple. The second experience is our vain attempt to hold together one another in thought, word, image: to remember. This practice is especially conscious when the person whom we attempt to hold together has died. "Time heals all" is a euphemism for "Sin kills love."

My inquiry into original sin and time leads directly to questions of predestination, individual freedom, divine foreknowledge, and universal salvation, presented in the final chapters of the book. By extension the argument could be applied to contemporary discussions of politics and culture, although I do not address these latter matters.

◆ ◆ ◆

It may have been possible to clean up this work, to make it appear respectable: third person, passive voice, footnotes. The book already has a few trappings of scholarship; it could have more, as some would prefer. Perhaps it could have made a contribution to the mountain of theological and philosophical knowledge that is our inheritance. But an air of dispassionate inquiry, fair-mindedness, and humble acknowledgment of its provisional status would only add more deception to a book that already possesses much of it. The book is not a subject of *intellectual* inquiry for me, although I have attempted to present these matters in a way that would be approachable, if not by many at least by any one. I am not trying out something, floating an idea that original sin and time are the same thing. *That* idea might be interesting, but, as Hegel observes in his *Encyclopaedia Logic*, "There is a host of interesting things in the world." Rather than interesting, I have an interest in sin. We all do.

In addition to disingenuous statements throughout, I should warn the reader about a prevailing sense of irreverence, inexcusable, but apparently irrepressible. Earlier versions of the book had Saint Augustine walk into a bar; a dedication to hypocrites and idolaters; and a claim that I was not trying to put psychologists out of business. Perhaps there is blasphemy here as well, at least in my passing consideration of a Hegelian God, responsible for both good and evil.

◆ ◆ ◆

Don Quixote observes that although he has been taught to think of pride as the greatest sin, he is most offended by ingratitude—the bitterest pill. I am grateful, truly grateful to all those people who have helped me along the way, especially Mary Barbera, simply to arrive at a point which although it may look like dotage to others, allows me some freedom of thought and reflection. But the freedom is chimerical. I have been formed, reformed, and perhaps even deformed a small amount, by the people I have known, the books I have read, and the things I have done.

I thank Eva Brann and Paul Griffiths, who were instrumental in very different ways in bringing this book to life. Indirect roles were played by friends, family, colleagues, students, and members of the Society of St. Vincent de Paul. Someone familiar with the Program of St. John's College will recognize its influence on this inquiry, perhaps not in my treatment of Augustine, Aquinas, Calvin, Kant, and Kierkegaard. But mention of Dedekind and Minkowski certainly reveals what my students, colleagues, and I have been reading for the past several decades.

I should also mention that this work comes from a position of great loss, so much so that I risk disrespecting memory by even mentioning it. Our children are present tacitly throughout the book. One in particular is present on nearly every page.

Annapolis
September, 2024

1

Original Sin and Time
The Problem

I TELL MY TALE backward. This is the only way it makes sense. In other words, it should eventually become clear why one must proceed in this fashion. The tale is an argument for equating original sin with time. It is my intent to present this argument methodically, systematically, and rationally, but the argument itself, at least as far as its nomenclature is concerned, depends upon revelation and belief. If the presentation is successful, there should be no need on the part of the reader to make a leap, no need to depend upon some arcane and mysterious truth, no paradox, no offense. Indeed, the reader should be able to follow the argument to the end and then, possibly, take it with a grain of salt or dismiss it entirely. This freedom of engagement is one of the many failings of this presentation. At every turn, it runs the risk of making sense. I am not preaching to the choir, although the choir may do well to pay attention to the sermon. The consequences of bringing together sin and time will pertain to divine foreknowledge, predestination, universal salvation, and most importantly to integrity.

Two entirely common experiences guide me and in effect provide clues for the argument that follows. The first is waiting, pure and simple. This we all do, and do so every day. We do it sometimes with eagerness, sometimes with dread. We wait with anticipation and frustration, imagination and annoyance. Context envelopes our waiting. Circumstances.

We wait for something, for someone. But here the concern is quite simply with the waiting itself.

The second experience is our practice of holding together one another in thought, word, image. This practice is especially conscious when the person whom we attempt to hold together is absent. Perhaps the person has died. Our task, individually, is to preserve the integrity of the missing individual, to keep whole that which is disintegrating before us.

◆ ◆ ◆

How are faith and works related? This question provided the impetus for *On Faith, Works, Eternity and the Creatures We Are*.[1] In the course of carrying out that inquiry, it became evident that the problem of time, or more precisely the problem of time and eternity, lay at the bottom of the investigation, and further that much about this problem had been presupposed in order to carry out that inquiry into faith and works. It was necessary to suppress consideration of this problem throughout. Are all theological studies reduced ultimately to questions of time and eternity?

What is the problem? In *On Faith, Works, Eternity and the Creatures We Are* there was one postulate or axiom: God is not bound by time. Many people would agree with this assertion, perhaps from a sense of piety, but what follows from such a claim? In the previous work time was presupposed but not defined. Little if anything was given to characterize time. What is it like? What are its aspects? Can one describe time sufficiently so as to give meaning to the expressions "non-temporal" or "a-temporal?" Although in this work on sin I may fare little better in terms of presuppositions and definitions, I intend to characterize time in such a way that makes it knowable, perhaps uniquely knowable by us, i.e., by us sinners because we are sinners. The problem is to come to see how time is sin originally.

Here at the beginning I shall specify the most important axioms of this inquiry, and in the course of development I shall present indirect arguments in behalf of their acceptance. These arguments are not demonstrations of the axioms. If the axioms were demonstrable then they would not be axioms. But axioms nonetheless need an argument for their acceptance, albeit provisional acceptance. At the very least, the reader must become interested in the world that the axioms describe, sufficiently interested to realize that the world so described is the one which the

---

1. My original title for this work was *Anxious Faith*.

reader inhabits. I hope to go beyond merely providing an account that is in some way interesting. I hope to provide an account in which each of us has an interest, perhaps an all-encompassing interest, theological nomenclature notwithstanding. But that remains to be seen.

The first axiom remains the same from *On Faith, Works, Eternity and the Creatures We Are*, although it might be expressed in various ways, and it has a two-fold expression, one concerning change and one concerning time. "For I the LORD do not change" (Mal 6:3). The axiom, however, is single, and accordingly silent on the matter of the difference if any between change and time. God is unchangeable. God is eternal, i.e., outside of time. God is time-less. God is in a sense impassive. God does not suffer, no matter how advantageous we may find it to express his sufferings: God's love for his creation; God's wrath; his mercy and so forth. "And the LORD said to Moses, 'I have seen this people, and behold, it is a stiff-necked people; now therefore let me alone, that my wrath may burn hot against them and I may consume them'" (Exod 32:9). "God so loved the world that he gave his only Son" (John 3:16). We may want a creator who is interested in his creation, who cares about it and about us. Most, but not all, of the stories that we tell ourselves about God describe a creator who is committed to that which has been created, and we know of no way to express this commitment without appealing to notions of change, especially change of feelings. The believer is so bold as to think that an intimate relationship exists between the individual creature and the creator, perhaps even a friendly relationship of give and take. "Thus the LORD used to speak to Moses face to face, as a man speaks to his friend" (Exod 33:11). What a friend! Our stories are stories of change, and in them God exists and lives in our lives. Regarding life and time, however, let me note that by eternal I do not mean everlasting in the sense of always *existing*, i.e., being for all time. Eternal indicates not temporal. In our stories, God is not eternal. The Hebrew Bible and a good part of the Greek Bible were not written by metaphysicists.

With this first axiom (God is eternal), I shall also persist in using the third-person, singular, masculine pronoun to refer to God. There is nothing objectionable to my mind if a reader prefers to substitute "she" for every appearance of "he" in this text when the referent is God, or for that matter when the referent is the indeterminate individual human being, but making this particular substitution would be awkward in many places where the argument relies on the Hebrew and Greek Bible and on Jewish and Christian biblical commentaries. Furthermore, this exchange, "she" for "he," would tend to draw attention to itself, possibly at the expense of what I am trying to express in the first place. Replacing "he" with "it" might lend emphasis to the impassivity of God, but at the expense of his alleged commitment to his creation. A sense of intimacy, whether or not it is defensible, would be lost with the neuter pronoun. There are, of course, other possibilities regarding the use of pronouns in reference to God. For example, a case can be made for using a plural pronoun. These matters, although they may be of great significance in certain contexts, are largely extraneous to this inquiry. Pronominal reference will be more of a concern when the matters of personal integrity and the individual are taken up, at the end of this study, although even there we shall not find justification for use of the plural. Eschatologically the singular "I" is regained, if not preserved.

A second axiom is that each human being has a soul. It is by possessing this soul that a human being, an individual, is able to say "I" meaningfully. (It would be dangerously presumptuous of anyone to conclude that another "person" was unable to say "I.") This defining characteristic, called apperception by philosophers and found so puzzling by David Hume, is apparent to all. The schizophrenic person, about whom others may perceive a truly divided mind and multiple selves, says "I," his inconsistent behavior notwithstanding. The person who desires to kill himself, to end his temporal existence, says "I." He says "*I* no longer want to exist. *I* have this desire. It is *mine*." What the en-souled being, the human being, cannot say meaningfully is "*I* do not want to be *I*." In other words, one can desire not to exist, but one cannot desire not to be. (*To be* and *to exist* do not mean the same thing.) This is why Leibniz writes that no one desires to be the king of China.[2] What one may desire is to be oneself *as* the king of China. One may even wish to have different characteristics, a more genial disposition, phlegmatic in the face of trouble and turmoil, kind to animals, but one wishes oneself to have these sterling traits. It may be misleading, however, to claim that a human being has a soul in the same way that a human being has two arms, a heart, or even a brain. Appendages, heart, and brain may be, to varying degrees, critical parts of the human being, and further may help to characterize humankind. But these possessions are exactly that, possessions, those things that normally belong to a human being. In this regard, a soul is different in that a soul does not belong to a human being. There is not some being, rational and

---

2. Leibniz, *Discourse on Metaphysics*, 34.

sentient, who says "I" *and* possesses a soul. The soul is not a possession of the human, it is a qualification. It is proper to the human being as human, but it is not a property of the human being.

There is much to be said about and in behalf of these first two axioms, most of which shall be postponed for later. Special and close attention will be given to the being who says "I" in the section on time as sin, chapter 7. It is worth noting, however, that people rarely act as though they believe the first axiom, no matter what they may claim rationally about a God who is omniscient, omnipotent, and eternal. Perhaps the most common purpose behind prayer is to get God to change his mind, to change somebody else's mind including our own, or in general to change the way things are. The second axiom, in contrast, is asserted by most people, a mountain of evidence to its contrary notwithstanding. The most common version of this belief is the claim that all human beings are created fundamentally equal to one another. One soul, in its soul-ness and its individuality, is not superior or inferior to another, regardless of circumstance, aptitude, and even effort. Because of the soul, the human being is irreducibly human. Differences and gray areas abound, which combine to underscore that this second axiom, if it is to be accepted at all, must be taken as an article of faith. Nonetheless, all praise and blame rest on acceptance of this axiom.

A third axiom is that mankind is fallen. This is the original sin axiom, and it asserts that there is a fundamental disorder in the world for which human beings bear responsibility and for which they are culpable. This axiom is denied by many people despite a similar mountain of evidence in its support. This third axiom is explored at length in this study. (Although the order of presentation is to move from time to sin, moving in the opposite direction more aptly characterizes this study, which is more a treatise on sin than a treatise on time.) One surprising consequence is that this axiom serves, at least in conjunction with the other axioms, for all that is wrong in the world, without exception. Indirectly it is an explanation for those occurrences and decisions that we commonly call mistakes or errors or failures. Most important, the original sin axiom attempts to reveal, at its most fundamental level, the character of blame. Just as the soul qualifies a human as human, so does blameworthiness. Only the blameworthy are worth saving. Blame in itself implies forgiveness and salvation.

To some degree this third axiom is derived or deduced in the course of my presentation, especially in chapter 7. Assuming some success in this regard, the axiom would not be properly axiomatic, but rather it would follow from what has come before. This third principle, however, remains axiomatic in its nomenclature. This is the axiom that posits fallen-ness. This is the axiom that calls this condition sin and opens this inquiry to the possibility of grace.

The second and third axioms, therefore, create a world, or more precisely they describe a world, one in which, according to the first axiom, God is lawgiver, judge, and executive.

Before moving on to a fourth consideration, if not axiom, let us consider the Bible (or Bibles, Hebrew and Greek). Claiming that the Bible is a source of wisdom, even a divinely inspired source, is just a weasely way of not confronting the word of God. The Bible contains the word of God revealed to man, although the Bible alone does not reveal the Word of God. The Bible (Hebrew or Greek) does not contain the words of God. This assertion is not as radically at odds with orthodox Judaic doctrine as it may at first appear. The Bible contains the words of men, but as Karl Barth has noted in various writings, it is from these words that the word of God attempts to break forth. The Bible is a witness to the Word of God. Can we let the word be revealed? If so, we receive revelation by engaging with the words of men, struggling with these words, suffering with apparent contradictions. (Jesus: he who is not with me is against me; he that is not against you is for you; Matt 12:30, Luke 9:50.) We begin with the words of men, but the words do not originate with men. This is so because the words, as the word of God, are revelatory and therefore necessarily come from without. The word of God is not a matter of man taking care of himself. There must be a bridge between the word of God and the words of men, a bridge over which or by means of which men can understand to some extent the word of God. Otherwise there would be no revelation. As meritorious as human beings may be, the word of God is not to their credit. Therefore, treatments of the Bible as literature, even as great literature, have the effect of degradation. The Word is not degraded, but the effort by the student of literature reverberates onto the student. The effort contextualizes the Word by locating the words, not only historically, but ultimately humanly. We poetize revelation.

If within the Bible is contained the word of God pointing to the Word of God, then this word is intellectually indigestible by any one man, by all men. This word necessarily remains incomprehensible, but, we hope and pray, not entirely unintelligible. We believe in a bridge, in transcendence. Barth even cautions that the Reformation's constant reliance on the Bible proved to be an insufficient safeguard against failure to interpret the fall of mankind strictly and ultimately in terms of the remedy, i.e., salvation effected by Jesus Christ, the Son of God become man.[3] These remarks about the Bible may amount to no more than acknowledgment that one never finishes with his encounter with the word of God.

Revelation, the word of God, might be considered axiomatic, but not here. This inquiry aims to unfold an argument in logical and reasonable fashion, i.e., backward. And yet at every turn there is appeal to Scripture, if not as support at least as resonance. At worst, it is a sign of education, bourgeois erudition. Thus one might "reasonably" expect an acknowledgment of the human indebtedness in the form of an axiom such as the word of God is revealed to mankind. Such would be axiomatic for those who have not heard the word of God, or for those who, following a suggestion by Aquinas, are willing to postulate the Bible as revelation in order to see what can be deduced from it in good, Aristotelian fashion. I shall not, however, place revelation on a list of axioms, as if it were one of several stipulations necessary in order to proceed with the argument. This refusal is not an act of piety but rather, ultimately, one of overwhelming confusion. *I* do not place the Word of God anywhere.

A fourth consideration, not presented here as an axiom but inextricably related to the axioms, is that man is free at least to some extent, or more properly speaking, at least in some regard or from some perspective. This freedom will in fact be presupposed in much of what follows, but I hope also to elaborate on ways in which freedom might be considered on the part of the individual and in the context of an omniscient God. Presumably freedom is entailed in culpability and just punishment, two aspects of sin. But freedom has long been questioned in the presence of an omniscient, omnipotent, impassive, eternal creator. Thus freedom is not asserted as an axiom per se, but we shall deal with it in the context of so-called divine foreknowledge and predestination. One might say that freedom, rather than being a possession of the human being, is an understanding of his sin. It is, however, also essential for an understanding of the fall of man as choice.

Connected to this fourth consideration is Kierkegaard's *possibility*, Kant's *ought*, and Augustine's and Calvin's *perseverance*, which combine to indicate the following additional subjects of inquiry.

---

3. Barth, *Church Dogmatics*, 4/1:388–89.

- As moral beings, we understand *ought* to mean that things might have been different, i.e., that we might have made things to be different.
- As temporal beings, we recognize the truth of the possibility and accordingly are made anxious.
- As temporal and moral beings, we recognize the virtue of perseverance and wish it for ourselves.

With these subjects in mind, I can assert that for those "Born okay the first time" there is nothing here. For those who are at ease with the pride, envy, avarice, anger, sloth, gluttony, lust, and cruelty of others as well as of themselves, there is nothing here. For those who are at ease with so-called natural disasters, there is nothing here. For those to whom the word *ought* is meaningless, because in fact things could not be otherwise, there is nothing here. For them, it is what it is. In the end, for them, there is no accounting in a meaningful way. For them, there is a list of things called life or being, but the list is in no particular order. For them, it is of no matter that the first shall be last and the last shall be first. For them, the first could be last and the last could be first, but in fact the first is first and the last is last. Order happens. These are those for whom facts are not merely meaningful, facts are supremely meaningful because that is all there is: facts. They do not agree with Kierkegaard that each fact is an approximation. These individuals are those who are blinded by the very sin that burdens them. For everyone else, even those who must proceed by accepting only provisionally the discomforting nomenclature of sin, grace, blame, and salvation, I tell my tale.

From the preliminary matter indicated above, I am led to conclude that time is sin. Sin is by definition missing the mark, disorder, and ultimately I hope to show that all disorder falls under sin, even those disasters and catastrophes that seem to be beyond our control. If time is sin, then time is disorder. But time is also the internal order of a rational, sentient being, a fundamental organizing principle of the soul. Since this being's order is also his disorder, there arises his culpability. Evidence for this culpability is man's future-oriented nature, Heidegger's futural man.[4] The argument, thus far, is admittedly circular, and much of what follows will be devoted, if not to disentangling and straightening out the circularity, at least to explicating and amplifying the claims made about time and sin.

---

4. Heidegger, *Being and Time* H325, "als zukünftiges."

After a full presentation of the preliminary material, we shall turn our attention to time and eternity, and especially to cause and effect.[5] Although this concern may seem to be abstract and tangential to the central argument, it should become clear that notions of eternity, necessity, permanence, and cause are needed to understand the argument itself. Only in the context of cause and effect can the subjects of freedom and culpability be broached. Furthermore, when we human beings consider the relationship between the temporal and the eternal, between time and eternity, we do so not from a position of disinterest. Quite the opposite: we participate in the relationship. It is our relationship and a very confusing one at that.

The case for the eternal must be made first, and in particular the case for our human—rational and sentient—access to the eternal. This will be done by displaying non-temporal action, and showing how rational beings understand such action. The action, simply, is one of cause causing an effect, and I shall argue that time or temporality does not underlie our understanding. Rather than this, the opposite is the case: that substance and permanence precede change, or to put it perhaps slightly more carefully, change entails or presupposes permanence, which surprisingly does not presuppose change. We shall see, however, that the presupposition of permanence can be called into question, and that it must remain a presupposition.

Ultimately the concerns are: (1) the intersection of (A) time and (B) eternity, and (2) the preservation of the individual. (1B) We know the eternal, at very least through necessity. This will be the section devoted to permanence, change, cause, and effect. (1A) We suffer time. This is an indisputable phenomenon. How we do this is worthy of inquiry, but the experience is undeniable. One need not be a phenomenologist to conclude that experience, quite simply, is. (2) *I* presupposes *I*, and according to the world *I* further presupposes encounter with others. This "I" is the apperceiving being, the being who says "I." Discovery of this *I* seems in a way to be unremarkable. Augustine did it in *On the Trinity*, Descartes did it again in his *Discourse on the Method* and *Meditations on First Philosophy*, but Hume questioned the ontological status of the one who says "I." This questioning is apt in one sense, since this is the *I* that disrupts

---

5. At the end of this first chapter there is also a guide to the following chapters.

by saying "I." This is *the* problem of self-reference, *the* confusion between comprehension and specification. This *I* is the source of original sin.

The gospels point to the concerns just listed, and Jesus speaks of them often, especially in the Gospel of John. One of his favorite expressions is "eternal life," which encompasses the concerns, for in eternal life we find the eternal expressed as living, i.e., metaphorically as temporal. Furthermore, it is the "I" who finds eternal life given to it by means of grace. This is the "I" that has been perfected by being fully integrated. Faith, hope, and charity are the instruments with which one engages the central concerns.

❖ ❖ ❖

In *On Faith, Works, Eternity and the Creatures We Are* the suggestion was made, with reservation, that time might be thought of as sin. With this study, I pursue that suggestion. Indeed, the entire study consists of developing this notion, of seeing how the two notions, sin and time, interpenetrate one another and ultimately can be understood only in relationship to each other. I intend to establish the relationship. This suggestion appears to be bold, curious, and to some perhaps even whimsical. It also runs the risk of impiety and blasphemy. If God is the creator of all, including time, as many assert, most passionately Augustine, then a consequence of this assertion about sin and time is that God is the author of sin. How so? God is the creator of man. All that belongs to man is ultimately traceable back to God. If sin originates in man, then its first cause is God himself. This much of impiety has often been voiced, and there are various attempts to refute this chain of reasoning. My impiety, if the assertion turns out to be impious, would then be a variation of the common one. Perhaps the names have simply been changed. Time rather than sin originates with man, or perhaps with the fallen angels. Then equate time with sin. Such is not my intent, or at least a change in nomenclature is not simply the intent, but we shall see several apologies offered by various theologians for the existence of evil. Perhaps most notable are the attempts, especially by Augustine, Anselm, and Aquinas, to explain why the fallen angels, the devil in particular, chose to sin. Can a cause be attributed to a creature, necessarily made to be good by God, who turns away from God? What made the rebellious angels rebel? May we even reasonably ask the question? According to pious doctrine, the angels' nature and they themselves were created entirely good. With regard to this inquiry, can time as an external phenomenon, something to be suffered, be interpreted as being both sinful and a creation of God, all of whose creative efforts are good? The apparent dichotomy is false. There is here neither contradiction nor paradox. Part of the argument for this claim will hardly be original or innovative, and will concern itself with the proper identification and understanding of terms such as "creation," "foreknowledge," and "freedom." I shall, however, make an attempt to delve into the fundamental existential act, the act of saying "I." This is the self-referential action, awareness, or knowledge that philosophers often call apperception, and from this action unfolds the relationship between sin and time.

Despite an inseverable connection, time and sin are not simply interchangeable. Furthermore, the impassive creator God who *loves* us, source of all that truly is, is good. (A pious Hegelian might find here evidence of religious piety. Why not simply accept the fact that God is also the source of evil? At this early stage I simply assert that I do not intentionally commit the sin of piety. A fuller consideration of God who is good must await the full exposition and development of the argument.) Fallen man, however, is interpreted in the context of time and sin. This interpretation requires that we give some attention to the well-known story that appears in Genesis, chapter 3, as well as to various interpretations of that story, not all of which lead to sin much less to original sin. But my treatment, influenced to some degree by Augustine, will emphasize both the sinfulness of mankind and the originality of this sinfulness, an originality that ultimately is negative. The origin is an undoing, the consequence of which is equally negative: waiting. The fall will be approached from several perspectives: literary, philological, biblical, and philosophical. The sum of these accounts will lead invariably to the same hellish waiting.

Let us begin with a consideration of the terms or words themselves, first individually, and then in combination: first, sin.

Sin is disorder between the creator and the created individuals who say "I." According to the First Letter of John, it is lawlessness (ἀνομία, 3:4). The act itself of saying "I" establishes the disorder; the act brings it about. The disorder is one of culpability on the part of the individual. It might seem that the individual, if by his very being as an individual necessarily brings about the disorder, cannot be held culpable either by the creator or by anyone else including the individual himself. This inference betrays a misunderstanding of how the disorder is brought about and furthermore a misunderstanding about the *being* of an individual. The individual who says "I" *wills* the disorder, i.e., the individual *responsibly* brings about the disorder. This is the act that Paul Tillich describes as the move from essence to existence. Individual human beings do not simply and merely *be* as does everything else. For human beings *to be* is *to act*. This is the act, the magnitude of which Karl Barth, Pascal, and others describe as requiring the sacrifice of the Son of God in order to reestablish order. This act constitutes the temporalizing of self. (My colleague Eva Brann might object at this point that the human being does not temporalize himself, but rather he is born temporal. My use of *act* includes birth. All human beings are born with original sin. This assertion could be distorted to claim that birth is sinful. "Behold, I was brought forth in iniquity, and in sin did my mother conceive me" [Ps 51:5]. I hope to correct such a misconception in the course of this study.) Most important here, however, is that sin is a relationship between creator and creature that is in fact described as *sin*, and not in some other way such as *failure* or *mistake*. Sin is not merely missing the mark.

The disorder originates with the saying of "I." In the language of philosophy and theology, this is an interpretation of apperception as sinful in character, at least to the extent and in the way that each and every one of us says "I." One might wonder if this origination occurs when a child is born, or when he reaches a certain age, or when he explicitly disrupts his relationship with the creator. But the disorder does not have a temporal origination in this sense. Although the disorder is fundamentally temporal in being, it is not so in occurrence. It is not an event. The disorder is in a way a qualification for all events, a necessary underpinning. The disorder originates in time only in the sense that it is inextricably bound up with time. More precisely, the disorder originates time. It does not occur at some time in the life of the individual, although it makes possible the individual's life. It does not occur within the so-called flow of time, in the time that attacks us and in the face of which we suffer. The disorder qualifies the life of the individual in that it qualifies the individual to have a life in the first place. This life is not the eternal life promised by Jesus Christ to the faithful. One might even characterize the qualified life as the life of the damned, something like eternal death, for surely it is the life of sin, although to assert this much requires a full exposition of the state of fallen mankind. In sum and most precisely, time does not cause sin nor does sin cause time. Sin and time, I hope to make clear, are aspects of the same thing but understood from different perspectives.⁶ A mark of our original sin and our temporal existence, our fallen-ness, is our bifurcated perspective, our disrupted "I."

From these few remarks, it should be evident that the term "sin" presupposes much. According to Kierkegaard, one sins before God.⁷ The term is used consciously, that is, in lieu of some other words like "vice" or "failure," and sin is definitely not a substitute for "mistake" as the latter word is sometimes used to soften the blow of culpability. Thus among the presuppositions are the notions of disorder, creator, and "I," in other words, the third, first, and second axioms respectively.

Disorder presupposes order. Justification, i.e., the act of making right, implies a condition of waywardness: the state of being un-right, the state in need of being made right, the state of being against the norm ($\dot{\alpha}\nu o\mu \acute{\iota}\alpha$). One is initially inclined to consider justification and waywardness as being mutually dependent and defined in relationship to one another. Justice, balance, order may seem all to be meaningful only in the contexts or possibilities of injustice, imbalance, disorder. We shall discover, however, that justice, balance, order are related to their opposites in similar fashion as permanence is related to change. In other words, we shall see that one (permanence, justice, etc.) of each pair truly comes first, or put more carefully, permanence can be presupposed independently of change.

The condition of unrighteousness is the wrongness, the disorder. There is here obligation, freedom, and violation, in effect the fourth consideration above. Things could be different, and they *ought* to be different. They *should* be right. We are in need of a fix. Anselm develops this notion of unrighteousness as a lack of original justice. Fallen man is deprived of original justice. Anselm's development will be used ultimately to drive a wedge between future Catholic and Protestant interpretations of original sin and of the corrupted or fallen state of mankind. These doctrinal distinctions will serve to elucidate the character of the sinfulness of time. The sinfulness of time, however, will not necessarily serve to resolve disputing interpretations unless the disputants acknowledge the truth of the apparently contradictory position. The dispute itself is evidence of the condition.

All this and more are presupposed by sin. How do we know of sin, or sin's existence? Can we inquire of ourselves about justification? Can we

6. Plotinus claims that eternity shines out ($\dot{\epsilon}\kappa\lambda\acute{\alpha}\mu\pi\omega$) from the substrate, being (*Enneads* 3.7.3). The converse is claimed here: time shines out from sin, non-being.

7. Kierkegaard, *Sickness unto Death*, 87.

seek within ourselves not correction but merely the conditions in need of correction? In short, would we be able to identify our own happiness and blessedness were we to be so fortunate? I believe that Kant's notion of "worthy to be happy" is related to these questions. *Worthy* in whose eyes? We shall see that, at least according to Karl Barth, our attempts to help ourselves by identifying our own problems are seriously misguided. These attempts are symptoms of the disease. They are the markings of the proud. There is a difference, however, between mere identification of a problem and its solution. The solution may require more than a human understanding, more than mere acknowledgment that each of us sins. The solution requires a full understanding of the problem, and the fullness is provided only by means of revelation. But even if the problem is unsolvable by us, we cannot stop being who we are, and that means that we cannot, or should not, cease to attempt to know and understand the problem.

Surely we do not need revelation to figure out, at least dimly, our sinful condition. Doubt may be a mark of imperfection—it was for both Augustine and Descartes—but is it sufficient? Might not doubt be merely a hint of disorder? Do we have an understanding of perfection adequate to conclude our own imperfection, adequate to take responsibility for imperfection?

There is the familiar bromide "We all make mistakes." The intention of this remark may be good, one of common misery. But the effect, the meaning, is hardly innocuous. To make a mistake is to choose door #1 when the car is behind door #3. A goat is behind door #1. The imperfection is evident, the ignorance. We are so ignorant that we cannot tell the difference between a new car and a goat if they are hidden behind doors. This inadequacy could be corrected. Our ability to see through doors could be vastly improved from its current state. Can this be the disorder we have in mind? Are we to take responsibility for choosing the wrong door? Perhaps, but if so we should also be willing to take responsibility for natural disasters—earthquakes, volcanic eruptions, killer storms. The burden of sin is unimaginably heavy.

"Original sin" is a good name for the sin in question, because it is sin that *originates* with human beings. Augustine, apparently relying on Irenaeus, has named it well. Arguably all sin is human sin—we exclude, at least for now, the fallen angels that figure prominently in the accounts of original sin by Augustine, Anselm, and Milton. But all other human sin is contextual. It is temporal. All other human sin *occurs*, not that it is not committed. It is committed, by human beings. And if it truly is sinful, then it truly is blameworthy. But all other human sin is committed at a time and in a place. This sin is sins. The commission is an event with a context. In short, about all other sin there might be some bickering regarding extenuating circumstances. Had things been different, poor upbringing, evil associates, dire need. Things were *not* different, but we could imagine them being so, and if so we could hope for a different outcome. With original sin, there effectively are no circumstances. Yes, there is God. Yes, there is man. Let us call man Adam and Eve. And if absolutely necessary, in order to get the story started, we might place Adam and Eve somewhere, in the garden for example, and we might introduce a subtle creature, the serpent. But not now, not yet. God, Adam, Eve, and a command. Nothing else. Not even Adam *and* Eve. No guile, no fruit that is a delight to the eyes and good for eating. All this (garden, fruit, serpent, etc.) is extraneous to the origin of sin, embellishment to the truth although captivating and enticing embellishment indeed. And so the command itself will seem to be trivial, of little significance and most especially of no great weight. (We shall see that if the command is given a temporal context, then it is impossibly severe and heavy, a monstrous and unbearable prohibition. In the temporal garden, even a garden without snakes, even a garden whose trees do not have interesting names like "the tree of knowledge of good and evil," only a malicious God, perhaps Hegel's God, would prohibit eating from one and only one tree, one tree just like all the other trees.) To obey will be no burden. This sin, original sin, is a sin that mankind can truly own. (Once the snake is introduced, then the bickering starts. He made me do it. She made me do it.) Original sin, if it were indeed something, would then truly be a creation of mankind, perhaps mankind's only creation, the only thing for which mankind could take full credit and responsibility. On one hand, this is entirely correct: all responsibility falls on man. But on the other hand, it assumes that original sin *is* something, that mankind has in fact produced something originally, that disobedience is substantial. And in this sense, "original" may be a misleading term since what it modifies, "sin," in a way is not. Sin has no substance. This is not a Manichaean treatise. At this introductory stage, however, I acknowledge the looseness with which I am using terms such as "original" and "creation." These are matters that will be considered more carefully and precisely.

Time as perceived by us is sin. Must we then conclude that time also has no substance? Time seems to reside both inwardly and externally, referred to as "phase time" and "succession time" respectively. (There are many other designations for kinds of time, several of which will be presented in the next chapter. But for our purposes, all of these designations can be reduced to two: phase and succession.) Inwardly time expresses the orientation of our being (perhaps Augustine's distension of mind, *distentio animi*). Externally time is a passion under which we suffer. According to some, it seems to flow. According to many, it seems to flow unevenly despite assertions to the contrary. That the inner and outer manifestations would both be considered time by us may at first appear to be confusing. Do we inflict the suffering of time upon ourselves? In a way this is exactly what we do. But the times are not confused; they are not mixed up. The times are one and point to our fundamental disorder: sin before God, and by extension sin before ourselves and before all others. The Catholic (and Lutheran) penitential prayer "Confiteor" makes the extension explicit, at least since 1970. "*Confiteor Deo omnipotenti, et vobis fratres, quia peccavi nimis . . .*" (I confess to almighty God, and to you, my brothers [and sisters], that I have greatly sinned . . .) By viewing time as suffering, we acknowledge our fallen-ness, our sinfulness, and our ingratitude. The sin is truly original. It originates with us. It is connected with our organization, with our very being, with our capacity to think. But this sin is not an accomplishment. We do not create sin. If anything, we un-create, and in so doing we originate sin. Hegel's determinate negation (*bestimmte Negation*) may be of some significance in this regard.[8] The sin begins with us. This is exactly what Augustine claims about the devil's fall. We begin the sin, by which I mean that we undo something. There is something, the goodness of God, godliness, creation, original justice, and we undo it. We transform our individuality and integrity, our soul-full-ness, as well as the individuality and integrity of others by means of division and degradation. Our individuality, our "I" is inextricably connected to dividing, to separation. Self-reference is inherently confusing, comprehensive and specific, and therefore a problem.

How are we capable of un-creating? Where does this negative power come from, if in fact it is a power or a capacity? Is destruction our delight? Is this an unintended consequence of God's creation? We are easily misled into thinking that because we are entirely responsible for our disobedience, that somehow we brought something into being. Disobedience presupposes obedience. We think of two states, and perversely take credit for one. Let there be a state of innocence and sinless-ness.

---

8. Hegel, *Phenomenology of Spirit*, 79.

We imagine a transference or movement from one state to the other. In other words, we presuppose the existence of time, a neutral template or measuring rod that backs up or contextualizes the movement. (This is the setting for most interpretations of Adam and Eve in the garden.) We proudly present to ourselves our creation of evil *ex nihilo*, and in so doing, the very assumption of the measuring device, we shall see, is clear evidence of our sinfulness.

The fact of the matter is that we are intrinsically and fundamentally confused, a fallen state that is characterized by the twofold nature of time. Furthermore, our attempts to engage with biblical statements—every sentence of Scripture is too hot to handle but too enticing to leave untouched—about eternal life, salvation, redemption, cause and effect, freedom, invariably involve additional confusion on our part, conflation where we attempt to understand by comprehending. But our attempt at comprehension, which amounts to holding two perspectives "at once," results in misunderstanding because we mistake the two perspectives for one. Accordingly we balk at the conditional sentence: if time is sin, and if sin has no substance, then time has no substance. The inference here, which effectively undermines the premises, may be logically correct, but effectively confused. The inference constitutes a misunderstanding of the terms involved.

My treatment of misunderstanding will include development of our encounter with mathematical models or systems, not the systems themselves, but our engagement with them, our understanding. We comprehend arithmetic or geometry, or so we think, and therefore we are capable of understanding a theorem. Here "understand" means that we are able to produce; we can work the system to obtain results, theorems. This will all be done in an effort to see cause and effect, both in temporal and in eternal or necessary senses.

Where sin is the subject, so is punishment the subject, in particular, hell. These are some of the terms (sin, punishment, hell), the nomenclature, that I beg the reader to accept provisionally. These *are* the terms that presuppose the resolution. More properly, these are the terms that follow upon that which we refer to as "resolution" or "redemption." There needs to be much argument and development, however, before one can assert that the "resolution" precedes the problem. Only by the end of this inquiry will I be able to show that notions such as "sin," "punishment," and "hell" result from salvation rather than necessitating it.

Hell is not eternal damnation. It is, in a sense, not even permanent. Hell would not be so frightening if only it were eternal. Go to hell and get it over with. Reject God's love in favor of creaturely autonomy, and do so once for all. No waiting. A single, irrevocable choice. Many theologians, Augustine, Anselm, and Aquinas notable among them, characterize the choice of the fallen angels in this way. I hope to show that their thinking is helpful only if one holds in abeyance any consideration of time and eternity. Otherwise, their arguments amount to a confusion of the temporal with the eternal.

Rather than this widely accepted interpretation, i.e., eternal damnation, hell is everlasting damnation. Although it is not quite correct to call it temporary, it *is* temporal, everlasting time. Accordingly many of the frightening characterizations of hell are accurate: never-ending fire; desire that the agonizing thirst be quenched. "Father Abraham, have mercy upon me, and send Lazarus to dip the end of his finger in water and cool my tongue; for I am in anguish in this flame" (Luke 16:24).

Hell represents the victory of original sin over redemption, and in that sense alone is it permanent and final. Hell is the myopic view that permanence presupposes change. It is the state chosen by the evil will, the state of separation chosen absolutely freely. But the state chosen is one of waiting. The time of sin has become the time of all, the time that is and is at all times. If hell is complete and final in any way, it is so in that desire has been perfected. The soul is perfectly dissatisfied. It must wait forever.

Dante's ice in the Inferno may be a good image to convey the permanence and finality of the state, but the image undermines the hellish indeterminacy. Only indeterminacy has been determined for the soul in hell. These souls are the infinite extensions of Heidegger's *futural* Dasein. In this regard, the vivid characterizations of hell—fire, ice, an annoying jingle played over and over—are misleading. They amount to distraction. Hell might better be described as time without sensation. Pure waiting. As if the damned soul could simply, merely, and only count.

◆ ◆ ◆

How do we understand the consequence of sin, as well as the hope for the expiation of sin, redemption, and reward or salvation? Intertwined with these subjects, especially given the connection of time to sin, are the matters of free will, foreknowledge, and predestination. Our understanding of predestination, at least as normally construed, results from confusion between comprehension and understanding. In particular, our natural and perhaps even rational attempt to comprehend the creature's sinfulness, *our* sinfulness, invariably leads to a misunderstanding of that sinfulness. By seeking to comprehend, we misunderstand. We proceed with our logical deductions, but without full knowledge of the terms involved. We proceed systematically with elements that lie outside of the system and with tools that extend beyond the system's boundaries. In misunderstanding, we offer a silent prayer for the redemption of the soul of Judas Iscariot. Indeed, we attempt to redeem the soul of Judas by our good intentions, and in so doing we attempt to help ourselves. Invariably we founder on the rock of self-help.

We stand in for God, comprehending God's foreknowledge, and then we fail to understand how or why Pharaoh's heart was hardened. How is Judas culpable for his betrayal and his despair, actions freely chosen by him but "foreknown" by God? There were extenuating circumstances. Are there not *still* extenuating circumstances? Part of our confusion is founded on the following mistake: We think that by God's foreknowledge that God knew that Judas would betray and despair at some point in time before Judas in fact chose to act. But surely this cannot be God's foreknowledge, for we have rendered it temporal. In comprehending the system, we have misunderstood what it means to foreknow, in particular, we have misunderstood "fore."

The term "foreknowledge" itself is misleading when applied to the divinity. In order to see this, we must first consider the ordinary use of the term.

What does it mean: to predict the future? What does it mean for someone, some being to say what will occur in the future? Let us take a common and seemingly simple example, the flipping of a coin. When a coin is flipped into the air, of the various outcomes, two are that it falls to the ground and lies motionless on the ground either heads up or tails up. We exclude all other possible outcomes: that the coin lands on its side and exhausts our patience while we wait for it to fall over either heads up or tails up; that the coin does not come down; that the coin apparently comes down but we cannot locate it; that the coin comes down and rolls away; etc. In common speech, then, we mean that to predict the future in this restricted case is to say with certainty, i.e., correctly that the coin will rest subsequently on the ground with, e.g., heads up. But more than just correctly, we mean also that there is no possibility of being incorrect. Apparently we distinguish between guessing correctly and foreknowledge.

If we have foreknowledge of the disposition of the coin, then we did not guess correctly how it would fall. We were not lucky. Prophecy is certain. Kierkegaard might object and counter that prophecy is merely approximation. But it is approximation in the same sense that a claim about the past, e.g., "Caesar crossed the Rubicon," is approximation. With respect to the coin, this approximation amounts to the prophet waiting for the coin to land, to inspect the coin, to see that it has landed heads up, and then to predict that the coin is to land heads up.

What do we mean? We predict in the sense that we say what will be, what must be. All this necessarily occurs in time. We are speaking of the future, i.e., an event, an outcome. By *pre*-dicting, we say before what will come after. Thus, assuming that we are absolutely certain of our prophecy, we can correctly speak of our foreknowledge. Such knowledge cannot be the knowing of God. It is not the certainty of God's knowledge that I am questioning, but rather the temporalizing of this knowledge. God knows, but not before or after anything. We, in contrast, are eager to transform our foreknowledge into cause. We are equally eager to degrade God's knowledge into ours. In a perverse alteration of experience, we contaminate the realm of contingency with our notions of necessity.

Even if the reader is persuaded of this condition, our condition of confusing our knowledge with God's, one might still wonder if there is any readily apparent or available evidence to support the consideration and juxtaposition of time with original sin, and various related notions. Is there common experience that one can point to in order to elicit provisional assent to my inquiry? Evidence for these various assertions is prominently found in the human being's battle for integrity, for it is in this fight that we stare our enemy, time, in the face. This is the time that originates as our sinfulness, our inner organization, phase time, that has come back to bite us as the alien succession time. This is the time that makes our existence corrosive to our very being, and corrosive to the being of all other human beings. We fight to hold ourselves together, and to hold together our understanding of other people, to hold together the very people themselves. Our fighting is an expression of love. The battle for integrity requires perseverance, but perseverance itself may be a chimera. Is perseverance a gift?

◆ ◆ ◆

This entire inquiry could be described as a Christian interpretation of time and eternity, of cause and effect, of freedom and necessity or foreknowledge. Here at the beginning, I offer no more enticement to follow my arguments than this description. Grant the author his nomenclature, and the reader may learn something, although probably not what the author is trying to convey. But surely some will think: Why bother? These topics have been considered by philosophers ever since there were philosophers, i.e., ever since man began to wonder about his world and about himself. Providing a Christian version of these inquiries has a decorative quality to it: both discursive and ornamental rather than investigative. Even so, some might be interested in the "parallels" between pagan interpretations and Christian, at least *this* Christian interpretation of these matters. My effort could then take its place, no doubt somewhere far down the list, among the legion accounts that attempt to explain and ultimately to justify Christianity: in short, to make sense out of Christianity.

Above, it was mentioned that the term "sin" presupposed freedom, obligation, disorder, God, and much more, among which is the following. Although many of the claims that I shall make in this pursuit may be preposterous, this next one seems to be especially so. The "Christian" expression of time, eternity, freedom, etc., is not a very good expression; it is not the best expression; it is the true expression. It is by means of Judeo-Christian revelation that we have access to the truth and accordingly to true statements about time, eternity, freedom. My claim, then, is that this inquiry is not a version of these matters, not even the best version of these matters, but the one, true, faithful expression of which all other accounts are versions. All other accounts amount to elaborations of the Judeo-Christian truth, the Word of God. Whether or not I shall succeed in establishing my claim is another matter entirely. It is quite reasonable here at the beginning for the reader to have doubts about the inquiry and argument. I share this doubt, but in this matter I am willing to be a fool.

Certainly one so disposed can read these remarks as a particular treatment of, say, being and becoming, a Christian version. This in fact may be a useful disposition or entry point into the inquiry, and it is possible and probably likely that no matter what I say or how I say it, one inclined to view these matters a certain way will persist in that way. Accordingly, this inquiry will be judged in light of the philosophical literature on time, being, and becoming, and very likely the verdict will be negative. My claim, however, is that Jesus Christ is the truth, the Word; thinking about being and becoming is an expression of that truth.

Christianity may well be Platonism (and Neoplatonism) for the masses in the sense of its common expression. In its particularity, however, Christianity supersedes Platonism. Although no one comprehends the Word of God, many have some understanding of Christianity, and these Christians believe in an eternal fact, which has a date and a place. Christianity as religion that concerns anything other than the relationship between the creator and creation, between God and man, is chit chat. But that is exactly what the Word of God is, the relationship of the creator to his creation. Knowledgeable explanations of Christianity, i.e., most biblical exegesis, are a taming—necessarily if we are truly dealing with the word of God—of what is revealed. The word of God is softened and sweetened into a saccharine gruel in order to make it more palatable. But the end of faith is not a neutered version of the truth. The end, the beatific vision, is the untamed, raw truth, and it is the end toward which the Christian strives. (It is the end of each and every person of faith, in a way, the end for each and every one of us.) The end is integrity. That one Christian or another expresses himself in terms of the masses does not alter the knowledge of God that consists of the vision. That the end is offered to all mankind—to the masses—does not degrade the vision. Indeed, the promise to all exalts and glorifies that which is so often meanly described. But consoling, presumably well-intentioned, bland expressions of the faith may well be those of the masses—it seems to me that they usually are. I hear the remarks coming from the preacher telling his congregation not to worry because God loves them, when what he should be saying is: Worry! God loves you! What greater burden could the creator place upon the creature?

◆ ◆ ◆

This first chapter has served as introduction to the entire inquiry, an inquiry that includes an argument. The following chapters spell out the argument in detail as well as entertaining some consequences of the argument.

Although sin and time are two aspects of the same thing, and although the origin of this argument stems from original sin, not from time, it will be pedagogically useful to take up time and eternity first (chapter 2). In some ways, that chapter may be the least satisfying—it certainly is the least comprehensive of the chapters—in that it sketches only very generally some conceptions and treatments of time and eternity as well as cause and effect. The purposes of the second chapter are twofold.

First, to appeal to our understanding of cause and effect, in particular succession, in a logical sense. I shall characterize this relation as "eternal act." The second purpose is to reduce the many descriptions of time to two, inner and outer, which, following Eva Brann's nomenclature, I call "phase" and "successive."

The third chapter begins with a reminder and a disclaimer that from a strictly Christian point of view the argument is being presented backward. In other words, a truly Christian expression would consist of reading this guide to the argument from bottom to top. Such an exposition, bottom to top, may masquerade as an expression of piety, but it would serve little or no purpose in my attempt to make the case for sin and time. The third chapter then provides an introduction to the biblical Hebrew notion of sin as missing the mark, the Christian adoption of this notion, and in particular the expansion of the evil inclination of man's heart (Gen 6:5 and 8:21) to become original sin.

The fourth chapter is about desire, which is central to both of the clues to this entire investigation: waiting and disintegration. The apostle Paul, Augustine, and Anselm provide particular descriptions of desire as concupiscence of the flesh and lack of original justice. The human condition of unrighteousness as understood in Christian context ensues from these descriptions, and this condition provides a hint toward the connection of originating sin, time, and apperception.

The fifth chapter concerns waiting, but not merely passive waiting. Active waiting, i.e., self-aware waiting, can be conceived as a virtue, in particular as perseverance. The problem of perseverance, quite simply, is duration. For how long must one act or refrain from action? What is the mental construct that enables one to conceive of continuation per se as virtue?

The sixth chapter constitutes circumstantial evidence for my central argument, that original sin and time are the same. The evidence is presented primarily in the form of narrative of the twin falls, by Adam and Eve, and by the devil. These two stories, myths, when analyzed according to the parameters of disobedience, waiting, and self-reference, surround my claim.

The seventh chapter, the most difficult for me to produce, is my attempt to deduce the central argument, and to do so from the defining characteristic of the individual, the capacity to say "I." This capacity, apperception, turns out to be inherently confused *and* blameworthy. The individual willfully confuses comprehension and understanding, inner and outer, totality and specification, and in so doing originates time as sin.

The eighth and ninth chapters apply the results of the argument, the deduction, to some of the principal concerns of freedom, knowledge, and eschatology as entertained in the Judeo-Christian tradition. I hope to show that the perennially vexing problem of predestination is nearly universally misunderstood. When understood in the context of time as original sin, predestination is no longer a problem.

The tenth chapter is the beginning of the inquiry, a treatment of the integrity that must be presupposed in order for the development of the argument. But this integrity, although necessary, is in no way deduced. It is revealed. My inquiry is most decidedly *not* a treatise on grace, but in lieu of the argument presented here, assuming that it holds, grace is all that we have.

2

The Eternal and the Temporal

THE PURPOSE OF THIS chapter is to make the case for the eternal, although some would argue that the case for the temporal is equally or more vexed and in greater need of establishment. By make the case, I mean to show, to demonstrate, to argue that we understand the eternal, and we do so solely because we are rational beings, and that this understanding is sufficient to establish the truth of the eternal.[1] In short, the eternal is. The eternal may be revealed to us in various ways, and its significance in an eschatological sense may be beyond demonstration. In this regard, the eternal may even have clear moral implications, although there may be a moral aspect to any recognition of the eternal. This would be the position of Christocentric theology for which revelation takes precedent over any attempt to argue rationally from the ground up. But let us leave these matters for later, and their moral components, although they may be imperatives, remain merely implied, not strictly deduced. At this point the argument is confined to rational demonstration.

We are engaged here in establishing a foundation, and the proceedings may seem to be both overly fastidious and dull, for there will be no appeal to stunning biblical exclamations, no reliance on evocative and poignant stories of human desire. Indeed, here there should be no appeal whatsoever to the imagination. This last demand is difficult to satisfy.

---

1. Plotinus argues that we understand the eternal because we are in contact with it, and through this contact we must have some share in it. *Enneads* V.3.7.7.

Hegel is right to decry in the *Phenomenology of Spirit* the role of picture-thinking in rigorous argumentation. The fact of the matter is, however, that most of us engage in such thinking most of the time. The vigor of our imagination is one of our greatest obstacles in trying to think about the eternal. Poets and artists may have an advantage over us in this endeavor in that they give themselves over entirely and willingly to their pictures, their feelings. As alternatives to painting, music, poetry, there are disciplines that attempt to steer clear of the imagination. Generally we recognize the success of logic and number theory, for examples, as relying very little if at all on pictures. The aim in this chapter is to proceed in that latter manner.

The eternal is a meaningful concept entirely independent of the notion of time, although much of the arguing here will require delineating the differences between the two, the eternal and the temporal. At this early stage even use of the word "eternity" to indicate the concept in question should be shunned. That expression has a factual sense to it, like "paternity," and this similarity, although merely linguistic and superficial, may mislead the reader. Furthermore, the necessary, if appealed to, would in no way involve fact. Eternity conveys a sense of status, one that is often referred to in theological discussion. But status or state connotes fixity and place, and these connotations are also likely to be misleading. Therefore, this state of eternity must await considerable development of the argument to be set forth, and it may be best to assert provisionally that eternity is not a state. Thus I attempt to ease into my presentation by using, perhaps hiding behind, the substantive adjective.[2]

One might begin to think about the eternal in an entirely negative manner, i.e., not temporal. Such an approach would be open to criticism that it does not establish the eternal, it does not make a case for the being of eternal, it merely indicates what the eternal is not. This is Hobbes's criticism of Descartes's assertion that he has a positive notion of the infinite. Hobbes responds that we understand the finite, and Descartes has merely attached the word "not" to this understanding. Such a negative approach is to be avoided if possible.

The eternal is real. Its reality is displayed by pointing to an instance of non-temporal action, which is sure sign of that reality. Of course, one set of words or accounts leads to another, and immediately we want to be clear about notions such as "real" and "action," and similarly to avoid

2. Plotinus expresses a similar concern about eternity (αἰών) and the eternal (αἰώνιος). *Enneads* V.3.7.2.

"non-temporal." We also want clarity regarding our relation to this purported action. Are rational beings required, and if so, how are they required? As participants? As those who know? For example, there may be much that is true or real about the world which we are unaware of or which we do not understand. Conversely, we may have images or expressions about which we might want to say that they were false or fictitious, i.e., not real. We call them illusions, delusions, chimeras, or phantoms. For Descartes, the measure of reality or truth was "clear and distinct." Was the thing in question clearly understood and in such a way that distinguished it from all else, i.e., from everything that it was not? Although there may be problems with Descartes's criteria, it is doubtful that this presentation will be of much if any improvement. This is so because I can do no better than to propose that what we know for certain to be real and to be true is real and true. This may seem to be an audacious claim. Of course, we, the knowers, are finite and fallible, and there is no accommodation made here for the theological notion of faith perfecting reason, but these limitations make sense only under the condition that there is truth against which they are measured. Our finitude and fallible nature presuppose truth. But even with "truth," as with "eternity," we must beware of thinking about it as a state or a judgment. By true or real we pursue here that which is. In his *Introduction to Metaphysics*, Heidegger attributes to some pre-Socratic Greeks, especially Parmenides and Heraclitus, an attempt to encounter and to speak about what is, but there the notion is *phusis*. It should become clear that such a notion, even if not interpreted as "nature," is not what is envisioned here.

Immediately one objects: What about the delusional person? Delusion is a relative term, and to apply it with absolute confidence, one needs a template or background against which to judge what another person claims to be real as a delusion. We are on the brink of solipsism with these considerations, or perhaps the opposite of solipsism, and it is not my aim whatsoever to make either of those arguments. Furthermore, how could anyone say that he or someone else was the arbiter of reality? This claim will be disappointing to the dedicated and determined epistemologist, but rather than obscure any further my rather simple assertion, I simply make it: that which we know and understand to be indubitably true and real is true and real, and it is true and real precisely because we understand it as such. It *is*. One can circle back and forth again, trying to get purchase on this understanding. One may engage in a critique of reason and perception or perhaps an exposition of the unfolding and development of consciousness, in an attempt to ground that which is. Without delving into subject and object, inner and outer, my claim is simply that we human beings understand, at least broadly, the meaning of the expression: It is. Unlike several languages that contain the subject within the inflected verb, English requires at least a pronoun, in this case "It." But the only word that is working here is "is." One can conduct a grammatical taxonomy at this point: third person, singular, present, indicative, etc. This sort of analysis is after the fact. Furthermore, our understanding of "is" is non-temporal. (Here again the Christocentric theologians will object, and there is no defense against their objection. One needs time and space to develop the rational argument.)

This looks like I have made the individual the arbiter, but note that my claim includes both knowing and understanding. That which is both *known* and *understood as real* is real. Known and understood by whom? By the one, or the who, or that which knows and understands. And what does this one or this who know and understand? This one or who knows and understands the truth and reality of something.

Real and *true* designate that which is. At this point some philosophers doubtless would want to use *being* and perhaps even *existence*. It will become very clear that the words "being" and "exist" are to be avoided if possible in this context. The purpose in this chapter is to demonstrate an action that both simply is and is non-temporal, or more carefully stated, *simply is*. "Action" might seem to be a complicated notion containing unintended and undesired consequences or suppositions, but by action is meant a simple instance of cause and effect. If one were to accept Paul Tillich's remark that "existence is always both fact and act," then our concern would be with *act* that is not *fact*.[3] In Thomist terminology, the ultimate object of concern would be God, pure act, but we are working well below the ultimate. If a non-temporal instance of cause and effect, an instance that is known and understood, can be given, then it will have been demonstrated that something is eternal, and we know it to be so.

Now one might object further that this chapter is attempting more than is necessary, since the action of a cause causing an effect may be overreaching. Would not a necessary relationship suffice, for example a primitive logical deduction, the syllogism, or an elementary equation of arithmetic? Perhaps, but a necessary relationship points merely to what might be called the "superficially eternal." What is needed in this study

---

3. Tillich, *Systematic Theology*, 2:78.

is something deeper, something "profoundly eternal," something which the immortal soul can encounter, but not in its immortality. In its immortality, the immortal soul is simply or merely not dying. Tillich gives a different meaning to immortality, "a quality which transcends temporality," but I reserve this notion for my comments at the end of this study on the integrity of the individual, where I hope to show that temporality is in need of transcendence only from a temporal perspective.[4] The soul under consideration here is still on the way to somewhere. This, according to Kierkegaard, is precisely the sickness unto death experienced by the despairing soul: hopelessness regarding the ultimate hope of death.[5] We need something that is profoundly eternal but not merely necessary. Hence the adoption of eternal action, specifically cause and effect. The search here is for something like Kant's synthetic a priori knowledge. For Kant, this kind of knowledge is a hallmark of reason and of the rational being. My endeavor, perhaps overly ambitious, is cosmological, at least in appearance, in that it seeks to say more than merely that there are rational beings, even though the discussion of the matter temporally takes place among rational beings.

The various objections raised to the use of *real* and *true* to characterize the eternal are in fact evidence that we understand the word "is." By asking about being, existence, and necessity, we betray our knowledge in the form of questions. These questions indicate on the one hand the complexity, subtlety, and interconnectedness of "is," but on the other hand that they are intelligent questions. They are pertinent. They can be asked only by one who understands what he is talking about.

For now, this is enough about the immortal soul, about knowing and understanding, about reality. My aim is to keep these remarks as general as they need to be. In this vein I use adjectives rather than nouns, or more exactly nouns constructed from adjectives. One speaks not of eternity and time, but rather of the eternal and the temporal. This chapter is not an inquiry into the concept of blessed eternity, Augustine's Sabbath rest, Aquinas's beatific vision, and it is for this state that the word "eternity" has been reserved. This blessed state is truly our end, especially in so far as the rest or vision consists in the fullness of time, the complete absorption and ultimate transformation of the temporal into the eternal, and the final integration of the individual in glory. This is the state of salvation,

---

4. Tillich, *Systematic Theology*, 3:410.
5. Kierkegaard, *Sickness unto Death*, 18.

which is the opposite of condemnation. Tillich notes that condemnation means "removal from the eternal."[6] This state is most definitely not a state. But here, near the beginning, the explicit article of faith is this one: some things can be truly known from consulting reason alone, even if we restrict *knowing*, almost tautologically, to that which a rational being does as a rational being. Let us guard, however, against the thought that this is a description of a being who is rational, some thing that is and that possesses reason among its various attributes or predicates. By rational being is meant strictly and solely one who or one that reasons, a reasoner. In particular, I assert that non-temporal action is a sure sign of the eternal, and that we rational beings merely to the extent that we are rational and in that sole capacity can verify the eternal. I assert further that the eternal is not produced by our knowing it, but rather that the eternal simply is. We, the rational beings, enter into a relationship with the eternal by means of our knowing it.

It must be acknowledged, also here at the beginning, that withholding appeals to traditional revelation as a source of our knowledge of the eternal is not a faithless act. Quite the opposite is the case. Here at the beginning, reason has been invoked. It is in reason, initially, that we place faith. As Kant famously articulates at the end of his *Grounding for the Metaphysics of Morals*, this ground of reason is without grounding. Again, Christocentric theologians would disagree, asserting that Jesus Christ is the ground of reason.

It turns out, of course, that almost everything written here will be about time, about that which the basic or rational eternal is not. I direct our attention to something that is, but it *is* not in time. It *is* a-temporal. In treating this matter, one is forced to use the language of privation, such as one does in speaking about atheism or non-being or the infinite. But the limitations of language need not determine the extent of the investigation. A radical materialist, or perhaps an intuitionist mathematician, or perhaps Thomas Hobbes, or perhaps even an Aristotelian might object to any and all things that cannot be finitely specified in number and detail. My hope is that the following remarks will dispel such obstinacy, that it can be shown that the eternal is truly significant in our lives. Kierkegaard writes that man "is a synthesis of the temporal and the eternal."[7] Man's inwardness or introspection is "the constituent of the eternal in man."[8]

6. Tillich, *Systematic Theology*, 2:78.
7. Kierkegaard, *Concept of Anxiety*, 85.
8. Kierkegaard, *Concept of Anxiety*, 151.

Kierkegaard goes on to characterize this inwardness as "earnestness," a conception that will recur at the end of this study where I deal with the integrity, and disintegration, of the human being, and attempt to show that our earnestness is a spark of divine love. But at this point I merely note my concurrence with Kierkegaard on this matter, that our inwardness is our relation to the eternal. We can be more specific, however, than simply referring to "inwardness," by studying an example in our understanding that posits the eternal within. This example is non-temporal action.

The instance of non-temporal action developed in *On Faith, Works, Eternity and the Creatures We Are* is a particular case of cause and effect. The causes of the Pythagorean Theorem, both in its geometric manifestation and in its algebraic generalization, are the definitions, common notions, and postulates of Euclidean geometry. Over the millennia, mathematicians have articulated notions and postulates in addition to those laid down in Euclid's *Elements*. It is immaterial here whether or not those specifications at the beginning of the *Elements* are sufficient for the unfolding of the subsequent propositions, and for many more unstated propositions. The point to note simply is that the postulates (or axioms) are necessary for the propositions. As is well known to students of geometry, the famous Fifth Postulate, or its systemic equivalent, is needed in order to derive Propositions I.47 and I.48, the full geometric expression of the Pythagorean Theorem. As can be demonstrated, without this postulate the Theorem cannot be deduced. Such is one of the remarkable developments of so-called hyperbolic or Lobachevskian geometry. The postulate in question concerns parallel lines. Rendered as Playfair's Axiom, it states that in a plane, through a point not on a given straight line, there is one and only one straight line parallel to the given straight line. "Parallel" here means that the line through the point does not intersect the given line in the plane no matter how far the two lines are extended. This is the version of the postulate that appears in most textbooks of Euclidean geometry.

Since the aim here is to give a non-temporal instance of cause and effect, one might wonder if space has been sneaked into our considerations by considering a problem of geometry, specifically consideration of extension. A geometric example affords ease of conception. We are not only rational beings but also sentient ones, as our sensation is, in Kant's terms, founded on our spatial intuition. Picture-thinking is often very useful. Therefore, we need to be certain that the example given, although it entails space and spatial intuition, is not dependent upon spatial intuition, and thus not dependent upon our imagination. If space were presupposed, then through a series of arguments contained in this book, one might deduce that there was space in heaven, a deduction that has no significance in the example being developed here. For Euclidean geometry, or at least a sufficient portion of it to include the Fifth Postulate and the deduction of the Pythagorean Theorem, can be rendered strictly algebraically. Much of what we normally think of as geometry can be transformed into other kinds of mathematical systems, leaving behind only the ghosts of spatial (or temporal) dimensions. The Euclidean system need not presuppose space at all, although such a system might be of scant interest to most of us when so rendered. Thus I shall continue by assuming ordinary spatial geometry, acknowledging the rhetorical and pedagogic advantage of using a limited case of cause and effect.

From this system, Euclidean geometry with suitable definitions, common notions, and postulates including the Fifth Postulate or its systemic equivalent, we can generate infinitely many propositions. We might say that infinitely theorems ensue. Some are "trivially" infinite in that they differ from one another only trivially. For example, in plane geometry:

1. The interior angle sum of a Euclidean trilateral rectilinear figure is two right angles.
2. The interior angle sum of a Euclidean quadrilateral rectilinear figure is four right angles.
3. The interior angle sum of a Euclidean pentagonal rectilinear figure is six right angles.
4. The interior angle sum of a Euclidean hexagonal rectilinear figure is eight right angles.

And so forth.

We "generalize" these theorems by asserting that the interior angle sum of a Euclidean rectilinear figure is equal to $(2s-4) \cdot \pi/2$, where s is the number of sides and $\pi/2$ designates a right angle in radians. Then if we want to say something about the angle sum of a 731-sided enclosed rectilinear figure, other than consulting a Greek grammar and lexicon in order to express "731-gonal," we would simply need to calculate.

One might reply that all I have done here is display in a confusing way the fact that I know how to count. Nonetheless, each of the propositions listed above *is* a proposition of Euclidean geometry, unique even if subsumed under a more general theorem. And there may well be infinitely many less trivial propositions of Euclidean geometry not specified in the *Elements*. For example, there is the parallelogram law: the sum of the squares on the two diagonals of a parallelogram is equal to the sum of the squares on the four sides.

In *On Faith, Works, Eternity and the Creatures We Are* it was suggested, fancifully, that we suppose there to be a mathematical creator who chose Euclidean geometry over alternatives out of a desire for universal incommensurability. For all squares, the side and the diagonal are demonstrably incommensurable, owing in part to the similarity of all squares. Aristotle cites this very example as a case of something that always (ἀεί) is and therefore cannot be temporal.[9] In the hyperbolic or Lobachevskian alternative, "squares" (equiangular, equilateral quadrilaterals) come in infinitely many varying sizes, no one being geometrically similar to any other "square" of different size. There would be, if the creator so chose, infinitely many "squares" where the side-diagonal ratio was commensurable, and infinitely many instances where it was incommensurable. I suggested labeling that state of affairs evil, and accordingly the creator might choose Euclidean geometry because it is good, or because the creator saw to it that it be good, and saw to it sufficiently so that we could understand it to be good. There is of course the possibility of the opposite interpretation regarding the goodness and evil of incommensurability, specifically that it may be evil. In the Lobachevskian case, at least some infinitely many "squares" have sides and diagonals that are commensurable. The point of this thought experiment, however, is to consider the knowledge of effects depending upon the causes. Evil will be taken up elsewhere along with the accompanying notions of disorder, sin, and culpability.

We human beings are logical and possess geometric knowledge, in part owing to intuition and in part owing to our rational soul. This knowledge may be rudimentary and primitive, but it is ours naturally. Does each one of us know about the case of universal incommensurability in Euclidean geometry? No, of course not. But Aristotle knew about it, and in fact many people know about it. Was there a time when we, each one of us, did not know about it? Yes! We came to know this relationship in the course of our lives, at a time before which we did not know it. *We are in time, at least in some ways.*

---

9. Aristotle, *Physica* IV.12.222a4.

Returning to the Euclidean case, the cause of each proposition is the system, *the* Euclidean geometry. Each proposition is an effect of the cause. The Pythagorean Theorem is not a free-standing fact of mathematics. Are the effects *foreknown* in the cause? We shall touch on the matter presently and in more detail much later in this study when considering foreknowledge, predestination, and freedom. But at this point, there is no need to delve any further into the geometric particulars, for the claim simply is the Fifth Postulate causes the Pythagorean Theorem, and many other theorems, as indicated. The Postulate is not the sole cause of the Theorem, but it is indispensable. In short, and perhaps in too many words, I have just given an instance of cause and effect. The effect is as real as the Pythagorean Theorem, i.e., as real as can be. But *real* here does not mean that the Pythagorean Theorem per se is real. (That requires an additional argument.) My claim is that the dependence of the Theorem upon the Postulate is real. It is truly derived from the Postulate. The dependence is evidence of cause and effect. How real are the Theorem and the Postulate themselves and independent of one another? They are as real as our rational thoughts, but in fact, they are not independent of one another. They are known by us, by reasoners.

Now surely it is not the case that the Fifth Postulate, simply because it is a coherent and understandable supposition, indeed one that many people are inclined to give assent to, is thereby real. Does thinking the Postulate make it real? Fortunately, this is a question that need not be answered here. All we need to do is to establish the reality of the cause *and* effect, i.e., that the Pythagorean Theorem *really* and *truly* follows from the Fifth Postulate. And yet, and this is important, the Theorem and the Postulate are not identical. The Postulate conceptually does not contain the Theorem, it causes it. The Theorem is the result of an eternal action.

One might still object that the reality of the combination of the Postulate and Theorem is confined to the realm of reason, that in a world without reason, the combination would not be. Initially such an assertion may ring true, but it is doubtful that the previous sentence has any meaning. When one tries to imagine a world without reason, one gets nothing but this world without rational beings. But *this* world is undeniably constructed with the aid of reason. Can we hold our imagination at bay and strictly think of a world without reason? In other words, without relying on the imagination, can we simply piece together in our mind the notions of "world" and "absence of reason"? The very thinking itself needed for this experiment renders the question moot. This is not to claim that the rational being creates the world. The world as a *world* is truly inconceivable without reason, but our rational conception is relational, not generative. Plotinus would agree, at least to the extent that the Intellect necessitates Being, i.e., the thing thought, but the Intellect does not generate Being.

Please note that the claim here is narrow. This is not an argument for a rational creator, a rational creation, or a *rationale* for the way things are. I am merely noting that there is reason. This much is phenomenally true. And there are rational beings—at least one and, I believe, many more—who encounter the world not as it is but as they are, i.e., as rational beings.

If we fully understand the cause, then do we know its effects? This is the kind of knowledge that is often attributed to God, i.e., it is said about God the creator. Augustine, seeming to reverse the relationship between things and knowledge, goes so far as to claim that things are because God knows them.[10] Such an assertion will lead us to consider the following apparent deduction. God foreknew that Judas Iscariot would betray Jesus of Nazareth and subsequently despair, and accordingly or nevertheless God created Judas. Augustine provides a rationale. "God foreknew but he created [sinners nonetheless] for the benefit of saints."[11] This line of defense will not be the one pursued when considering foreknowledge and predestination.

Would full understanding of the foundation of Euclidean geometry result in knowledge of all the propositions or theorems? We might easily answer "no" if we consider a single, finite individual, no matter how well the individual human being understood geometry. We might also conclude that a machine would not "know" all of the theorems. One of the startling outcomes of Gödel's incompleteness theorems is that for any system as rich as arithmetic (number theory) or geometry, if the system or theory is consistent (no contradictions are derivable within the system), then there is a true statement of the system that cannot be derived. The "truth" of any such statement is determined in advance by a finite, decidable method. Thus there is a theorem of the system that cannot be proven by using the proof methods of the system. In other words, there is a true statement that cannot be deduced. Presumably this theorem is an effect of the system. But we would conclude that the machine did not "know" the theorem because it could not deduce it.

---

10. Augustine, *On the Trinity* XV.22.
11. Augustine, *Literal Meaning of Genesis* XI.22.29.

Is the existence of such a theorem a sign of freedom? Furthermore, is it a sign of freedom in a system or environment or world in which the cause foreknows all the effects? These are matters for the consideration of divine foreknowledge, predestination, and freedom. (Gödel's famous theorems are complicated versions of the problem of self-reference.)

Let us return to the central point of inquiry, cause and effect. The Fifth Postulate and the Pythagorean Theorem are real on the supposition that there is reason, and the latter supposition, in true Cartesian fashion, in undeniable. Put another way, reason is phenomenal, and it reveals the truth of the mathematical relation of cause and effect in this case. Hence the instance of cause and effect is undeniable. Furthermore, the effect is not explicitly contained in the cause. There is no mention of the Pythagorean Theorem in Playfair's Axiom. This is so in part because the Axiom is necessary but insufficient to produce the Theorem. I bring up this distinction to anticipate and counter a concern about eternity. Could it possibly be a state of mere logical deduction? Even worse, could it be a state where, in the language of philosophers, all "judgments" are analytic and none are synthetic? The eternity of revelation is much more interesting than mere analysis. It is revealed to be wonderful and filled with joy. Analogously, here the specific action of cause and effect is not merely or simply analytic. We must, therefore, look for a moment at cause and effect to determine explicitly that the relationship is not temporal.

Several writers have questioned the non-temporal status of cause and effect, either directly or indirectly, and there is considerable scholarly commentary on the subject. Thomas Hobbes questions the status indirectly by acknowledging a materialist world that depends entirely on motion and desire. All effects in a Hobbesian world necessarily come after their causes in time. Presumably the Epicurean philosophy of Lucretius would also fall into this category. Slightly more directly, David Hume also locates action in time. Hume recognizes the philosophical relationship of cause and effect, but he grounds it strictly in a temporal succession of impressions. The effect *is* the impression that occurs in time following upon another impression which is the cause. The sentient being then attributes the philosophical relation of cause and effect to the succession of impressions. In a way, the sentient being produces the relationship. The temporal is the template against which all judgments are made. The most direct assault on the eternal, however, occurs in Martin Heidegger's *Being and Time*.

THE ETERNAL AND THE TEMPORAL

We consider the relationship between the temporal and the eternal, between time and eternity, but not from a position of disinterest. Quite the opposite: we participate in the relationship. Heidegger would have us believe, at least in *Being and Time*, that *Dasein*'s relationship to the eternal is fictitious. His position is similar to that of Hobbes, who claims, in contrast to Descartes, that our notion of the infinite is entirely negative, and consists in fact and merely in a meaningless concatenation of words. According to Hobbes, we comprehend the finite (do we?) and simply add *not* to that word and understanding, thus forming *infinite*. But, he claims, we have no direct understanding of the infinite. Descartes on the other hand thought that we had a positive notion of the infinite. The eternal, then, for Heidegger, is *Dasein*'s unfounded belief in the reality of combining the *temporal* with *not*.

According to Heidegger, all succession is rooted in temporality.[12] We (*Dasein*) are the ones who make sense out of succession because we are temporal beings. Heidegger asserts, "It is often held that there is a 'cleavage' between 'temporal' entities [natural processes and historical happenings] and the 'supra-temporal' eternal [spatial and numerical relationships], and efforts are made to bridge this over."[13] "Even the 'non-temporal' and 'supra-temporal' are 'temporal' with regard to their Being and not just privatively by contrast with something 'temporal' as an entity 'in time', but in a *positive* sense."[14]

According to Heidegger, *Dasein* is always anxious, because there is always something in the future that needs to be settled.[15] This is the soul who is always on the way to somewhere, the soul who suffers from the sickness unto death. *Dasein* is tempted, however, to attribute permanence—an absolute requisite for cause and effect; see below—or thing-hood to its experiences. Heidegger identifies a pernicious "ancient ontology" that insists on inventing "thing-concepts," i.e., being, in a world of time.[16] He calls it reifying (*Verdinglichung*). And as long as Heidegger can traffic in the world of *sein* and *Dasein*, with this connotation of existence, then his arguments seem to have force. This is so because the temporal has been presupposed in existence itself. Having placed time in the equation, Heidegger, and we along with him, discover time in the equation.

12. Heidegger, *Being and Time* H18–19, 227.
13. Heidegger, *Being and Time* H18.
14. Heidegger, *Being and Time* H19.
15. Heidegger, *Being and Time* H325, 79, 266.
16. Heidegger, *Being and Time* H437.

Before going further, it should be pointed out that these claims regarding cause and effect all concern experience, in particular, the experience of the human being. Modern physics, relativity and quantum mechanics, will present challenges to what seem to be the parameters of ordinary experience. Here, however, we find Hobbes, Hume, and Heidegger making claims about cause and effect under the condition of our attributing the relationship to our experience.

Experience itself entails time, and thus if experience is allowed to be the fundamental datum of consideration, then there will be no extirpating of time. In the *Critique of Pure Reason*, Kant gives conditions for experience that argue for it, and these conditions require substance and the relationship of cause and effect to serve as foundation. They will also serve as the foundation for time or temporality.

Kant notes that the succession of perceptions in experience is contingent. By this he means that one appearance follows another without, as part of the experience, the necessity that one "occur" before the other. He concludes, "Therefore determination of the existence of objects in time can come about only through the linking of perceptions in time as such, and hence only through concepts connecting them a priori."[17] Kant's aim is to show the rule, the a priori conditions under which two perceptions are linked in time. This is the rule according to which one experience precedes the other.

He begins with what he calls the "Principle of the Permanence of Substance."[18] "In all variation by appearances substance is permanent, and its quantum in nature is neither increased nor decreased." The argument for the rule goes thus. Time does not vary, nor can it be perceived. That which presents time, the *substrate* in Kant's words, must be found in the appearances, and this is *substance* itself. Therefore, substance is necessary for something to exist such that it is experienced.[19] We must keep in mind that the things that Kant is speaking about are the appearances. He goes to great length to distinguish the appearances—all that we perceive—from the things in themselves, about which he claims that little can be said other than that they are objects.

Kant concludes, "Hence all time relations . . . are possible only in the permanent. I.e., the permanent is the *substratum* of the empirical presentation of time itself; all time determinations are possible only in the

17. Kant, *Critique of Pure Reason* B219.
18. Kant, *Critique of Pure Reason* B224.
19. Kant, *Critique of Pure Reason* B225.

substratum.... Solely through the permanent does sequential *existence* in different parts of the time series acquire a *magnitude*, called *duration*."[20] Thus time is not the backdrop against which we encounter things. There is no encounter of things (plural) unless there be permanent substances, that which makes the encounter possible. In this context, the term "permanent," of course, cries out to be misunderstood. The mind very easily thinks of the permanent as ever-lasting, i.e., as preserving itself through the passage of time. But this is exactly what the permanent is not. The permanent does not exist. Rather the permanent is the condition for existence. The permanent simply is, and accordingly makes existence possible.

With his next principle, Kant connects the permanent with change. The "Principle of Temporal Succession according to the Law of Causality" states, "All changes occur according to the law of the connection of cause and effect."[21] For two appearances to be distinct from one another, there must be a rule or principle, and objective relation by or according to which they are distinguished. "Now in order for this objective relation to be cognized as determinate, the relation between the two states must be thought as being such that it determines as necessary which of the states must be placed before and which after, rather than vice versa. But a concept carrying with it a necessity of synthetic unity can only be a pure concept of understanding, which therefore does not reside in perception." The claim here is that we do not perceive the concept of succession, but rather our perceptions (plural) are made possible by the rule to which the concept refers. "Here this concept is that of the *relation of cause and effect*; ... Therefore experience itself—i.e., empirical cognition of appearances—is possible only inasmuch as we subject the succession of appearances, and hence all change, to the law of causality."[22] According to Kant, therefore, all experience presupposes both permanence and the relationship of cause and effect.

It is not surprising that Kant's claim about permanence is not the last word regarding substance and things in time. Commenting on Kant's treatment of succession, Paul Ricoeur states: "Permanence somehow includes succession and simultaneity. The 'aesthetic,' not yet having to deal with specific objects, or objective phenomena, recognizes only the oneness and infinity of time. But now it happens that phenomenal objectivity gives rise to this unexpected feature, permanence, which participates in

20. Kant, *Critique of Pure Reason* B226.
21. Kant, *Critique of Pure Reason* B232.
22. Kant, *Critique of Pure Reason* B234.

the same a priori character of all the aspects of time acknowledged by the 'Aesthetic.'"[23] A few pages later, Ricoeur counters Kant's assertion.

> We were not entirely persuaded by the argument that the third "mode" of time, permanence, also called "time in general," is rendered completely intelligible by its correlation with the schematism of substance and the principle of permanence. The idea of the permanence of time seems richer in meaning than the permanence of something in time. In fact, it seems to be the ultimate condition of possibility for all such things.[24]

Ricoeur's position is similar to the ancient claim attributed to Heraclitus that all is in flux. More modern interpretations might accord primacy to "continuance."[25] At first sight, these claims giving priority to flux, continuance, and permanence of time over and against things in themselves or substances, the Kantian substrate, seem to invite ridicule. One might ask: What is in flux? What continues? What is in time? Modern physics, however, provides unsettling examples concerning these questions, especially in the particle-wave duality. Quantum mechanics shows that the curious collection of phenomena that had been attributed to light is also applicable to subatomic "particles." The wave-like behavior of the electron, the individual "particle," undermines the very name of particle.

The purpose of this brief excursus is simply to acknowledge that at the deepest level it may be necessary to admit that the Kantian substrate is an article of belief: things first. Permanence does not presuppose change, provided that permanence itself is presupposed.[26]

Later in the *Critique of Pure Reason*, Kant applies this argument to his solution of the third antinomy regarding freedom by claiming that there has occurred a dialectical illusion between the competing arguments, one for the natural law and the other for spontaneity. The latter, a genuinely free act, unconditioned, is a product of reason, whereas *the* natural law, that is the very conditions for experience, are in the understanding.

---

23. Ricoeur, *Time and Narrative*, 3:251–52.

24. Ricoeur, *Time and Narrative*, 3:266.

25. See for example Husserl's comments on "the unity of the flux of consciousness itself" (*Phenomenology of Internal Time-Consciousness*, 106); "eine, einzige Bewußtseinsfluß" (*Zur Phänomenologie*, 80).

26. Barth makes a similar comment regarding election and rejection. "The Yes cannot be heard unless the No is also heard. But the No is said for the sake of the Yes and not for its own sake. In substance, therefore, the first and last word is Yes and not No." Barth, *Church Dogmatics*, 2/2:13. Also in this vein see Augustine's remarks about the existence of good things without the existence of evil. *City of God* XIV.11 and XIX.13.

"Pure reason, as a merely intelligible power, is not subjected to the form of time, nor consequently to the conditions of temporal succession. The causality of reason in its intelligible character by no means *arises*, or starts at a certain time, in order to produce an effect. For otherwise it would itself be subjected to the natural law of appearances in so far as this law determines causal series with regard to time, and the causality of reason would then be nature, not freedom."[27] Thus reason, as cause, does not precede its effect in time. This may seem analogous to the argument above regarding the cause of certain propositions of Euclidean geometry. The Fifth Postulate does not precede the Pythagorean Theorem in time. But here there is a difference. The Pythagorean Theorem, effect that it is, is no more or less eternal than the Fifth Postulate. Kant's spontaneous act, the act of freedom, however, results in a succession of effects that all are empirical. The non-temporal enters into time. (This presumably ordinary relation, the entrance of the non-temporal into the temporal, has the most splendid manifestation in the Son of God become man, Jesus Christ. But that entrance is decidedly not ordinary, i.e., not ordered or ordained as a necessary condition for experience. The incarnation is an act of love, freely engaged in, and antithetical to ordinance. It is an action for which there is no accounting. In fact, it is the action from which follow all accounts. If one chooses to, however, one could look through the wrong end of the telescope and see this splendid manifestation as a necessary stage in the emptying out of God into the world, a *kenosis* apparently evident by the existence of spirit.)

The argument for the eternal is now complete. The sign of the eternal is non-temporal action. Such action requires the relationship between cause and effect. At this point we need not be any more specific about what constitutes a cause or an effect. In other words, there is no need to define cause here other than in relationship to effect, and vice versa. I have provided a mathematical example from geometry that shows cause and effect. Furthermore, I have summarized the Kantian argument that the relationship of cause and effect supports the notion of time or, more precisely, temporal succession. The reality of cause and effect makes experience possible, and this we can determine merely by means of a careful investigation of experience itself.

This analysis of experience also supports the claim that there cannot be an endless succession of claims to priority between the permanent

---

27. Kant, *Critique of Pure Reason* B579–80.

and change. Superficially, the permanent presupposes change, and change presupposes permanence. But the latter presupposition, as was noted above, is the myopic view from hell. The apparent paradox is a chimera. Vacillation between permanence and change requires the underpinning of the concepts between which the argument takes place, the Kantian substrate.

No doubt some, not Heidegger, would say that thus far we have undertaken the easy part of the problem, i.e., the establishment of non-temporal action of cause and effect. What has not been shown, one might object, is the existence of time. Marilynne Robinson writes, "The eternal as an idea is much less preposterous than time, and this very fact should seize our attention."[28] In a way, the idea of time is a simple matter, since we can easily show that time does not *exist*, but this is playing with words, in particular using the word "exist" to mean "be in time." As many writers on the subject, including Augustine and Kant, note, if time were to exist in that way, then there would be infinitely many times, each existing within infinitely many times.

There are, of course, very many books and articles about time per se, various kinds of time, various understandings of time, various treatments of time, various denials of time. The introduction to Richard Sorabji's study may be taken as typical. "The central theme of this book is time. Is time real? Does it depend on consciousness? Could it exist without a universe full of change? Did the universe, or did time itself, have a beginning?"[29] A few pages later we read, "Of course, we know that time exists."[30] I shall not attempt to survey opinions on a subject that has seized the attention of many thinkers all over the world for as long as there have been thinkers. One can even read books with quasi-self-referential titles such as *The History of Time*. There are, however, some interpretations that are worth mentioning. In some cases these interpretations are quite common and often of practical use, although they do not stand up very well to scrutiny into the nature of time, what time really is. Some other interpretations, however, present aspects that shall be considered in more detail.

The word "temporal" is an adjective that refers to time. Omitted here are the various smart remarks and jokes regarding time, some of which are famously attributed to Augustine. They all amount to the same thing:

28. Robinson, "Psalm Eight," 243.
29. Sorabji, *Time, Creation*, 1.
30. Sorabji, *Time, Creation*, 7.

We think that we know what time is, but it is very difficult or impossible to put into words what we think that we know.

The most common understanding of time, one that is practical in much of our life, reveals itself in fact as an understanding of space. Space is the ultimate container to which is attached an immaterial clock. Paramount to this understanding, and perhaps to all understandings of time, is a notion of an *event*. (Events lurk in *Dasein*.) That is not to say *the* notion of an event, but *a* notion. An event is a material occurrence, and it *is* or *exists* solely in relationship to another material occurrence and in fact in relationship to all other events. As we just saw, events are possible according to the Kantian substrates of permanence and the relationship of cause and effect. The event entails a place, the location in the container where the event "occurs." By "occur" we usually mean that the event is related to other events in more ways than by relative place. The clock is that other way which relates the events to one another. Indeed, that is all that the clock does. It orders places or locations in the container, one to another as well as one to itself. Both the container and the clock are absolute in their information. There are of course many other assumptions about the container and the clock: that they measure things according to place and duration, that they have a seemingly continuous and perhaps infinite backdrop against which they make these measurements, and so forth. (Continuity and infinite expansion or infinite division are not absolutely necessary.) Material things (including force), then, *exist* somewhere in the container, i.e., they are located, and they have an identifying marker supplied by the clock. The marker is called "when" and often is further specified as "before," "simultaneous," or "after." This, supposedly, is all that the clock does; it puts a time stamp on each and every place, and in principle it does so one-dimensionally. Given three times no two of which are the same, the times are ordered by the clock in such a way that only one of the three is said to be between the other two.

Problematic exceptions immediately rush to mind. What about emotion? What about thought? Let us stick to the material or physical world for a moment, the world of particles and force fields, for we shall see that this pragmatic but rather dull understanding of time is both undermined and preserved by the theory of relativity and the development of spacetime.

In recent centuries, physicists have developed a mathematical representation of the container and clock, consisting of three spatial dimensions and one temporal dimension. The dimensions strictly speaking are mathematical in that they entail the notion of "between-ness," a notion which in some cases can be given a strict definition. For any three members or elements of a single dimension, if they are truly distinct, then in that dimension one and only one is between the other two. (Other possibilities could occur if dimensions circled back on themselves.) This is what was just assumed about the action or work of the clock. Between-ness, in fact, is synonymous with the notion of distinct. The spatial dimensions accord with our common sense of space and usually are described or represented by Cartesian coordinates, with the three axes conveniently but not necessarily established orthogonally to one another. These dimensions are interchangeable, which simply means that a mathematical representation of location is not altered by rotating the axes. A fourth dimension, time, is also often conceived as spatial, specifically as a straight line, continuous or not, but this dimension is absolutely distinct from the other three dimensions.[31] The "time" line in no way intersects the axes of the Cartesian co-ordinate system, although mathematically it intersects every point in three-dimensional space. No element or member of the time dimension is a member of one of the spatial dimensions, although they may have the same name. The time elements, however, *are* dimensional in that they are governed by between-ness. (Again, there may be alternatives in a cyclic theory of time.)

One of the remarkable results of the theory of special relativity, and later general relativity, is the inadequacy of this mathematical representation. Albert Einstein's discoveries and theories are rightly celebrated. Hermann Minkowski provided a fuller mathematical representation of the theories concerning special relativity. Most remarkable is to consider two of these four-dimensional systems in uniform translation or movement with respect to one another. (This consideration itself needs greater specification since it contains within it a conventional spatial disposition. For convenience, let the translation be along one of the spatial dimensions.) By representing these relative systems with the appropriate coordinates (numerical quaternaries), the spatial and temporal dimensions, when translated, infiltrate one another. In short, all four dimensions are

---

31. Even sophisticated attempts to represent combinations of different kinds of time, for example phase time and succession time—see below—depend upon spatial imagery. See Husserl's diagrammatic presentation that attempts, in two spatial dimensions, to display the combination or union of phase time and succession time. *Zur Phänomenologie des inneren Zeitbewusstseins*, 28; *Phenomenology of Internal Time-Consciousness*, 49. Both Ricoeur and Brann comment on Husserl's diagram. Ricoeur, *Time and Narrative* 3:28–30; and Brann, *What, Then, Is Time?*, 134–39.

placed on the same mathematical footing, with spatial considerations being a part of temporal expressions and vice versa. The result is spacetime, Minkowski's absolute world. In this world, there are regions in which the relationship of two events is uncertain with respect to time (and to space). One event might be the cause of another event, the effect, but under some interpretations the effect will "occur before" the cause.

Therefore, in the world of containers and clocks, the two cannot be kept separate. One might always have wanted to answer the question "What time is it?" with "Where?" Now, for mathematical physicists, one must. But matters are even worse than this. Along with the development of quantum mechanics came the theory of indeterminacy. One way of thinking about this is to consider a particle in motion with a velocity. (The velocity can be zero.) Werner Heisenberg's principle of uncertainty shows that the location of the particle and its momentum *cannot* both be known. The very measurement of one of these, location or momentum, has an effect on the other. Mere measurement influences the future of the particle. The particle has as part of its very being our understanding of it. One might say that we know more about the particle than we care to know.

Physicists have made various mathematical accommodations for general relativity and quantum mechanics, although it would seem that the two theories may be in conflict. The "block universe" of relativity treats all time, actually spacetime, as the same. This *is* Minkowski's absolute world. Accordingly, the spacetime of any particle is determined by the particle's world line. With quantum theory, the "future" of the particle is not determined.

Especially intriguing is the idea that mathematical physics errs in treating so-called *real* numbers as real, i.e., as truly signifying physical and material relationships. On the intuitionist assumption that only rational, finite numbers are truly real (at any given time), the indeterminacy of quantum theory can be represented or captured by the unfolding of finite numbers as measures of material being. But, as is the case with all such mathematical accounts, the unfolding presupposes a backdrop against which it takes place. In short, the accounts presuppose time, at least when interpreted, and they do so in order to give an account of time.

On the one hand, there is nothing wrong with presupposing the being of the thing being studied. Such is phenomenology. I did it above when I insisted upon using the adjectives eternal and temporal "merely" to refer to the things, eternity and time. On the other hand, it is absurdly tautological to use the being—I avoid the term "existence"—of a thing as an explanation for the being of the thing. One would do better to ask one's mother why he should obey her command.

Modern physics, of course, is not the only place to read and learn about time. There is a long and rich philosophical conversation in the West, stretching back at least to Plato and Aristotle and somewhat before, that attempts to make the case for time: specifically, to say what time is. Furthermore, there are seemingly countless other ways of attempting to express time, and these expressions vary according to place, according to, yes, time, and according to temperament. Poets may be of some help here, since all are trying to say something about something that truly is, or at least, what seems to be. Those who make no pretense to think without images, artists, and who may not even claim to *think*, are free to move directly to a representational mode of presentation.

From among the myriad books and articles on time, I have cited two recent studies, by Sorabji and by Ricoeur. Here I consider one more.

Eva Brann provides an enlightened, useful, and clear summary of major, Western philosophical accounts of time in her *What, Then, Is Time?* She begins with what she calls "External Time." This she and I shall eventually refer to as succession time. (A far more ominous description of it is forthcoming.) Under this heading she considers those who think of time as motion (Plato [moving heavens] and Einstein), and those who develop time from space (Hegel and Bergson). All of my discussion above of the physicists' accounts falls into the first classification: time as a clock. It is a kind of thinking about time to which Brann is not especially sympathetic. She calls it a fallacious notion,[32] and when she gives her own account of time, she prefers to derive succession time out of what she will call phase time.

It is not my intent to summarize Brann's work, but it should be noted now that this first kind of time is the time that later shall be treated as the alien. The alien is sin, our sin. This may result in my agreement with Brann, but only for the most odd of reasons.

> If time be sin,
> And sin be evil,
> And evil be nothing,
> What, Then, Is Time?
> This *is* the time that we suffer.

---

32 Brann, *What, Then, Is Time?*, 19.

Brann's second category is the "Counting Soul," where she groups Aristotle and Kant.[33] The Kantian notion of time is taken up below, but here note the fundamental role played by the soul in counting. We might say that time is within us, and further as rational, sentient beings created by God, we count. According to Plotinus, this ability to count is reflective of our ultimate origin, the One. Access to our immortal soul as *one* is by means of its relationship to the One. (But see below, the connection of Plotinus with the ground of time.)

Do we count using the natural or counting numbers? We understand in that realm the notion of successor. Proofs of mathematical induction rely on this understanding. Is this an order which, although known by the human mind, is independent of that mind, perhaps in such a way that time would form the foundation of counting? Richard Dedekind denies the possibility. "In speaking of arithmetic (algebra, analysis) as a part of logic I mean to imply that I consider the number-concept entirely independent of the notions of intuitions of space and time, that I consider it an immediate result from the laws of thought. . . . numbers are free creations of the human mind."[34] Thus for Dedekind, although we remain within the realm of human thinking, we are free from dependence upon time. Accordingly, we might find time to be an expression of our counting soul, and according to both Aristotle and Brann, the soul must originate time.[35] Brann, however, claims a difference between the numbers of arithmetic and those generated by counting, "psychic counting."[36] I understand the latter to be a radically myopic or constricted notion of successor. One produces another and no more, but of course, another is also one. Accordingly it produces another, and no more. And so forth. We shall see, eventually, that our so-called psychic counting is partly responsible for our fallen state, for our original sin.

Brann's third group contains the discussions of time by Plotinus and Heidegger. These are the philosophers who seek to ground time. For Plotinus, the One yields the Intellect, which in turn yields the Soul, and the Soul is identical with time. Time falls out of and is grounded in eternity.[37] Heidegger grounds time in *Dasein*, the human being who exists, i.e., who is somewhere. The human being is *being there*. This group or pair use an

---

33. Ricoeur agrees with this grouping. *Time and Narrative*, 3:58.
34. Dedekind, "Nature and Meaning of Numbers," 31.
35. Brann, *What, Then, Is Time?*, 46.
36. Brann, *What, Then, Is Time?*, 73.
37. Brann, *What, Then, Is Time?*, 97–98.

expression—fallen—that will play a crucial role in the development of my treatment of time.

The fourth and final group is called "The Stretching of the Mind." Here we find Augustine and Husserl.[38] It is with this group that Brann seems to find most sympathy. Augustine's distension of the mind (*distentio animi*) plays a crucial part in the argument for the primacy of phase-time.[39] Augustine's comments on the subject have been seminal for my own thinking. Key to his understanding is the present, or perhaps we should say the three presents: the past which is present to us in memory; the experiential present; and the future which is present to us, largely in hope, fear, and anticipation.

Let us return now to Kant in order to adopt an aspect of his understanding of time. Kant proposes to consider time in one of three ways: (1) subsistent and independent of things (Newtonian), perhaps the most common conception; (2) relational and inherent in things (Leibnizian), i.e., as things truly stand, in relationship to everything else; (3) as intuition, in particular *our* intuition of order or succession of appearances (Kantian), that which makes sequence possible.[40] The container with a clock, described above, is an example of the first kind of time, so-called absolute space and absolute time. I mentioned above that the disruption of this notion by relativity preserved in a way the thinking that underlies the classical or Newtonian conception. This is so because even with Minkowski's spacetime we are dealing with an absolute world, a world *in* which we are, i.e., a world in which we find ourselves. Events are primary and given for both Einstein and Minkowski. Kant, however, presents an alternative to the common understanding.

Neither space nor time is an empirical concept that has been abstracted from experience.[41] Instead of positing space and time as absolutes independent of us, Kant begins with our intuitions, i.e., our means of cognition. "All our intuition is nothing but the presentation of

---

38. The scholarly literature treating Augustine's conception of time, especially in book 11 of *Confessions*, is enormous. For example, Paige Hochschild adds a footnote to her comment that opinion is varied regarding Augustine's theory of time. The note cites more than twenty books and articles. *Memory in Augustine's Theological*, 157–58.

39. A subset of the voluminous literature on Augustine's notion of time is devoted to these two words, *distentio* and *animus*. For example, see: Dusen, *Space of Time*; Hochschild, *Memory in Augustine's Theological*; Nightingale, *Once out of Nature*; Wetzel, *Augustine and the Limits*, ch. 1; and of course Ricoeur.

40. Kant, *Critique of Pure Reason* B49–50.

41. Kant, *Critique of Pure Reason* B38, 46.

appearance.... What may be the case regarding objects in themselves and apart from all this receptivity of our sensibility remains to us entirely unknown."[42] For us to perceive simultaneity or succession, time must be present a priori in us.[43] "Time is not something that is self-subsistent.... Time is nothing but the form of inner sense."[44] Strictly speaking, "time is the formal *a priori* condition of all appearances generally."[45] Space, of course, is the name we give to our outer intuition. (The non-Euclidean geometers will attack Kant on this count, claiming that there is an outer reality into which the rational, sentient being is thrust, or born.) Therefore all appearances, and accordingly all knowledge about the appearances, depend upon our intuitions of space and time. Other beings may have another relationship to all that is, but we as human beings must begin with our intuitions. Surely "simultaneous" is one of the most presumptuous of all notions.

Above we saw a brief summary of Kant's argument regarding the permanent and cause and effect, that they are necessarily presupposed by experience. Experience in turn is an indisputable phenomenon. The connection of this to time is straightforward. The constituents of experience are events. Events entail, in part, time. Time then becomes the necessary organizing medium for all experience. Kant refers to it as inner intuition. This is the intuition that makes so-called phase time possible: past, present, future, or according to Augustine, present past, present present, and present future. This is the intuition that I refer to as our inner principle of organization, and it is in the face of this principle that succession time appears as an alien.

There are various pairings of terms for the complex temporal reality. For my purposes I have simplified and reduced the various terms to two used by Eva Brann (she uses more than two), i.e., phase time and succession time. These two characterizations are perceived, perhaps over simply, as inner and outer, or subjective and objective, or spiritual and physical. Ricoeur uses several terms for the former, such as psychological, phenomenological, and mortal. He tends to use cosmological in each pairing to designate the outer time. Heidegger has time of care and time of science, or being-toward death and world-time. Pelikan has continuity of memory

---

42. Kant, *Critique of Pure Reason* B59.
43. Kant, *Critique of Pure Reason* B46.
44. Kant, *Critique of Pure Reason* B49.
45. Kant, *Critique of Pure Reason* B50.

and continuity of self.[46] Nightingale prefers psychic time and earthly time, and describes Augustine as offering "a heterochronic theory of time."[47]

This confrontation between one and only one time expressed both as the foundation for all our cognition while also expressed as the alien under whom we suffer, endure, persevere, constitutes *the* evidence of our original sin. Augustine writes, "You are my eternal Father, but I am scattered in times whose order I do not understand."[48]

This is the case for both the eternal and the temporal, and it is a case limited to the understanding of a rational, sentient being, to a human being. As Kierkegaard notes, the human being is a synthesis of the two, eternal and temporal.[49] It now remains to develop notions of sin and culpability, the related notions of concupiscence and perseverance, to connect these notions to the fall of mankind, and to point, if possible, to the ultimate resolution and transformation of the fallen state in Jesus Christ by which the individual is fully integrated. For with Jesus Christ we have the ultimate elucidation of the fallen state.[50] Kierkegaard goes to great length to depict the life of Christ as a life of abasement. This is so because the life of Christ refers to the life of Jesus of Nazareth, a human life, a temporal life, and "temporality in its entirety was suffering and abasement" for Christ.[51] In other words, it remains to present in subsequent chapters the meaning and significance of the rational understanding of the eternal and the temporal.

In anticipation of the ultimate resolution, I observe that waiting will be critical to understanding the connection of sin to time. Brann quotes Richard Feynman on the subject, "time is what happens when nothing else happens, when we are just waiting."[52] Brann observes that this remark is tossed off nonchalantly, and that Feynman soon abandons any real inquiry into what time is in lieu of his real interest, i.e., speaking about how to measure time. Perhaps inadvertently, he has pointed to the very key, the reason why perseverance might be considered a virtue. Poetry is found in unusual places.

---

46. Pelikan, *Mystery of Continuity*, 26.
47. Nightingale, *Once out of Nature*, 56.
48. Augustine, *Confessions* XI.xxix.39.
49. Kierkegaard, *Sickness unto Death*, 13.
50. See also my comments on Karl Barth's "Doctrine of Reconciliation" at the beginning of my treatment of sin and culpability, in the next chapter.
51. Kierkegaard, *Practice in Christianity*, 182.
52. Brann, *What, Then, Is Time?*, 13.

3

Sin and Culpability

A SIN IS AN event. In the course of this study, I shall develop the notion that sin is *the* event, that man the sinner encounters time and does so sinfully, by way of his sin. Kierkegaard might object because he understands sin to continue. "Every state of sin is a new sin."[1] This line of thinking ultimately will be subsumed by the connection between original sin and time. For the continuance of un-repented sin is temporal extension; it is sin being itself. The "newness" of each un-repented sin is simply the sin itself. Now, however, the aim is to work on a definition of sin. More important than the definition per se, which could pose a danger by closing off questions, it is necessary to emphasize the work to be done. Ideally, one works with a definition, or perhaps, one works *on* a definition. One defines. One sets limits and then gets to work on that which has been delimited, working within the limits, pushing the limits, challenging them, leaping over the boundaries.

As a preliminary observation, I should also mention the line of argument developed by Karl Barth in his *Church Dogmatics* regarding sin.[2] This observation constitutes a digression from my argument. It amounts to getting off topic before ever getting on topic, but the digression is critically important. By indicating the path not taken, the path chosen will be more clearly disclosed.

1. Kierkegaard, *Sickness unto Death*, 105.
2. Barth, *Church Dogmatics*, 4/1:358–513.

Barth argues that one truly comes to know sin only by first considering original sin, the origin of sinfulness. And this origin can be understood fully only by inquiring into the fall of mankind. But most important, the fall of mankind is meaningful ultimately and solely through an understanding of its remedy, Jesus Christ. Thus, according to Barth, we never really begin to come to grips with our sinfulness until we first view the entire matter, by which is meant all human being, through the lens of salvation. We are obstructed from true understanding because of who we are. "Access to the knowledge that he is a sinner is lacking to man because he is a sinner."[3] Only by encountering himself through the divine judgment of Jesus Christ, the Son of God become man, does the human being see correctly who he really is. A true understanding of sin requires revelation.

Pascal and others have pointed in this direction, and one might reasonably conclude that this approach is truly logical, theological, and analytical. In short, assume the problem solved. Mankind is redeemed by Jesus Christ, the Son of God become man. Man is elected, and the human being is thereby justified. This is the price of redemption: that the creator become a creature, and not some enhanced god-man hybrid, but rather a truly hopeless human being, condemned to fear abandonment on the cross. "For our sake, he made him to be sin who knew no sin, so that in him we might become the righteousness of God" (2 Cor 5:21). By measuring the so-called descent, from God to man, we begin to come to a realization of our abysmal state.

Barth's treatment of the matter is well-developed, beautiful, powerfully persuasive, and extends further than previous claims which amount, in effect, to a cost-benefit analysis. Barth insists that any attempt to inquire into man's fallen state that does not begin and end with Jesus Christ is bound to fall short, and not by a small amount. Such attempts will completely miss the mark. They will fail because of their false premises and foundations. Such attempts begin with man, and from there they determine the state of disorder. The inquirer along these lines "may be aware of the problematic nature of his existence as man. But this does not mean even remotely that he is aware of his being as the man of sin, at odds with God and his neighbour and himself."[4] The knowledge of sin obtained in this way "will finally prove to be only a dramatised form of the

---

3. Barth, *Church Dogmatics*, 4/1:360–61.
4. Barth, *Church Dogmatics*, 4/1:360.

self-knowledge of man left to himself, and that in the confrontation there can be no knowledge of the real sin by which man is accused by God and of which he is guilty before him."[5] This kind of knowledge is inadequate.

Thus God judges man to be the man of sin and this judgment becomes clear to man only by his becoming aware of Jesus Christ. According to Kierkegaard, man sins before God.[6] All other knowledge of man's wayward state is "self-knowledge." We might even call it self-help knowledge, the knowledge of someone who truly believes that he can help himself if only he inquires deeply into his own being, seeking to "know thyself," if only he tries hard enough. Barth then goes on to ask, "But what if the knowledge of faith from Holy Scripture and knowledge in the form of immediate self-knowledge do not compete with one another? What if the true and basic form of all man's knowledge of the Law and sin is immediate self-knowledge?" Then man will be "easily satisfied with the hope and peace which we can have and know without the resurrection of Jesus Christ and the verdict of the Holy Spirit, except perhaps in a symbolical and illustrative form. He will then very quickly find himself in the sphere of a general philosophy of religion or life or existence." And accordingly, "sin takes on the appearance of something which is quite comfortable."[7] Such a person will in fact be rid of Jesus Christ, and rid of any need for transcendent remedy. If he cannot succeed in helping himself, perhaps he can find a therapist.

Barth's analysis provides not so much a solution than an elaboration of the persistent and unanswered question of Neoplatonism as expressed by Plotinus. Why does the One, by means of emanation, produce the Intellect, and in turn why does the Intellect produce the Soul? In short, why is there a fall to begin with, and how can the descent of the Soul ever be reversed? Hence Augustine can claim that in the books of the Platonists he had read much of the first chapter of the Gospel of John, of course in different words. But he did not read that the Word "came to his own and his own did not receive him; but as many as received him, to them he gave the power to become sons of God by believing in his name." Nor did he read, "the word was made flesh and dwelt among us."[8]

One might conclude at this point that Barth's argument is firmly and exclusively rooted in Holy Scripture. But even here, he warns that

5. Barth, *Church Dogmatics*, 4/1:387.
6. Kierkegaard, *Sickness unto Death*, 77, 87.
7. Barth, *Church Dogmatics*, 4/1:372–73.
8. Augustine, *Confessions* VII.ix.13–14.

scrupulous adherence to the text of the Bible may be misleading. Barth seems to take a supra-biblical position vis à vis sin and redemption. It is through the fact of Jesus Christ, the Son of God become man, that man learns what it means to be a sinner. Narrow and strict focus on the biblical text can and will obstruct the true significance of redemption. The Word of God is not equivalent with the words of the Bible.

Barth's position is archly Christocentric. Other writers who have strongly influenced me and my argument, such as Hans Urs von Balthasar, also put Jesus Christ at the beginning of all theological inquiry. In Jesus Christ, God is revealed as he is, at least to the extent that mankind can receive revelation. All discussion not only of sin but of all creation begins with Christ. I concur in principle but not in practice. As stated at the beginning, mine is a tale best told backward.

These remarks, however, are preliminary, and thus I have chosen not to follow Barth's logical, theological, analytical approach to the problem, because for all its merit and profundity the approach may be poor pedagogy. And if one is disposed to a sort of perverse Aristotelian analysis, one can form a conclusion that may be both true and unhelpful: Jesus Christ is the final cause of man the sinner, and *a fortiori* the final cause of the fall of man, of original sin, and of sin in general. Accordingly, I proceed "rationally" while fully acknowledging that this method is the hallmark of a sinner. And I aggravate the sin by noting that from my position the approach advocated by Barth looks like the easy way, even if it is unobtainable. Reduced to simplest terms, the argument is since Jesus Christ is the answer, why not skip to the answer to begin with, and then work backward? Perhaps some fortunate ones, not I, can start from their own salvation and integrity, and then proceed to know thyself. Despite the uplifting words of the Christocentric approach, it is I who shall have rhetoric as an ally.

These matters will be taken up at length in the sections on redemption and reintegration of the individual, but here we proceed more synthetically.

◆ ◆ ◆

The very notion of sin is attested widely in all kinds of writing. As was the case with time, the writing about sin is voluminous. Whereas the general philosophical appeal of sin vis à vis time may not be as great, this deficiency is more than compensated for in the field of self-help literature.[9] We shall consider the words from the Hebrew, Greek, and Latin Bibles that are translated by the English "sin." First, however, let us begin with Augustine's definition, a definition that Aquinas found worthy of extended treatment.

"Sin, then, is any transgression in deed, or word, or desire, of the eternal law."[10] This is the lawlessness (ἀνομία) of the First Letter of John (3:4), but "violation of the law" may express better Augustine's intent than "lawlessness." Although many of the words in the definition are worthy of scrutiny, the first aim must be to inquire about eternal law. Augustine continues, "And the eternal law is the divine order or will of God, which requires the preservation of natural order, and forbids the breach of it."[11]

The natural order in man, his disposition, consists of a body and a soul. Unlike beasts, the human being has a soul that includes reason. The soul therefore is naturally superior to the body, because reason is superior to the absence of reason. Reason in itself is good. Furthermore, reason has both a pure contemplative and a practical function. The highest object of contemplation is the beatific vision (Aquinas's term) and accordingly this use of reason is the highest function to which all other human activity ought to be directed and subject. The beatific vision is man's final cause, although this specific, Aristotelian term should not be attributed to Augustine.

Augustine then combines his notion of natural order, ordained by eternal law, with the actions of man. "A man, therefore, who acts in obedience to the faith which obeys God, restrains all mortal affections, and keeps them within the natural limit, regulating his desires so as to put the higher before the lower. If there was no pleasure in what is unlawful, no one would sin. To sin is to indulge this pleasure instead of restraining it. And by unlawful is meant what is forbidden by the law in which the order of nature is preserved."[12] A sinner, therefore, confuses greater and lesser goods by acting in such a way as to favor the lesser, and does so because there is some immediate or superficial pleasure in favoring the lower

---

9. Recent examples of the former include Taylor O'Neill, *Grace, Predestination, and the Permission of Sin*, and Thomas H. McCall, *Against God and Nature*.

10. "*Ergo peccatum est, factum vel dictum vel concupitum aliquid contra aeternam legem.*" Augustine, *Contra Faustum* XXII.27.

11. "*Lex vero aeterna est, ratio divina vel voluntas Dei, ordinem naturalem conservari iubens, perturbari vetans.*" Augustine, *Contra Faustum* XXII.27.

12. Augustine, *Contra Faustum* XXII.28.

desire. Augustine goes on to wonder if there are any rational creatures for whom all action contrary to eternal law would be unpleasant, and notes that certainly for man and for the fallen angels this is not the case. These angels "were so made, that they had the potentiality of restraining their desires from the unlawful; and in not doing this they sinned. Great, then, is the creature man, for he is restored by this potentiality, by which, if he had so chosen, he would not have fallen. And great is the Lord, and greatly to be praised, who created man." Neither beasts nor the righteous angels henceforth sin. "But man, whose life on this earth is a trial on account of sin, subdues to himself what he has in common with beasts, and subdues to God what he has in common with angels; till, when righteousness is perfected and immortality attained, he shall be raised from among beasts and ranked with angels."[13] Unlike man, the angels have made their bed for all time and must lie in it, in joy or misery as the case may be. We shall return to the state of angels, fallen and loyal, at the end of this section with a consideration of evil, and again in the chapter on the fall of mankind. Man, however, is in time and on trial. Faith is on trial at all times.

Aquinas takes up the matter of sin as violation of eternal law, and he provides an important elaboration regarding eternal law. All law is directed to the common good, but "eternal law is nothing else than the exemplar of divine wisdom, as directing all actions and movements."[14] Only God knows fully the eternal law, but rational creatures can know about the eternal law from how it is reflected in the natural world. They can detect orderliness in the created world. At this point, Aquinas cites Romans (1:20), "Ever since the creation of the world his invisible nature, namely, his eternal power and deity, has been clearly perceived in the things that have been made."[15] Creation itself is testimony to the power and godliness of the creator. (Christocentric theologians would be quick to note that the God being pointed to here by creation is the "God" of Aristotle.) All law, to the extent that it partakes of right reason, comes from eternal law. Rational creatures are subject to this law in two ways, by knowledge and by way of action and passion.[16] Thus the human being, simply by being a part of creation, participates in eternal law in the same way that a heavy object tends to move toward the center of the earth. But human beings are also capable of discerning the existence of eternal law

---

13. Augustine, *Contra Faustum* XXII.28.
14. Aquinas, *Summa theologica* I-II, Q.93, A.1.
15. Aquinas, *Summa theologica* I-II, Q.93, A.2.
16. Aquinas, *Summa theologica* I-II, Q.93, A.3, A.6.

as well as many of its precepts and manifestations. The reason for the order of creation, not simply the order itself, is seen by man, although perhaps only as in a mirror dimly. The sinful man is one who adheres only imperfectly to the eternal law in these two ways. His thoughts, words, and deeds vary from the truth.

One more elaboration or clarification is needed in order to establish a working definition, and that is regarding law itself. Aquinas writes, "Law is a rule and measure of acts, whereby man is induced to act or is restrained from acting."[17] We restrict our attention to human beings, leaving angels and other beings for later. "Now the rule and measure of human acts is the reason, which is the first principle of human acts . . . . For it belongs to the reason to direct to the end, which is the first principle in all matters of action."[18]

Thus according to Augustine and Aquinas, sin is a violation of the eternal law, which in turn is that divine directive which governs the whole world, both according to the very motions and actions of things and according to reason. Reason, in turn, is that faculty that enables certain of God's creation to know of, to understand sufficiently clearly, and therefore to be bound by eternal law. Thus "the wrath of God is revealed from heaven against all ungodliness and wickedness of men who by their wickedness suppress the truth. . . . So they are without excuse; for although they knew God they did not honor him as God or give thanks to him, but they became futile in their thinking and their senseless minds were darkened. Claiming to be wise, they became fools" (Rom 1:19-22). The obligation or binding here assumes the possibility of transgression. To some extent, the rational being is free, but the predicament of this being is estrangement. Subsequently I shall inquire into this estrangement as it is characterized by Augustine as concupiscence. Here, the inquiry and comments are more general. According to Paul Tillich, man's "estrangement is sin. It is not a state of things, like the laws of nature, but a matter of both personal freedom and universal destiny."[19] To transgress is to act, and thus "sin as an individual act actualizes the universal fact of estrangement."[20]

◆ ◆ ◆

17. Aquinas, *Summa theologica* I-II, Q.90, A.1.
18. Aquinas, *Summa theologica* I-II, Q.90, A.1.
19. Tillich, *Systematic Theology*, 2:46.
20. Tillich, *Systematic Theology*, 2:56.

It is hardly my intention to provide a history of writing and thought about sin. I do not even intend to give a brief and relatively even-handed summary of the subject. But it is incumbent upon me to attempt to say what sin is in order to develop the driving question of this entire investigation, and hence to have a working definition or at least a notion of sin.

With the notion of sin come the matters of occurrence, responsibility, freedom, culpability, and punishment, but these matters must be held in abeyance temporarily. Sin is our subject. Those words that are used, primarily in the Western biblical tradition, to express the condition or state of sin are set forth below.[21] By consulting a good dictionary or lexicon, one can read a great deal about each.

Hebrew	*chata* verb Strong #2398	to miss (the mark), to go wrong, to sin
	chet masculine noun Strong #2399	sin, guilt of sin
	chatta'ah feminine noun Strong #2403	sin, sin offering
Greek	ἁμαρτάνω verb Strong #264	to miss (the mark), to fail of doing, to go wrong
	ἁμαρτία feminine noun Strong #266	sin, guilt, sin offering
	ἁμάρτημα neuter noun Strong #265	sin, sinful deed
Latin	*peccatum* neuter noun	sin, moral offense
	sons masculine noun	criminal, guilty
Old English	synn	
Middle English	sinne	

The first appearance of the word sin in the Bible is in Genesis (4:6–7). Cain was disappointed because the Lord had shown respect for the offering of his brother, Abel, but not for his offering. The farmer Cain offered "the fruit of the ground," whereas the shepherd Abel offered "the firstlings of his flock and of their fat portions." The Lord counseled Cain, "Why are you angry, and why has your countenance fallen? If you do well, will you not be accepted? And if you do not do well, sin is couching at the door; its desire is for you, but you must master it." The phrase of particular interest is:

21. Several more terms, Hebrew and Greek, are describe by McCall, *Against God and Nature*, 34–39.

| *lappethach hattaat robets* | At the door sin makes its lair.[22] |

Sin is depicted as a predator or perhaps a lover who has a longing (*tshuwqah*) for Cain. Sin is simply sitting there, lurking. Where did it come from? Kierkegaard writes that sin presupposes itself. Sin came into the world by sin, and it did so in a leap.[23] What sin really presupposes is grace, but that is getting ahead of ourselves. Thus one thinks of sin as being substantial, perhaps an embodiment of evil. The many subsequent appearances in the Bible of various words to indicate sin make evident the connotation of guilt. The term occurs more than 1,600 times in the Hebrew and Greek Bible including the Apocrypha.

Sin is disorder of a specific kind, for sin is relational. Kierkegaard: sin before God. In this sense, sin really does presuppose grace and forgiveness; it presupposes a powerful judge, perhaps an authority who can pardon an offender. One can easily imagine many kinds of disorder and confusion that seem to be truly adventitious. Because of the external source of the disorder, assuming there is a source or cause, we do not sincerely identify a relationship between ourselves and the disordered state. We might curse fate or bemoan *our* misfortune, but in so doing usually we are expressing disappointment and frustration. We are not linking the cause of the disorder, e.g., fate, with ourselves. To attempt to do so would lead to a seemingly never-ending determination of material cause and effect. Quite to the contrary, we are solving the problem of responsibility, at least vis à vis ourselves, by breaking the relationship and removing ourselves from the causal chain.

In the case of sin, however, matters are different in that we explicitly make the connection between our thought, word, or deed and some other entity. For Augustine and Aquinas, that entity is eternal law, ordained by God, and known fully by him, but dimly by human beings. For some, the entity might be loosely and vaguely identified as God, and this is the God who judges. For others, the entity might be another expression for ourselves, an entity or rule that we call conscience. Drawing on the Hebrew verb, Karl Barth notes that in all sin there is loss, man "loses himself," for sin "seems to be that of 'missing'—of the right way."[24] Regardless of the judge, the judgment is the same. The sinner of his own doing has missed the mark. And missing the mark presupposes the mark in the first place,

22. Brown et al., *Brown-Driver-Briggs*, 918 s.v. *rabats*; Strong #7257.
23. Kierkegaard, *Concept of Anxiety*, 32.
24. Barth, *Church Dogmatics*, 4/1:406.

and "the mark has not been set up for the purpose of missing the aim."[25] Straying from the path of righteousness presupposes the existence of a path to begin with. There is eternal law, and we violate it. There is no disputing that the mark has been missed.

For most of us, for most of the time, the two kinds of disorder, adventitious and sinful, are kept distinct, at least in principle. On the one hand, when a storm wreaks havoc in our lives and damages our property, we become dismayed, perhaps even angry, but we think of ourselves as victims. On the other hand, the thief who thinks of himself as a thief knows that he is a sinner. Eventually these two kinds of disorder will be brought under a single heading, i.e., original sin.

At this point, however, the subject is sin in general, and not *original* sin. Sin is *the* disorder between the creator and the creature with apperception, i.e., the creature who meaningfully says "I." The act itself of saying "I," as an event, brings about the very disorder. Saying "I" is *the* event, that which qualifies us for all subsequent events. The act establishes a temporal relationship. The act is willful and hence blameworthy. The question remains, however, to what extent the act is made freely. It will be necessary to give an account of how and why the expression of oneself, the saying of "I," is related to the opening claim of this chapter: a sin is an event. For in a way, although this expression is essentially connected with time, it does not occur at some time in a person's life. The distinction will turn out to be one between sin and a sin. Our tendency to think categorically, perhaps according to genus and species, can obscure in the case of sin the activity, albeit in a way negative activity. These matters will be taken up principally in chapter 7. For the moment, however, we restrict our attention to the second kind of disorder, the kind brought about by thieves, adulterers, and liars. "But as for the cowardly, the faithless, the polluted, as for murderers, fornicators, sorcerers, idolaters, and all liars, their lot shall be in the lake that burns with fire and Sulphur, which is the second death" (Rev 21:8). The judge will exercise his authority and impose punishment on the offender.

Let the creator be he who creates all that there is. (I shall not dally with consideration of *ex nihilo*, with thinking about something from nothing. This very thought of nothing in fact presupposes something, and vice versa, as Heidegger argues.[26]) An account of disorder in the

---

25. Epictetus, *Enchiridion* 27.

26. Heidegger, *Introduction to Metaphysics*, 1. "Why are there beings at all instead of nothing?" I am not entirely persuaded that the thought of something presupposes

world, both adventitious and willful, must then address the relationship of the creator to the earthquakes, tsunamis, lies, and murders of our lives. Such an account may be difficult to provide, but it becomes only more so if one thinks or imagines that the creator is good. This problem is hardly new, and there are writings from all times and places that take up the matter of a good God connected with a world that seems to be filled with misfortune, cruelty, and deceit. This problem is the problem of evil, which Tillich characterizes as destruction.

> If one is asked how a loving and almighty God can permit evil, one cannot answer in the terms of the question as it was asked. One must first insist on an answer to the question How could he permit sin?—a question which is answered the moment it is asked. Not permitting sin would mean not permitting freedom; this would deny the very nature of man, his finite freedom. Only after this answer can one describe evil as the structure of self-destruction which is implicit in the nature of universal estrangement.[27]

Tillich's assertion will receive further scrutiny in chapter 8 on foreknowledge, predestination, and freedom, where we shall see that the claim for freedom is an intermediary one.

Augustine's "solution" to the problem is appealing. Identify all that truly is, all that is good, with God. God then becomes both all being and the only being. "[God] is called being (*essentia*) truly and properly in such a way that perhaps only God ought to be called being."[28] Tillich identifies essence with the eternal, and accordingly "the appearance of evil vanishes in the face of the eternal."[29] In the face of personal injury caused by another person, Augustine's assertion and Tillich's elaboration appear to be both un-consoling and preposterous.

Much is presupposed by the notion of sin, a notion which is distinct from vice and failure. Aquinas goes to some length to distinguish between vice and sin. In his mind, vice is a habit whereas sin is an individual thought, word, or deed. Vice is a way of life that is conducive to committing sins, but the virtuous person can sin in thought, word, or deed. Each sinful act is an event. And the vicious person need not live a

nothing. Permanence precedes change.

27. Tillich, *Systematic Theology*, 2:60–61.
28. Augustine, *On the Trinity* VII.5.10.
29. Tillich, *Systematic Theology*, 3:399.

life of continuous sinning, his disposition notwithstanding.[30] According to Kierkegaard, the opposite of sin is not virtue, but rather faith.[31] Virtue and vice are opposites.

To substitute the notion of failure for sin is undoubtedly cowardly and evasive. Yes, our lives are filled with failure. We often do not achieve what we set out to achieve, and in at least some cases, our will seems to be entirely set on achieving success. The failure comes about, then, because of something outside of our control, or so we claim. We fail to achieve x because we are unable to do y, and we are absolutely certain that under the present circumstances y is necessary and sufficient to cause x. We may be perfectly willing and desirous to do y, but its execution is beyond us. It would be quite unusual to refer to this failure as a sin. Such a characterization is not entirely out of the question once the theory of original sin as time has been fully developed. But the evasion occurs when we reverse the designations: when the thief calls his theft a failure. Even more evasive and irresponsible is to call the failure a mistake.

We all make mistakes, and we often attempt to mollify our bad feelings over failures by reminding ourselves of our limitations. We are fallible. We are finite. Why do we all make mistakes? As with failure, mistakes may be subsumed eventually under sin, but at this point the subject is sin in general. What mistake did the thief make? If the act was indeed theft, then the thief stole something. He saw an object that he believed to be another person's property, and he took it for his own enjoyment and with the intent or at least the knowledge that his action would deprive the other person of that person's enjoyment of the property, enjoyment that was proper to the other person *as* a person.

Certainly there are gray areas between sin and failure and between failure and mistakes. Individual thoughts, words, and deeds may fall into these areas. But the distinctions, in principle, are clear. Sins are not mistakes. That mistakes might be sins is the thrust of the entire argument of this book.

Disorder presupposes order, as is also the case with other privative notions such as atheism and God, non-being and being, change and permanence, and alas a-temporal and time. (This last presupposition depends solely upon sinfulness.) Sin presupposes grace and forgiveness. God's wrath is his love. The theological terms for the need to reestablish

---

30. Aquinas, *Summa theologica* I-II, Q.71, A.1.
31. Kierkegaard, *Sickness unto Death*, 82.

order are fraught with connotations of punishment and damnation: justification, righteousness, imputation. Disorder, strictly speaking, might be in need of correction. Justification, however, usually implies the correction of sin and error. Error, narrowly conceived, is in the realm of mistakes. We might say that someone by choosing a particular number in hopes of winning the lottery and having not won has made a mistake; he has erred in his choice of numbers. Is the person who has chosen incorrectly guilty of choosing the wrong number? Is he guilty of not being able to predict accurately the outcome of the lottery? At this point, one must say no, although ultimately it will be shown that he is indeed guilty.

The disorder that we seek in the realm of sin is willful disorder. Someone freely has chosen to commit a sin, to violate eternal law in thought, word, or deed. For that transgression, the person is blameworthy, and we do blame him. Kant would have us believe that our condemnation is rooted in reason. He cites the example of someone who tells a malicious lie and does so voluntarily. In investigating the circumstances leading up to the lie, we discover that the person had a bad upbringing, was subject to the bad influence of equally malicious acquaintances, and even had a wicked natural constitution. We further discover immediate circumstances that might have influenced the person to lie.

> But although we believe the action to be determined by these causes, we nevertheless blame the perpetrator. We blame him not because of his unfortunate natural makeup, nor because of the circumstances influencing him—indeed, not even because of his previous way of life. For we presuppose that we can set aside entirely how this way of life was, and that we can regard the bygone series of conditions as not having occurred, and can regard this deed as entirely unconditioned with respect to the previous state, as if the perpetrator starts with it a series of consequences completely on his own. The blame is based on a law of reason; and reason is regarded in this blaming as a cause that, regardless of all the mentioned empirical conditions, could and ought to have determined the person's conduct differently.... The action is imputed to the agent's intelligible character: now—at the instant when he is lying—the guilt is entirely his.[32]

This is Kant's analysis of blameworthiness. To clarify, the blame is based on reason and its orderliness, not on understanding. Understanding exists in the lawful world of appearances.

---

32. Kant, *Critique of Pure Reason* B582–83.

Whether or not we ground this blame in reason, as Kant does, the effect and significance is the same. There are those actions of thought, word, or deed which we deem blameworthy, and not just the action itself. We blame the individual, often ourselves, who performed the action. Here we might reasonably say that we blame the individual who committed the act. In these instances, we are not deterred in our condemnation by extenuating circumstances. These considerations may lessen the severity of our judgment, and in some cases such considerations may eliminate entirely any imputation of guilt or wrongdoing, but not in every case. For this very reason we refer to some of our lies as "white lies." If lying were truly blameless in the latter case, we would not refer to the lie at all.

In those instances where we determine that the actor deserves blame, we suppose that the individual acted freely, or at least sufficiently freely to deserve the amount of blame that we attribute to him. His culpability is directly proportional to the disorder of his action compounded with his freedom. He *could* have acted differently, and he *ought* to have acted differently. The individual is guilty. He is culpable (*culpa*, Latin, fault or blame). The mark has been missed. The individual has deviated from the path. Justice, or at least our sense of justice, has been disturbed, and justice demands that the wicked be punished. More precisely, our sense of justice impels us to want and to seek to reestablish the order or balance that is implied by the notion of justice itself. Sin consists in bringing about a state of imbalance willfully.

The very notion of sin entails an imbalance in need of correction. Eternal law has been violated, but eternal law is the ultimate directive regarding how things are and how they go or ought to go. And it is a *law*, which means that it is more than a tally of events past, present, and future. It is an account for those events. It is orderly, directive, and purposive. Therefore, at least according to Augustine and Aquinas, we creatures have a duty to try to conform to the law. We incur the obligation because we are rational beings. (We may incur many other obligations and responsibilities owing to revelation, but we postpone those concerns for now.) We ought to be law-abiding. In our physical actions and in our passions, we invariably do conform, but that is strictly in a material or physical sense of cause and effect, according to the Kantian law of appearances. To the extent that eternal law has been violated, our sense of justice demands justification, but alas, in the case of us sinners, we are largely at a loss as how to reestablish justice. The apostle Paul famously exclaims: "I do not understand my own actions. For I do not do what I want, but

I do the very thing I hate" (Rom 7:15). We are, however, at least dimly aware of eternal law, at least to the extent that we are sinners. To this limited extent, however, we here are the "self-help" sinners that Barth would exclude from serious and ultimate consideration. This law exerts its lawful force upon us because we are spiritual beings. As Kierkegaard notes, sin is "a qualification of spirit." But we are more than merely spiritual. We are creatures. Thus Kierkegaard writes that sin is "the intensification of despair" before God.[33] Moreover, admittance to Christianity "is only through the consciousness of sin."[34] In this claim, Kierkegaard explicitly moves beyond eternal law and into the realm of Christianity, and in this regard, the move is one of ultimate hope. That things have gone awry and that they are awry because of us are undeniable. Nevertheless, there is hope for complete justification.

At the very end of this study, I shall return to this matter, for it is the truth of Christian revelation that mankind is justified ultimately as well as initially. This is the action of Jesus Christ performed in the fullness of time. This is the action that reintegrates each individual and enables him to say "I" without sinning. The descent described by Plotinus from the One through the Intellect to the Soul is not merely corrected; it is fully absorbed in the correction and dissolved of its consequence. But here, the subject is simply sin. The disruption of balance, however, points to an important development in the understanding of original sin. In the next chapter on concupiscence and original justice, I shall present the thinking of various theologians, primarily Augustine and Anselm, that original sin left a permanent disorder in fallen man. The evidence for this, identified by Paul and Augustine as concupiscence, is transformed by Anselm into a loss of original justice.

The state of sin, therefore, simply and perhaps hubristically understood, is one of imbalance. The condition is one of fallen-ness, one of suffering, wherein the individual seeks to persevere endlessly. The individual undergoes this state; it is a passion. It seems to happen to him, but we shall see that fallen man also wills the passion. We shall see further, in the section on time as *original* sin, that this sinful state is one that the individual, with a corrupted nature, is incapable of rebalancing. More precisely, the individual is unable, even after achieving a momentary balance or re-justification, to preserve the readjusted state. Some may

33. Kierkegaard, *Sickness unto Death*, 81, 77.
34. Kierkegaard, *Practice in Christianity*, 67–68.

discern the influence of the Reformers Luther and Calvin in this assertion. As influential as they have been on my thinking, I maintain that similarities between our positions are somewhat coincidental.

The disordered state that we will, sin, deserves punishment. Hell is one name for this punishment, the ultimate state, or condition, or activity of punishment. Hell is intrinsically and deeply connected with our disorders, both with original sin and with so-called personal or subsequent sin, a connection that will be demonstrated in another section. The hellish conditions present us with an apparent paradox. It too in a way is in the fullness of time since it constitutes something like eternal temporality. Hell is waiting, and the waiting never ends. Perhaps paradoxically, eternal damnation does not await the damned, just as salvation does not await the saved. Hell and heaven are not future (or past) states. Our birth is in the past and our death is in the future, but not heaven or hell. These states, however, as one would expect, are antithetical. One is eternal and the other is temporal. With hell, the seeming paradox occurs between its inherent, temporal nature and its eternal being relative to us. Thus ultimate temporality is a-temporal; it is a life of perfect contradiction. The waiting, the looking to the future, never ends because it never advances, but it fails to advance fully in the context of advancement: desire without satisfaction. The person who always arrives early for appointments is eager to get a head start on eternal damnation. This person finds it unbearable to wait to start waiting.

By sinning, do we bring upon ourselves this ultimate sentence? Do we stand guilty before God, or before one another, or before ourselves, thereby condemned to suffer punishment? If so, should not we repent of our transgression of the eternal law? Should not we beg forgiveness from any and all whom we may have offended and from those who might be able to forgive us? This is exactly what a character in *The Brothers Karamazov* does. In a section entitled "The Russian Monk," we read about the Elder Zosima, an old monk at the end of his days. Zosima has been a spiritual advisor to Alyosha, whom the narrator refers to in the first sentence of the book as "my hero."

While lying on his deathbed, Zosima says that he has blessed Alyosha in his thoughts and tells him that he resembles his own brother Markel, not in appearance but spiritually.[35] Markel was some eight years older than Zosima and a self-avowed atheist. One Lenten season, when Markel

---

35. Dostoevsky, *Brothers Karamazov*, 285–86.

was about seventeen years old, he became seriously ill with consumption. To the amazement of his family, the boy suddenly started fasting and attending church. The doctor's prognosis, which turned out to be correct, was that Markel would live for only a few more weeks. Zosima, however, cites these final weeks of Markel's life as providing the ultimate direction for his own, a life which was widely but not universally recognized as holy and devoted to prayer, discernment, and spiritual guidance.

During his final days, Markel's disposition was transformed from his former feisty and irreverent self to one of total confession in which he embraced all of God's good creation. The doctor claimed that the boy had fallen into madness. Markel, however, sought to console his mother. "Mama, do not weep, life is paradise, and we are all in paradise, but we do not want to know it, and if we did want to know it, tomorrow there would be paradise the world over."[36] He continued that "we must all serve each other . . . . And I shall also tell you, dear mother, that each of us is guilty in everything before everyone, and I most of all. . . . Each of us is guilty before everyone, for everyone and everything. I do not know how to explain it to you, but I feel it so strongly that it pains me. And how could we have lived before, getting angry, and not knowing anything?"[37] Having acknowledged his guilt, and indeed universal guilt, Markel sought forgiveness from all of God's creation. Lying in his bed and looking out at the garden where the birds were chattering, he spoke:

> Birds of God, joyful birds, you, too, must forgive me, because I have also sinned before you. . . . Yes, there was so much of God's glory around me: birds, trees, meadows, sky, and I alone lived in shame, I alone dishonored everything, and did not notice the beauty and glory of it at all. . . . Dear mother, my joy, I am weeping from gladness, not from grief; I want to be guilty before them, only I cannot explain it to you, for I do not even know how to love them. Let me be sinful before everyone, but so that everyone will forgive me, and that is paradise. Am I not in paradise now.[38]

In so saying, Markel echoes the words of the apostle Paul. "We know that the whole creation has been groaning in travail until now; and not only the creation, but we ourselves, who have the first fruits of the Spirit, groan

---

36. Dostoevsky, *Brothers Karamazov*, 288.
37. Dostoevsky, *Brothers Karamazov*, 289.
38. Dostoevsky, *Brothers Karamazov*, 289–90.

inwardly as we wait for adoption as sons, the redemption of our bodies" (Rom 8:22–23).

Markel understands his offense to be against all of creation, and he seeks forgiveness from all of creation. This is what Kierkegaard understood about anxiety, that it brought up "the individuality to providence," for anxiety discovers guilt. "Whoever learns to know his guilt only by analogy to judgments of the police court and the supreme court never really understands that he is guilty, for if a man is guilty, he is infinitely guilty."[39] Kierkegaard has dispensed with self-help guilt and replaced it with true guilt, guilt before God.

We have here the fundamental ingredients of all sin. An individual with both the knowledge and the capability to adhere to eternal law willfully transgresses that law. The transgression, the sin in the mind of the sinner, is deemed blameworthy, culpable, and deserving of punishment at least in so far as punishment is corrective according to eternal law. Most important, there is a need to reestablish balance, justice, and that need is recognized by the individual who has committed the sin. In a sense, the reestablishment of justice takes precedence over the efficacy of corrective punishment. To return to a just or balanced state, the individual must receive forgiveness from all whom he has offended. Specifically the individual needs to be forgiven by God, who is all being, and hence the individual requests forgiveness from all creation, that is, from all that truly is, for his sin has been an offense against all that truly is, all that accords with eternal law.

This is the state with sin in general. All sin is offense against eternal law, which is the directive for all that is. Accordingly all sin entails universal imbalance and is universally culpable. Sin, as so understood and as described thus far, is often referred to by theologians as personal sin. Critical to this designation is the willfulness of the thought, word, or deed that proved to be offensive. Kierkegaard notes that "sin is not a negation but a position."[40] And willfulness indicates the possibility that things might have been otherwise. The sinner had a choice and, to the extent that he is culpable, he *freely* exercised the choice to offend. Furthermore, the sinner inevitably remains resolute in his choice. Kierkegaard is arguing against the Platonic notion that sin is really error, a misunderstanding.

---

39. Kierkegaard, *Concept of Anxiety*, 161.
40. Kierkegaard, *Sickness unto Death*, 96.

What remains to be considered in this study, but not in this chapter, is in what way so-called original sin might be sin at all. The willful choice to offend eternal law must be found in each and every fallen creature, if there be any such fallen creature, and the punishment exacted against each and every fallen creature must be accounted for. That there is disorder in the world, at least from an emotional perspective, is undeniable. This is so not merely because of the destruction and damage caused by natural events such as hurricanes and earthquakes. Nor is it necessarily because of similar destruction and damage caused by war, famine, and neglect. Nor is it solely because of the injury that we inflict upon one another and upon ourselves because of our cruel and hateful actions. The indisputable disorder is lodged in our souls. We understand the tsunami to be destructive and disruptive. We understand the carnage of war to be horrible. We feel guilty for the harm we cause to other people, for our injurious ways. We, it turns out, are the true barometer of worldly disorder. Even if we narrow our concerns strictly to our own uncertainty, our own capacity to doubt, our own absence of grounding, therein we find evidence of something less than orderly. With a suitable interpretation, still to be made, therein we shall find evidence of sin. In a non-Christocentric sense, revelation, the Bible, only seems to confirm something that we know already and know very well.

Let me make explicit that this is the evidence of conscience. We stand accused of sin directly before ourselves, and this comes about because we ourselves make the accusation. Some may account for the accusation in greater detail than others. Some, like Kant, may base the accusation in contradiction, acting against the categorical imperative and thereby offending reason. Others arrive at the same state, the same condition, by a route less clearly delineated. Regardless of the path acknowledged, this sad condition is decidedly not the woeful state of sin to which I referred at the beginning of this chapter. Knowledge of that state of sin comes about through revelation. We must be told about the divine judgment, the unique act of love wherein the creator becomes the creature, the purpose being to reorder creation, to expiate all sin. No, that is the sin of Christians. It is true that I have had that sin in mind all along, and it is true that the sin of the judgment and of revelation is the sin for which we have been absolved. But the sin primarily explored in this chapter is the sin contrary to eternal law, the sin identified by Augustine. This is the sin that Anselm and Aquinas elucidate. This is the sin of Romans 1:20, the sin that we all must acknowledge.

Are these two sins possibly different? Of course not. There is but one man, the sinner, but we come to know this man in various ways. As mentioned earlier, there are rhetorical and pedagogic advantages to beginning with the knowledge that is immediately accessible to reason and to reason alone. I persist in telling my tale backward. It is the only way it makes sense.

To conclude, let us return to the subject of evil. In Genesis, we read about a terrible indictment of humankind. "The LORD saw that the wickedness of man was great in the earth, and that every imagination of the thoughts of his heart was only evil continually. And the LORD was sorry that he had made man on the earth, and it grieved him to his heart" (Gen 6:5–6). In response to this observation, the LORD flooded the earth and wiped out all animals, beasts, birds, and insects. Only Noah and those living and breathing creatures that were with him in the ark survived. When the waters ebbed, Noah went out, built an altar, and sacrificed to the LORD a sacrifice that was pleasing to the LORD, who said to himself, "I will never again curse the ground because of man, for the imagination of man's heart is evil from his youth; neither will I ever again destroy every living creature as I have done" (Gen 8:21).

We learn from these remarks that even though Noah found favor with the LORD, mankind is fundamentally unchanged by the flood. His heart remains evil continually and from his youth. The two words and phrase involved are these.

yetzer masculine noun	form, framing, purpose, imagination	Strong #3336
ra' adjective, masculine noun	bad, evil	Strong #7451
yetzer hara	evil inclination	

This inclination is the source of much Jewish and Christian theological commentary, especially concerning its possible connection to original sin. The evil inclination is not necessarily sinful. We shall see that Augustine's adoption of concupiscence is also, in the minds of some, not necessarily sinful, although it is fundamental to the state of fallen mankind. Calvin and Luther, in turn, will carry Augustine's concupiscence to a kind of completion by determining it to be sinful and necessarily so. At this stage, I do not mean to equate the evil inclination of Gen 6:5 and 8:21 with the sin that is lurking desirously by Cain's door (Gen 4:7). And it will take yet another step to link the carnal desire that is developed by Paul and Augustine to man's imagination.

The beast at Cain's door seems to be substantial. One might give a Manichaean interpretation to this substance, thereby identifying an evil entity, one that is in conflict with the good. Augustine certainly was enthralled by this notion, and he wrote extensively in ultimate repudiation of the idea of substantial evil. But if man is inclined in his heart, surely we want to know toward what he is inclined. Is there some thing, a pole to indicate the direction of this inclination? If man exists in a moral and ethical force field, we want to know about the center of force and its nature.

Augustine famously dispenses with the entire problem by equating evil, and now we must say so-called evil, with nothing, with non-being. In a world, God's creation, where to be is to be good, the opposite of good is *not* something, for the opposite of the good is nothing at all. Indeed, one is careless with words by concatenating "opposite" with "good," because the combination is inherently a contradiction. There is no thing referred to when we say "the opposite of good," and we further confuse the matter by assigning a name, "evil," to that which is not. Sinfulness is required to come up with an expression such as "the opposite of good."

Such a claim must come as a surprise to all of us, at least in terms of our everyday conversation and practical thinking. To those of us who suffer, i.e., to all of us, the claim even seems offensive because it apparently reduces our trials and agony to be about nothing at all. And what about the devil? What are we going to do with him? Many theologians, notably including Augustine, have written about the reality of the devil.

Treatment of this matter belongs properly in a forthcoming section on the fall and on the connection of time with sin, but it is worth noting here that there is a traditional theological understanding that the angels who rebelled against God have been fixed in their rebellion. The good angels are equally fixed in their loyalty. The devil, therefore, seems to partake of both sin and evil, for in turning against God he has sinned. But in remaining permanent in his opposition, he assumes the character of evil, or so it seems. It is as if choice of both the fallen angels and the loyal angels has had the effect of annihilating time, at least for themselves. Their actions, from our perspective, have the quality of endurance and permanence. From their perspective, however, their decision is truly irrevocable. Their wills are fixed, and the wills of the fallen angels are fixed on nothing. They turn continuously toward that which is not. They turn continuously away from all that is.

It has not been my intention to write a treatise on evil, and now I have rushed ahead to the association of time with sin. My purpose here has been to distinguish between sin and evil or so-called evil. Even if evil were substantial, it would not be sin, for sin is an occurrence, an event. Evil is not an event. It remains to be seen if time is evil.

When we describe an act as evil, what we mean to say is that someone has committed a sin.

According to Jaroslav Pelikan, Augustine comes close to equating time with evil. "There are passages in Augustine in which he does seem to have been at the point of equating transiency and sin, and therefore time and evil." Pelikan cites *Confessions* VII.v.7, where Augustine searches for the origin of evil, but claims that Augustine "was rescued from drawing the potential consequences of his view of time and transiency by his hostility to the Manichean heresy."[41] Further association of time and evil can be found in *On the Trinity*. In drawing the distinction between wisdom and knowledge (*sapientia* and *scientia*), Augustine notes that Job referred to the abstinence from evil things as knowledge, "because it is in terms of time that we are in the midst of evils."[42]

---

41. Pelikan, *Mystery of Continuity*, 30–31.

42. Augustine, *On the Trinity* XII.14.22. "*Quoniam secundum tempus in malis sumus.*" Augustine, *De Trinitate* XII.14.22.

4

Concupiscence and Original Justice

THAT THE HUMAN BEING taken in entirety is fallible and finite is indisputable. To what extent these limitations and flaws are proper to the human being is the subject of this chapter. If there is a human nature, how are we to think of it in the abstract, and how do we compare this abstraction to the individual human beings of our lives, to ourselves?

In his presentation and development of the notion of original sin, Augustine emphasizes the word *concupiscentia* as it appears in Latin translations of the letters of the apostle Paul. The purpose in taking up the matter of this expression, and its subsequent modification and extension by Anselm and Aquinas, is to see how it relates to our central inquiry regarding original sin and time. There is an important affinity between these old expressions and the interpretation of sin being developed, important but perhaps limited. The purposes here are not to provide a broad etymological summary of the use of *concupiscentia*, much less an exhaustive review of the doctrine of original sin and its historical reception. There exists much scholarly writing on the subject.

The matter of the fall itself, the origin of original sin, will be treated in later chapters. It may seem that the logical sequence has been inverted. It may seem that I have chosen to deal with the effect without dealing with the cause. In a way, this is correct. The intent is to extend the inquiry into sin and culpability from the last chapter, to consider evidence of mankind's so-called sinful nature. Of course, one might deny this characterization of human nature. One might deny that man is a sinner, is *the* sinner, abundant evidence to the contrary. One might object to the nomenclature—sin, fallen, redemption—while assenting to the condition described, but not in so many words. One might even deny human nature itself, preferring to believe in a continuous array of life forms. In a dramatic expansion of Darwin's argument regarding the origin of species, one might deny all lines of demarcation within the kingdom of life, and thus discover toward one extreme an especially plastic concentration called "man." Traveling along this path, one might work through the writings of Nietzsche and arrive at the existentialist works of the twentieth century. As misdirected as the path may be, there are many intriguing and provocative suggestions along the way, not the least of which is transcendence in lieu of immanence (Kierkegaard, and then de Beauvoir, *The Second Sex*).

Rather than argue any of these points, I simply assume as manifest that man is a sinner, although as of yet I have not adopted the extreme position of Karl Barth, specifically looking to the remedy, the judgment and condemnation of mankind that is entailed in the supreme act of love, in order to understand the sin. The procedure has been rational, i.e., thus far I have explicitly placed faith primarily in reason. The approach here, however, is similar to Barth's in the following respect. I am proceeding analytically to the extent that I propose to study the symptoms in an effort to learn about the disease, holding in abeyance the screams from those who claim that although the patient is dying at an early age he has no disease. In this chapter, rather than constructing a synthetic argument that leads to original sin, I presuppose its existence. These methodological concerns, however, do not exclude the need to inquire into the characteristics of the sinful man, at least those delineated by great thinkers who have deemed mankind to be fallen. Hence the concern with concupiscence.

Regarding the word, in general there has been no attempt to determine exactly which Latin version of the Bible Augustine had before him when making various comments on concupiscence and original sin. He was familiar with the ongoing work of his contemporary Jerome in translating nearly the entire Bible into Latin, a version now known as the Vulgate and widely adopted by the Western church. But Augustine's access to the manuscripts of the so-called Vetus Latina, predating the Vulgate, is a scholarly, historical matter outside the scope of these considerations.

There is one case, identified below, where it seems likely that Augustine's text pertinent to this inquiry differed from Jerome's.

We must, however, locate the term sufficiently precisely to understand better how it informs the notion of original sin. Furthermore, it is this term along with its modified understanding as the lack of original justice that has established the framework for varying Christian interpretations of original sin itself. After the expansion and modification of Anselm and Aquinas, Luther and Calvin reaffirm the significance of *concupiscentia* itself, and the interpretation of the latter theologians becomes a critical element in the doctrinal division between Protestants and Catholics in the sixteenth century, so much so that the Council of Treat explicitly rejected the understanding of the term as put forth by Luther and Calvin. Even some authors such as Kierkegaard, who do not necessarily fit simply and neatly into the Catholic-Protestant division, recognize the fundamental role played by concupiscence in conceiving of original sin. Kierkegaard replaces concupiscence with sensuousness, which "is not sinfulness, but since sin was posited and continues to be posited, it makes sensuousness sinfulness."[1] Kierkegaard essentially is following the same method as the one employed here. For Paul Tillich, along with unbelief and hubris, concupiscence is a mark of estrangement, "the unlimited desire to draw the whole of reality into one's self," to reach unlimited abundance.[2] Tillich sees as symbols of concupiscence Kierkegaard's treatment of Nero and Don Giovanni, Goethe's Faust, Freud's notion of libido, and Nietzsche's "will to power."[3]

Of course, there are more interpretations than those of the Reformers and of Roman Catholics. The Orthodox Church has its own take on the significance of the episode in the garden, the fall. Even more generally, Jews and Christians are not in agreement regarding the significance, i.e., the meaning of the disobedience of Adam and Eve. I touched on this matter in my comments on the evil inclination mentioned in Genesis (6:5, 8:21),[4] and shall return to it when considering the fall per se. It is not the aim here, or anywhere in this study, to attempt directly to adjudicate among these various positions. I wish simply to ground our consideration of concupiscence and justice in the writings and thinking of those theologians who have introduced and employed these words in

1. Kierkegaard, *Concept of Anxiety*, 76.
2. Tillich, *Systematic Theology*, 1:47, 52.
3. Tillich, *Systematic Theology*, 2:52–55.
4. Ch. 3.

connection with original sin, i.e., in the thinking of those who recognize the sinfulness of mankind and who accordingly seek to analyze this state.

Throughout his life, Augustine developed the expression of his theory of original sin. From the fairly late work *On Marriage and Concupiscence* one can read a succinct statement connecting original sin to concupiscence. "Our purpose . . . is to distinguish between the evil of carnal concupiscence from which man who is born therefrom contracts original sin, and the good of marriage. For there would have been none of this shame-producing concupiscence, which is impudently praised by impudent men, if man had not previously sinned."[5] Augustine explicitly connects his thought about concupiscence to Paul. Augustine continues, "But if, in like manner, the question be asked of the concupiscence of the flesh, how it is that acts now bring shame which once were free from shame, will not her answer be, that she only began to have existence in men's members after sin? And, therefore, that the apostle designated her influence as the law of sin [Rom 7:23], inasmuch as she subjugated man to herself when he was unwilling to remain subject to his God."[6] For example, how are we to understand sexual attraction, stimulation, and pleasure? To be explicit and blunt, what is the difference between orgasms among married couples and fornicators?

Especially pertinent are Augustine's comments regarding chapters 6 and 7 of Romans, where he addresses the transmission of concupiscence. This "law of sin" which righteousness forbids us to obey and "which is cleansed only by the sacrament of regeneration, does undoubtedly, by means of natural birth, pass on the bond of sin to a man's posterity, unless they are themselves loosed from it by regeneration."[7] The thinking here, at least in part, is that if concupiscence is truly a characteristic of man and furthermore is evidence of the fall and its consequential sin, then this state is in a way passed on from human to human naturally.

Subsequently, Augustine writes:

> Let not sin therefore reign in your mortal body, that you should obey the lusts thereof [Rom 6:12]. [Paul] does not say, that you should have the lusts thereof, but that you should obey the lusts thereof; in order that (as these desires are greater or less in different individuals, according as each shall have progressed in the renewal of the inner man) we may maintain the fight of holiness

---

5. Augustine, *On Marriage and Concupiscence* I.i.1.
6. Augustine, *On Marriage and Concupiscence* I.xxi–xxii.24.
7. Augustine, *On Marriage and Concupiscence* I.xxiii.25.

and chastity, for the purpose of withholding obedience to these lusts. Nevertheless, our wish ought to be nothing less than the nonexistence of these very desires, even if the accomplishment of such a wish be not possible in the body of this death. This is the reason why the same apostle, in another passage, addressing us as if in his own person, gives us this instruction: For what I would, says he, that do I not; but what I hate, that do I [Rom 7:15]. In a word, I covet. For he was unwilling to do this, that he might be perfect on every side. If, then, I do that which I would not, he goes on to say, I consent unto the law that it is good [Rom 7:16]. Because the law, too, wills not that which I also would not. For it wills not that I should have concupiscence, for it says, You shall not covet; and I am no less unwilling to cherish so evil a desire. In this, therefore, there is complete accord between the will of the law and my own will. But because he was unwilling to covet, and yet did covet, and for all that did not by any means obey this concupiscence so as to yield assent to it, he immediately adds these words: Now, then, it is no more I that do it, but sin that dwells in me [Rom 7:17].[8]

Note that this is not quite the clarification that it appears to be in English since Augustine's Latin for concupiscence and for coveting is the same word, *concupiscio*.

Augustine is trying to locate or quantify the tipping point in the apostle Paul where evidence of original sin becomes explicit, contemporary sin. The desire that concupiscence gives evidence for is present in each of us, and although the evidence may be a sure sign of an original failure, a fallen-ness, the desire in itself as manifest in the apostle is not the sin, at least not according to Augustine and to most interpretations. The extent of the desire that results in covetousness, that in a sense goes too far, constitutes sin. Desire itself contains an aspect of expectation, a condition of waiting. And waiting is the sure sign of mankind's fallen state and original sin, for it is in waiting that we become aware of the connection of our sin with time itself. In other words, Augustine's notion of concupiscence, in its most rarefied and fundamental sense, is precisely the mark of original sin, but such is my interpretation and does not seem to be explicitly what Augustine had in mind.

In another place, Augustine elaborates on his understanding of fleshly desire, at least as it appears in Paul's letter to the Galatians.

---

8. Augustine, *On Marriage and Concupiscence* I.xxvii.30.

> It is certainly true and trustworthy as can be, the text that runs: *The flesh lusts against the spirit and the spirit against the flesh* [Gal 5:17]; but still everyone, I think, would agree, educated and uneducated, that the flesh cannot lust after anything without the soul. And thus the cause of fleshly lust is not to be found in the soul alone, but much less in the flesh alone. It arises, after all, from both; from the soul, that is, because without it no enjoyment can be felt, and from the flesh because without it there cannot be felt any specifically fleshly enjoyment. And so what the apostle is calling flesh lusting against spirit is undoubtedly fleshly enjoyment, which the spirit has from the flesh and with the flesh, lusting against the enjoyment which the spirit has alone. The sort it has alone, if I am not mistaken, is that kind of desire, unmixed with the pleasure of the flesh or with a passion for fleshly things, with which *the soul is longing and fainting for the courts of the Lord* [Ps 84:2]. Alone it also has that about which it is told: *You have lusted after Wisdom; keep the commandments, and the Lord will grant her to you* [Sir 1:26].[9]

Thus the two "lusts," flesh against spirit and spirit against flesh, according to Augustine, are not strictly symmetrical. In order for the flesh to desire in a "fleshly" way requires a soul, requires spirit, to experience and perhaps act on the desire. The spirit or soul, on the other hand, has no need of the flesh in its desire for the wisdom of the Lord. The desire in this latter sense is non-corporeal not only in its end but also in its substance.

Augustine is well aware that Paul has a broad notion of "flesh," indicated by the famous list of works of the flesh in this passage from Galatians (see below). Thus Augustine writes, "The phrase *the flesh is lusting*, you see, means that the soul is doing that in its wake, and here the word 'flesh' is being used in much the same way as one talks about the ears hearing and the eyes seeing; can anybody, I mean to say, be unaware that it is rather the soul which hears with the ears and sees with the eyes?"[10] Aquinas agrees: "The soul is the subject of original sin, and not the flesh."[11] We might go so far as to say that the flesh is always and everywhere entirely obedient to eternal law. It is the human being, rational and sentient, who acts against God's law.

The connection that Augustine and Aquinas make from the flesh to the soul is apt in the sense that sinfulness seems to reside principally and

---

9. Augustine, *Literal Meaning of Genesis* X.12.20.
10. Augustine, *Literal Meaning of Genesis* X.12.21.
11. Aquinas, *Summa theologica* I-II, Q.83, A.1.

perhaps entirely within the domain of the soul and the spirit. The flesh itself is an instrument or medium by means of which the soul lusts. It takes the imagination of an animist to ascribe merit and blame solely to material. These remarks by Paul, Augustine, and Aquinas, however, point to the never-ending source of wonder that we call the flesh, a wonder that pertains to the origin and purpose of the material world.

With this much in place, let us turn to the word in Romans that Augustine has in mind. The Latin *concupiscentia* is a translation of the Greek ἐπιθυμία. According to Strong's *Concordance* (#1939), ἐπιθυμία appears thirty-eight times in the New Testament (excluding the Apocrypha), nineteen of which occur in Paul's letters. Its most common meanings are desire, yearning, longing; and of course the noun has a verbal form. The Greek word evidently is a combination of θυμός with the prefix ἐπι-. θυμός is widely commented upon, especially in philosophical literature. The most common meanings given are soul, breath, life, heart, spirit, courage. An especially popular translation is *spiritedness*. ἐπι- is a ubiquitous prefix with many meanings, common among which are on, upon, to, over. Thus *desire* is an unremarkable signification for the combination of *on* with *spirit(ed)*.

Concupiscentia is the substantive form of the verb *concupisco*, which means to desire strongly, to covet, to aim at. Here we have the prefix *con* (with) attached to *cupisco*, to wish or desire. The latter verb is formed from *cupido* (Cupid), the Latin counterpart to the Greek god of desire, Eros.

The biblical contexts in which ἐπιθυμία appears support a variety of translations, including concupiscence, covetousness, desire, lust, and passion. Some uses of ἐπιθυμία signify no special desire other than *want* and do not pertain to Augustine's interpretation, at least as regards the flesh. The pertinent appearances occur largely, but not entirely, in the letters of Paul, and the Vulgate most often translates the word as *concupiscentia*, but at times as *desiderium*. Here we consider only those appearances that inform and at least agree with Augustine's interpretation.

Regarding those men who knew about God from his creation but failed to give him honor, Paul writes, "Therefore God gave them up in the lusts [ἐπιθυμίαις] of their hearts to impurity, to the dishonoring of their bodies among themselves, because they exchanged the truth about God for a lie and worshiped and served the creature rather than the creator, who is blessed for ever! Amen" (Rom 1:24–25).

Jesus Christ died to overcome sin, and so "Let not sin therefore reign in your mortal bodies, to make you obey their passions [ἐπιθυμίαις]. Do not yield your members to sin as instruments of wickedness, but yield yourselves to God as men who have been brought from death to life, and your members to God as instruments of righteousness" (Rom 6:12–13).

To the extent that the law specifies and delineates sin, it has been conducive to a certain kind of sin. "What then shall we say? That the law is sin? By no means! Yet, if it had not been for the law, I should not have known sin. I should not have known what it is to covet if the law had not said, 'You shall not covet' [Οὐκ ἐπιθυμήσεις]. But sin, finding opportunity in the commandment, wrought in me all kinds of covetousness [ἐπιθυμίαν]. Apart from the law sin lies dead" (Rom 7:7–8).

There is also the critical Pauline passage that Augustine cites in *Confessions* regarding his conversion, that in which the voice told him to take up and read in Romans (13:12–14). "Let us then cast off the works of darkness and put on the armor of light; let us conduct ourselves becomingly as in the day, not in reveling and drunkenness, not in debauchery and licentiousness, not in quarreling and jealousy. But put on the Lord Jesus Christ, and make no provision for the flesh, to gratify its desires [ἐπιθυμίαις]." The Vulgate does not translate ἐπιθυμίαις here as *concupiscentiis*, but rather as *desideriis*, but there is reason to believe that Augustine's version of the Bible may have had the former term. Elsewhere he makes the following passing remark about this passage. "Let us walk honestly, as in the day; not in rioting and drunkenness, not in chambering and wantonness, not in strife and envying: but put ye on the Lord Jesus Christ, and make not provision for the flesh, to fulfill the lusts thereof [Rom 13:12–14]. Now if the passage were translated thus, *et carnis providentiam ne in concupiscentiis feceritis*, the ear would no doubt be gratified with a more harmonious ending; but our translator, with more strictness, preferred to retain even the order of the words."[12]

In Galatians (5:16–17) we read, "But I say, walk by the Spirit, and do not gratify the desires [ἐπιθυμίαν] of the flesh. For the desires of the flesh are against the Spirit [ἐπιθυμεῖ: the flesh desires or strives against the spirit], and the desires of the Spirit are against the flesh; for these are opposed to each other, to prevent you from doing what you would." We shall return later to the subject of desires of the Spirit. And following the extensive list of the works of the flesh, Paul writes, "And those who belong to Christ Jesus have crucified the flesh with its passions [παθήμασιν] and

---

12. Augustine, *On Christian Doctrine* IV.20.40.

desires [ἐπιθυμίαις]" (5:24). The Vulgate has *desiderium* in verse 16, the verb *concupiscit* in verse 17, and *concupiscentiis* in verse 24.

Finally from Paul's letters there is his reference to the old man and the new man. "Put off your old nature which belongs to your former manner of life and is corrupt through deceitful lusts [ἐπιθυμίας], and be renewed in the spirit of your minds, and put on the new nature, created after the likeness of God in true righteousness and holiness" (Eph 4:22–24). Here again in the Vulgate we find *desideria* instead of *concupiscentias* but it is coupled with *erroris* (erroneous desires).

Although Augustine relies on Paul in expressing his understanding of concupiscence, at least in *On Marriage and Concupiscence*, there occurs in the Letter of James a remarkably succinct statement connecting concupiscence with sin and death (Jas 1:13–15). "Let no one say when he is tempted, 'I am tempted by God'; for God cannot be tempted with evil and he himself tempts no one; but each person is tempted when he is lured and enticed by his own desire. Then desire when it has conceived gives birth to sin; and sin when it is full-grown brings forth death." The Vulgate has *concupiscentia*. It is not evident from this passage that James is referring to the sin of humankind that Augustine will label "original." We do see, however, that the sin that is born from concupiscence is entirely the responsibility of mankind. One might say it arises from his nature.

Finally I cite the Second Letter of Peter, where again concupiscence is directly associated with corruption in the world. "His divine power has granted to us all things that pertain to life and godliness, through the knowledge of him who called us to his own glory and excellence, by which he has granted to us his precious and very great promises, that through these you may escape from the corruption that is in the world because of passion, and become partakers of the divine nature" (2 Pet 1:3–4). The Vulgate has "*in mundo est concupiscentiae corruptionem.*"

These are the sources that helped to shape Augustine's understanding of original sin as expressed by desire innate in human nature. To be precise the expression is *concupiscence of the flesh*. Augustine acknowledges another kind of concupiscence, that is, desire of the spirit. We saw this above.[13] In another place, he refers explicitly to the expression "desires of the Spirit are against the flesh" (Gal 5:17) in rebuking the Pelagians for claiming that God aroused concupiscence in Abraham and Sarah as a gift from heaven.

---

13. Augustine, *Literal Meaning of Genesis* X.12.20.

> He [Pelagius] has much also to say, though to no purpose, concerning Abraham and Sarah, how they received a son according to the promise; and at last he mentions the word *concupiscence*. But he does not add the usual phrase, of the flesh, because this is the very thing which causes the shame. Whereas, on account of concupiscence there is sometimes a call for boasting, inasmuch as there is a concupiscence of the spirit against the flesh [Gal 5:17], and a concupiscence of wisdom.[14]

In response to a critic who had labelled Ambrose and Cyprian as Manichaeans, Augustine writes, "Do you, he [the critical writer] asks, repeat your affirmation, 'There would be no concupiscence if man had not first sinned; marriage, however, would have existed, even if no one had sinned'? I never said, There would be no concupiscence, because there is a concupiscence of the spirit, which craves wisdom."[15] Augustine is referring to the Book of Wisdom. "So the desire [ἐπιθυμία] for wisdom leads to a kingdom. Therefore if you delight in thrones and scepters, O monarchs over the peoples, honor wisdom, that you may reign for ever" (6:20–21). The Vulgate has *concupiscentia*.

This broader understanding of concupiscence or desire, not linked exclusively to the flesh, will be significant for the evaluation of the terms with respect to time, the ultimate endeavor of this entire section. For with these spiritual desires we encounter a non-material imbalance, a pointing to the future devoid of flesh and material but nonetheless full of expectation and waiting, perhaps a longing for wisdom. Before engaging in this analysis, however, we should complete the grounding of concupiscence in theological commentary, especially as it is transformed vis à vis original sin by Anselm and Aquinas, and also as it is reaffirmed by Luther and Calvin.

At the beginning of *On the Virginal Conception, and On Original Sin*, Anselm seeks to characterize how the nature of prelapsarian man was transformed by the fall. He writes, "But it does not appear that original sin derives from the beginning of human nature, since the origin of human nature was just [*origo illius justa fuit*]; for our first parents were created just, without any sin." Anselm's aim initially is to distinguish between original, i.e., corrupted nature's sin and personal sin. He continues:

---

14. Augustine, *On Marriage and Concupiscence* II.ix.23.
15. Augustine, *On Marriage and Concupiscence* II.xxx.52.

That which is received in one's origin is called "original"; it could also be called "natural," not because it derives from the essence of the nature, but because it is received along with the nature on account of the nature's corruption. By contrast, the sin that all human beings commit once they are persons can be called "personal" on the same grounds. Thus, Adam and Eve were "originally" (that is, at their very beginning, as soon as they were human beings) and without delay just together. [*Adam et Eva originalis . . . sine intervallo justi simul fuerunt.*][16]

Anselm is careful here to distinguish between essential human nature that is created by God and therefore entirely good and the so-called natural transmission of original sin to all mankind. This latter natural transmission is in a way uncreated by man; what was in balance has been tilted.

Anselm has characterized the prelapsarian nature of man as one possessing original justice, an order or balance of his being that was within his capacity to preserve. Anselm is thereby addressing a problem or question that faces all commentators on the matter who have assumed that the creator is not only entirely good but also that all he has created is consequently good. How can man, who was created good, have a corrupt nature? According to Anselm, Adam and Eve, by acting individually and personally, transformed their natural state. Anselm writes, "But since they sinned personally, even though they were originally strong and uncorrupted and had the power always to preserve justice without difficulty, everything they were became weakened and corrupted: . . . subject to corruption and carnal appetites, while their souls were infected with carnal affections."[17]

In so doing, their "natural" state, and ours, was left in debt, but through no defect or imbalance in their original creation. Anselm continues:

> And because the whole of human nature was in them, and nothing of human nature was outside them, the whole of human nature was weakened and corrupted.
>
> What was left in human nature, therefore, was the debt of the justice, whole and sound and without any injustice that human nature had received, and the debt of making recompense

---

16. Anselm, *Virginal Conception*, ch. 1.
17. Anselm, *Virginal Conception*, ch. 2.

for having abandoned justice, along with the corruption that it had incurred on account of sin.[18]

Anselm extends the debt to all born of our original parents, and names the justice lost as "original justice." "It appears to be necessary that in infants human nature is born with the debt of making recompense for the first sin, which it had the power to avoid always, and with the debt of having original justice, which it had the power to preserve always [*et cum debito habendi originalem justitiam, quam semper servare valuit*]."[19] Adam and Eve have in effect created a new man, and this new man turns out to be Paul's "old man."

Therefore, the fallen state has been re-characterized. Augustine, relying on Paul, had identified this state as concupiscence of the flesh, a newly "natural" condition of mankind that inclined him toward sin. Anselm, by describing the prelapsarian state as original justice, has rendered Augustine's concupiscence of the flesh into a debt, an absence. That which had been positive, an urge, has been transformed into something negative, a lacking. Desire has been reinterpreted as imbalance. Accordingly in mankind, as created by God, there is no positive natural inclination to evil. Rather the inclination is negative, an absence of grace initially bestowed upon Adam and Eve. God is therefore acquitted of creating evil, which all along, since Augustine, has been characterized by some as a lacking, indeed a lack of being. By directing their God-given and therefore good desire improperly, preferring the lesser good over the greater, Adam and Eve have chosen non-being, specifically the order of things that is not. Their misdirected urge has had the effect of annihilation, in this case, annihilation of justice. Adam and Eve somehow have reversed God's creation *ex nihilo*.

Aquinas adopts the statements of both theologians regarding original sin, and he does so explicitly, citing them by name, Anselm and Augustine, respectively with original justice and concupiscence. On the question of the essence of original sin, Aquinas distinguishes between formal and material causes and thus combines the two notions. Concupiscence is a general term for the many material causes of original sin, but the formal cause is the absence of original justice. In answer to the question "Whether original sin is concupiscence," he writes:

---

18. Anselm, *Virginal Conception*, ch. 2.
19. Anselm, *Virginal Conception*, ch. 2.

I answer that, Everything takes its species from its form: and it has been stated (Article 2) that the species of original sin is taken from its cause. Consequently the formal element of original sin must be considered in respect of the cause of original sin. But contraries have contrary causes. Therefore the cause of original sin must be considered with respect to the cause of original justice, which is opposed to it. Now the whole order of original justice consists in man's will being subject to God: which subjection, first and chiefly, was in the will, whose function it is to move all the other parts to the end, as stated above [I-II:9:1], so that the will being turned away from God, all the other powers of the soul become inordinate. Accordingly the privation of original justice, whereby the will was made subject to God, is the formal element in original sin; while every other disorder of the soul's powers, is a kind of material element in respect of original sin. Now the inordinateness of the other powers of the soul consists chiefly in their turning inordinately to mutable good; which inordinateness may be called by the general name of concupiscence. Hence original sin is concupiscence, materially, but privation of original justice, formally.[20]

Of course, original justice is not the formal cause of original sin. Original justice is the subjection of man's will to God, a will that accordingly would direct all the powers of the soul to align themselves with the divine order. The deprivation of this original justice left the powers of the soul disordered, i.e., imbalanced, or at least lacking governance. One imagines the just and balanced arms of a scale having been tilted. These powers of the soul, although disordered or imbalanced, are powers nonetheless, and they are able to choose, but their disordered state causes them to turn toward mutable goods and consequently away from that which is truly good, God. Concupiscence, then, is the name for the material state of fallen man, the state where, according to Paul, sin "reigns in your mortal bodies, to make you obey their passions" (Rom 6:12). Here is a fuller version of the famous passage from Romans that Augustine quoted above.

> [15] I do not understand my own actions. For I do not do what I want, but I do the very thing I hate. [16] Now if I do what I do not want, I agree that the law is good. [17] So then it is no longer I that do it, but sin which dwells within me. [18] For I know that nothing good dwells within me, that is, in my flesh. I can will what is

---

20. Aquinas, *Summa theologica* I, Q.82, A.3.

> right, but I cannot do it. [19] For I do not do the good I want, but the evil I do not want is what I do. [20] Now if I do what I do not want, it is no longer I that do it, but sin which dwells within me. (Rom 7:15–20)

In Kant's terminology, the apostle Paul is discovering that he is noumenal to himself.

To the extent that the modifications of Anselm and Aquinas amount to a defense of the innate goodness of human nature, even after the fall, the Reformers Luther and Calvin reject those modifications. Indeed, they adopt Augustine's notion of concupiscence and intensify it to the point of obliterating the distinction between formal and material cause. Luther is famous, perhaps infamous, for his claims about reason as an impediment to faith. Reason is the whore who must be killed by the faithful Christian. In his *Commentary on Galatians*, Luther remarks, "We have received the first fruits of the Spirit, but not yet the tenths [a security deposit but no annual tithe]; neither is reason utterly killed in this life. Which may appear by our concupiscence, wrath, impatiency, and other fruits of the flesh and of infidelity yet remaining in us."[21] Thus concupiscence is a remnant of reason, and reason one infers is a mark of fallen mankind. No part of the human being is exempt from corruption.

In commenting on Gal 5:17 Luther writes:

> When Paul saith that the flesh lusteth against the spirit, and the spirit against the flesh, he admonisheth us that we shall feel the concupiscence of the flesh, that is to say, not only carnal lust, but also pride, wrath, heaviness, impatience, incredulity, and such-like. Notwithstanding he would have us so to feel them, that we consent not unto them, nor accomplish them: that is, that we neither think, speak, nor do those things which the flesh provoketh us unto. . . . But if ye forsake the guiding of the Spirit, and follow the flesh, ye shall fulfil the lust of the flesh, and he shall die, as Paul saith in the eighth to the Romans. So this saying of the Apostle is to be understood, not of fleshly lusts only, but of the whole kingdom of sin.[22]

Luther has expanded the concupiscence of the flesh to pride, wrath, heaviness, impatience, and incredulity. In short, the lusting of the flesh extends well beyond what one might think of as ordinary concupiscence. It is in this very passage of Galatians where Paul gives his famous list

21. Luther, *Selections*, 127.
22. Luther, *Selections*, 145.

of the works of the flesh: "fornication, impurity, licentiousness, idolatry, sorcery, enmity, strife, jealousy, anger, selfishness, dissension, party spirit, envy, drunkenness, carousing and the like" (Gal 5:19–21). Augustine had given a favorable interpretation to the spirit lusting against the flesh, one in which the spirit seeks the wisdom of God. Luther, however, remains stuck on the word "lust," which must have a negative connotation.

In his *Disputation against Scholastic Theology* (1517), Luther asserts several of his tenets of faith that he claims are in opposition to traditional and misguided theology. Among these are "21. No act is done according to nature that is not an act of concupiscence against God. 22. Every act of concupiscence against God is evil and a fornication of the spirit. 23. Nor is it true that an act of concupiscence can be set aright by the virtue of hope."[23] According to Luther, the nature of fallen man has been radically transformed, not into one where there is merely a lack of original justice, a debt. Rather than this, Luther's fallen man has a nature that entails concupiscence. This much Augustine would readily agree with. But Luther's concupiscence is not confined to the flesh, nor is it simply an inclination, an urging in one's bones. Fallen man *is* concupiscent and thereby sinful, and his sinfulness extends to all or nearly all of his desires, fleshly or otherwise. Fallen man becomes synonymous with evil desire. If one is permitted to speak about reason as if it had desires, the way Kant and Kierkegaard speak about it, then no doubt Luther would include reason under his all-encompassing concupiscence. Reason is the pride of man, and pride is a sin.

Following the letters of Paul and the writings of Augustine, Calvin concurs with Luther's assessment of original sin. "Original sin, then, may be defined a hereditary corruption and depravity of our nature, extending to all the parts of the soul, which first makes us obnoxious to the wrath of God, and then produces in us works which in Scripture are termed works of the flesh. This corruption is repeatedly designated by Paul by the term sin [Gal 5:19]; while the works which proceed from it . . . are also termed sins."[24] The corruption, according to Calvin, has occurred in all parts of the soul. Human nature is thoroughly corrupt. Calvin mentions Augustine by name in this section, but then refers again to him obliquely as he expands the notion of a nature "utterly devoid of goodness." "Those who term it concupiscence use a word not very inappropriate, provided

23. Luther, *Disputation against Scholastic Theology*, 21–23.
24. Calvin, *Institutes* II.1.8.

it were added (this, however, many will be no means concede), that everything which is in man, from the intellect to the will, from the soul even to the flesh, is defiled and pervaded with this concupiscence; or, to express it more briefly, that the whole man is in himself nothing else than concupiscence."[25] Calvin has thus made explicit the full expansion of Augustine's concupiscence to express the whole of human nature. In so doing, he has effectively rejected Anselm's original justice or notion of debt as the lingering sign of man's fallen state. No longer need the theologian waste time trying to distinguish between the sexual pleasure that occurs among married couples from that of fornicators.

The Council of Trent addressed the interpretations of human nature and sin of Luther and Calvin. "If any one denies, that, by the grace of our Lord Jesus Christ, which is conferred in baptism, the guilt of original sin is remitted; or even asserts that all that which has the true and proper nature of sin is not taken away, but says that it is only erased, or not imputed,—let him be anathema."[26] This of course is exactly what Luther and Calvin had claimed, that is, that although the guilt of original sin is not imputed to those who receive baptism, the nature of mankind remains in a state of sin.

The Council's decree continues, acknowledging the state or condition of concupiscence in fallen man. "But this holy synod confesses and is sensible, that in the baptized there remains concupiscence, or an incentive [to sin]; which, since it is left for us to strive against, cannot injure those who consent not, but resist manfully by the grace of Jesus Christ; yea, he who shall have *striven lawfully shall [be] crowned*." But this incentive to sin, this inclination is, according to the Council, not sin itself. "This concupiscence, which the apostle sometimes calls sin, the holy synod declares that the Catholic Church has never understood to be called sin, as being truly and properly sin in those *born again*, but because it is of sin, and inclines to sin. And if any one is of a contrary opinion, let him be anathema."[27] Concupiscence is *sin-ly* but not sin itself. Baptism along with a continuous infusion of God's grace restores the human being to a state of goodness.

The dispute here between the Reformers and the Roman Catholic Church has elicited the attention and comments of many theologians, and doctrinally the difference in understanding of the nature of fallen

---

25. Calvin, *Institutes* II.1.8.
26. Buckley, *Canons and Decrees*, session V, sect. 5.
27. Buckley, *Canons and Decrees*, session V, sect. 5.

man continues as a mark of distinction between Protestant and Catholic theology. Nonetheless, the term *concupiscence* continues to be employed by both traditions. The Augsburg Confession of 1530 states the foundational Lutheran position. Article II on original sin asserts:

> [Our churches] teach that since the fall of Adam all men begotten in the natural way are born with sin, that is, without the fear of God, without trust in God, and with concupiscence; and that this disease, or vice of origin, is truly sin, even now condemning and bringing eternal death upon those not born again through Baptism and the Holy Ghost. They condemn the Pelagians and others who deny that original depravity is sin, and who, to obscure the glory of Christ's merit and benefits, argue that man can be justified before God by his own strength and reason.[28]

A similar claim about the error of the Pelagians along with an insistence on the sinfulness per se of concupiscence is found in the Ninth Article of the *Thirty-Nine Articles* of the Anglican Church.

> Original sin standeth not in the following of Adam, (as the Pelagians do vainly talk;) but it is the fault and corruption of the Nature of every man, that naturally is engendered of the offspring of Adam; whereby man is very far gone from original righteousness, and is of his own nature inclined to evil, so that the flesh lusteth always contrary to the Spirit; and therefore in every person born into this world, it deserveth God's wrath and damnation. And this infection of nature doth remain, yea in them that are regenerated; whereby the lust of the flesh, called in Greek, φρονημα σαρκος, (which some do expound the wisdom, some sensuality, some the affection, some the desire, of the flesh), is not subject to the Law of God. And although there is no condemnation for them that believe and are baptized; yet the Apostle doth confess, that concupiscence and lust hath of itself the nature of sin.[29]

Again the Pelagians are condemned, but the sinfulness of concupiscence is asserted. Furthermore, this article notes the elaboration of Paul regarding lusts of the flesh, as interpreted by the Reformers. "To set the mind [φρόνημα] on the flesh is death, but to set the mind on the Spirit is life and peace. For the mind that is set on the flesh is hostile to God; it does not submit to God's law, indeed it cannot; and those who are in the flesh

---

28. *Augsburg Confession*, art. 2.1–3.
29. *Thirty-Nine Articles*, art. 9.

cannot please God" (Rom 8:6–8). Following Paul, concupiscence has become the mind, wisdom, sensuality, affection, desire of the flesh. There is no mention here of the spirit lusting against the flesh. Lust in its entirety has been subsumed by the flesh.

The Catechism of the Catholic Church also condemns the Pelagian heresy, but it distinguishes between the Reformers' position of concupiscence as intrinsically sinful and the Catholic Church's claim regarding inclination to sin.

> Although it is proper to each individual, original sin does not have the character of a personal fault in any of Adam's descendants. It is a deprivation of original holiness and justice, but human nature has not been totally corrupted: it is wounded in the natural powers proper to it, subject to ignorance, suffering and the dominion of death, and inclined to sin—an inclination to evil that is called "concupiscence." Baptism, by imparting the life of Christ's grace, erases original sin and turns a man back toward God, but the consequences for nature, weakened and inclined to evil, persist in man and summon him to spiritual battle.[30]

Here the descendants of Adam have not been totally corrupted. Presumably reason per se is not corrupt, although human pride in reason no doubt remains sinful. Baptism and grace are the remedy. The Catechism continues.

> The Church's teaching on the transmission of original sin was articulated more precisely in the fifth century, especially under the impulse of St. Augustine's reflections against Pelagianism, and in the sixteenth century, in opposition to the Protestant Reformation. Pelagius held that man could, by the natural power of free will and without the necessary help of God's grace, lead a morally good life; he thus reduced the influence of Adam's fault to bad example. The first Protestant reformers, on the contrary, taught that original sin has radically perverted man and destroyed his freedom; they identified the sin inherited by each man with the tendency to evil (concupiscentia), which would be insurmountable. The Church pronounced on the meaning of the data of Revelation on original sin especially at the second Council of Orange (529) and at the Council of Trent (1546).[31]

The Catholic Catechism elaborates further elsewhere on the nature of concupiscence. "Etymologically, 'concupiscence' can refer to

---

30. *Catechism of the Catholic Church*, part 1, sect. 2, art. 1, §7, no. 405–6.
31. *Catechism of the Catholic Church*, part 1, sect. 2, art. 1, §7, no. 405–6.

any intense form of human desire. Christian theology has given it a particular meaning: the movement of the sensitive appetite contrary to the operation of the human reason. The apostle St. Paul identifies it with the rebellion of the 'flesh' against the 'spirit'. Concupiscence stems from the disobedience of the first sin. It unsettles man's moral faculties and, without being in itself an offense, inclines man to commit sins."[32] It is as if man's spiritual immune system has been compromised. The original justice that would have been operative in a fully healthy immune system is lacking. Nevertheless, the system and man himself, created by God, are inherently good.

To summarize the historical information, I note that Augustine adopted the Latin translation *concupiscentia* of the Greek ἐπιθυμία in the letters of Paul, especially Romans and Galatians. Augustine interpreted the desire of the flesh, carnal concupiscence, as evidence of original sin. The evidence in Augustine's thinking was either the sin itself or an inclination in fallen human nature to sin. (The Reformers see concupiscence as sin whereas the Council of Trent sees it as an inclination.) This tendency or state of imbalance was characterized by Anselm as a lack of justice, a debt. Adam and Eve had been graced with an original justice that they lost by means of their personal transgression. The Reformers Luther and Calvin, while not rejecting the notion of imbalance or disorder introduced by Anselm, reemphasized the concupiscence of the fallen state of mankind. They did, however, reject the fallen nature of man as that of being solely negative, i.e., in debt. They also expanded, or perhaps made clear, Paul's intention regarding concupiscence to include all desire of the fallen human being, and they underscored that this condition was the actual state of sin and not merely an inclination toward sin. Man's condition is worse than merely lacking a governor, for his nature actively and spontaneously inclines toward evil. The *yetzer hara* of Gen 6:5 and 8:21 has returned. Since the time of Luther and Calvin, the Roman Catholic Church and most Protestant churches have been in disagreement regarding the fallen nature of mankind.

It is worth noting that all commentators cited here are attempting to describe and define human nature, both before and after the fall. One must wonder if they thought that the world changed when Adam and Eve disobeyed, or perhaps just the world of human beings. Perhaps they would argue that there is no difference. It is also worth noting that all of

---

32. *Catechism of the Catholic Church*, part 3, sect. 2, art. 9, no. 2515.

these commentators treat the fall as an event. Specifically, there was a time before the fall during which lived Adam and Eve, whom God had created and whose nature, according to Anselm, was created just. There *occurred* the transgression, in time, and thereafter the nature of humankind was altered. Some more recent theological commentary, especially that of Barth and Tillich, is much more circumspect regarding the temporal or event-laden quality of the fall of mankind.

All of the theologians that have been mentioned in this section would be eager to continue the story, to speak of baptism and either the remission of sins themselves or at least relief from the imputation of guilt from original sin. They would also be eager to speak about the redeeming act of Jesus Christ, the son of God. But these matters, although of ultimate significance, are not my concern here. Furthermore, I have not attempted to develop other opinions about original sin, for example the Jewish notion of *yetzer hara*, an evil purpose or inclination among mankind. ("The LORD saw that the wickedness of man was great in the earth, and that every imagination of the thoughts of his heart was only evil continually," Gen 6:5). This is the inclination associated with evil and its relationship to sin and culpability that was mentioned in the previous chapter. But there is no attempt here to follow Jewish commentary on what in human nature constitutes evidence of this inclination. Nor have I dealt with the Orthodox Church's teaching on ancestral sin. Furthermore, in the Judeo-Christian tradition there are some Protestant denominations that reject entirely the doctrine of original sin, and there are several religious societies only weakly or tangentially related to the Judeo-Christian tradition for whom the doctrine of original sin is entirely foreign or absent. The concern here, in this section, is not with original sin in general but rather with desire, its characterization as concupiscence, and the emendation of Anselm regarding original justice.

In order to see how concupiscence and time might be related, it might seem expedient to determine first whether the relationship was with phase time (inner organization) or succession time (that which we suffer and perceive as alien). Such a determination at this stage, however, may cut off significant parts of the inquiry. Therefore I shall concentrate initially on concupiscence as imbalance, thereby combining Augustine's notion with that of Anselm. Imbalance implies balance. Two states are so identified, and one naturally wonders about the passage from one state to the other. With passage, we think of change and tend to give a temporal order to the succession. Very generally we associate time with desire, although this general association will need to be clarified.

Physical desire seems to be a passion, something that we undergo and suffer. We have an urge or a straining, a nisus toward some other state and away from some present state. How physical is physical desire? Augustine notes in *The Literal Meaning of Genesis* that physical desire, be it to see, hear, smell, taste, or touch, is not strictly a desire of the flesh. As he puts it, the eyes do not see, but rather the soul sees by means of the eyes. It is perhaps conceivable that one might restrict attention solely to physical stimulus and response, thereby conducting a strictly material investigation. One might even introduce biochemical and electro-neurological considerations. In doing so, one would have entered the realm of neuro-science and consequently rendered any common notion of desire moot. We might describe the future path of a heavy object let loose from above the surface of the earth as one marked out by the desire of the object to move toward the center of the earth. But such language is merely a human way of description. Carried to an extreme, one might view all material as en-souled and accordingly filled with desires. Alternatively one could describe certain physical responses to stimuli as love. I shall not pursue this course, one in which God is not merely a useless concept but rather a notion that amounts to clatter.

Let us follow Augustine at least to the extent of attributing the desire of the flesh ultimately to the soul (or mind or intellect). The urge, then, that Paul locates in the flesh is experienced by the human being; it is felt or thought. It is undergone. Immediately the question arises regarding the possibility of non-fleshly desires. Paul mentions the desires of the spirit against the flesh, and Augustine writes of concupiscence of the spirit and of wisdom. So let us inquire in general regarding desire of reason, or to personalize slightly the inquiry, desire of a rational being as a rational being.

What are the desires of a rational being separate from sensation of any kind? Surely there are some things each of us would like to know that do not seem to be sensory. For example, one might like to know if there are infinitely many perfect numbers. Furthermore, whether or not there are infinitely many, one might like to know each of them. We can follow a fairly straightforward demonstration that there are infinitely many prime numbers in Euclid's *Elements*.[33] One might want to scru-

---

33. Euclid, *Elements* IX.20.

tinize each step of the demonstration, which ultimately would lead to questions about counting and about thought itself. And one might object to the expression "infinitely many" where the proposition asserts merely that prime numbers are more than any assigned multitude. But my reply is simply that *that* is what I mean by "infinitely many." In other words, this is not the place to enter into a discussion of what it means to "know" or "comprehend" a series with infinitely many elements or members; for example: the sum of the series each element of which is in the form $1/2^n$ = 1 for all positive integers *n*. I beg the indulgence of the reader as I investigate this desire further, trivial though it may seem.

A perfect number is one whose divisors add up to the number itself, divisors including the number 1 but excluding the number itself. The first perfect number is 6 (1 + 2 + 3 = 6). The second perfect number, in ascending order, is 28 (1 + 2 + 4 + 7 + 14 = 28). The third perfect number is 496, and so on. How many are there?

Euclid concludes his number books, VII–IX of the *Elements*, with a demonstration of how to produce a perfect number, but he does so without giving any examples. His demonstration, in modern or algebraic terms, amounts to looking for a prime number in the form of 2^n-1. If a number in that form turns out to be prime, then Euclid demonstrates that the product of this number and the number in the form of 2^{n-1} is perfect. All such perfect numbers, however many there may be, will be even. Euclid does not address the possibility of there being an odd perfect number. Accordingly, we shall temporarily confine our attention to the following question: Are there infinitely many Euclidean perfect numbers?

At this point, we are not even asking to know each one of these perfect numbers. (Perhaps I fear that, knowing the number of them to be infinite, I would know the individual numbers in the same way that I know all the even numbers, or, as presented in chapter 2, the knowledge would be akin to the knowledge of the angle sum of the internal angles of a rectilinear figure.) We would like to know about perfect numbers what we know about prime numbers. We know that there are infinitely many prime numbers, although certainly no one knows each one of them, at least not by name. This assertion means to say: We understand the demonstration that there are more prime numbers than any assigned number, and we believe that we have an understanding of what that demonstration depends upon, i.e., counting and thinking. (As arcane as this knowledge may be, I enjoy it.) And so we desire to obtain an understanding about perfect numbers equivalent to our understanding about prime numbers.

In short, we know a proposition of number theory about prime numbers and can state it, but although we can state an equivalent proposition of number theory about perfect numbers, we do not know if it is true or false.

The question about perfect numbers, Euclidean perfect numbers to be precise, can be reduced to the following: Are there infinitely many Mersenne prime numbers? Prime numbers in the form of 2^n-1 are named after Marin Mersenne. We know that if a number in the form of 2^n-1 is prime, then n must be prime, for $2^{pq}-1$, where p and q are integers, is composite.[34] But n being prime is insufficient to produce a prime number. $2^{11}-1 = 2,047 = 23 \times 89$.

There are, of course, more mathematically sophisticated treatments of Mersenne primes and Euclidean perfect numbers. As of this writing, approximately fifty Mersenne primes have been identified, and consequently about fifty Euclidean perfect numbers. This is enough detail. I *want* to know if there are infinitely many perfect numbers. If a mathematician were to discover a demonstration that there were or were not infinitely many perfect numbers, and assuming that I could understand the demonstration, then my desire would be satisfied (at which point I could turn my attention and desire to the Goldbach conjecture).

Having provided a few of the particulars of this particular desire of reason and of a rational being, first let us ask if sensation is involved. It would not seem so in any obvious way, but perhaps the notion of numbers, the ability simply to count entails sensation. Numbers require the notion of the unit as well as the notion of same and other. Are we now in the realm of space, Kantian outer intuition? This is idle inquiry since we have been presupposing all along that sensation entailed temporal succession. The purpose in going this far down what must seem like a side street is to investigate whether rational desire presupposes time.

I shall use the language of temporality to recapitulate progress thus far. There exists a state of knowing and not knowing. Specifically we can compare our knowledge about the number of primes with our knowledge about the number of perfect numbers. At least in one articulation of the proposition, for each case, the comparison yields different results. Now of course there is the history of one's understanding of these matters, which necessarily is temporal. There was a time when *one* did not know if there were infinitely many prime numbers. But that is not to claim that there was a time when it was unknowable how many primes there were.

---

34. This can be derived from Euclid's previous proposition in the *Elements* IX.35.

Now we can imagine the existence of a future state in which one knows about perfect numbers what we know about prime numbers, i.e., there are infinitely many of them. But even a demonstration that the number of perfect numbers was finite would satisfy the desire, for then we would understand a different proposition. We could compare our knowledge about prime numbers with our knowledge about perfect numbers, and in a sense the comparison would be positive in that one would positively understand the differing cardinality of each collection of numbers. But in these current considerations, we have explicitly introduced a temporal framework, both by referring to the history of learning, but also by writing about the *existence* of numerical propositions, as if they were events.

We have yet to entertain the notion that the number of perfect numbers is undecidable, that there may be neither infinitely many nor finitely many of them. There are surprises in mathematics, but such a surprise would seem to undermine the very logic of mathematical thought and to contradict the principle of non-contradiction, which of course can be "contradicted" only by presupposing it. But even in a very general and unreflective way, certainty about the undecidable nature of the question would satisfy the desire of reason.

The states of conditions described above are different, and if one possessed one state of knowing and possessed the other state of knowing, the two states of knowing being incompatible and thereby violating the principle of non-contradiction, one would be forced to say that one state succeeded the other. One state followed the other. An alternative, perhaps, would be to know a paradox, not as a paradox, but as compatible propositions. In this case, the propositions would not constitute a paradox.

The a-temporal possibility of succession remains, but that possibility concerns logical entailment and freedom, neither of which apply here to the question about desire. I conclude here, tentatively and with some diffidence, that desire entails time, or to put it another way, concupiscence is subsumed under time. This does not preclude an investigation of the notion of a-temporal satisfaction, which might be thought of as the heavenly state or beatific vision. Such consideration, however, is for another place and will require a treatment of the possibility of satisfaction without desire. Hobbes, no doubt, would shudder at the thought. In fact, he would call it no thought at all. When this matter is taken up formally, at the end of this study, one must take care, as one should throughout the entire study, to distinguish, or at least to attempt to distinguish between bad poetry and theological insight, a case example being satisfaction without desire.

Not only does desire entail time, and time—at least according to my argument—entail sin, but sin in turn entails a being capable of sin. Sin is a relationship with God. According to Kierkegaard, sin is a position. For our purposes here, we can restrict our attention for one side of the relationship to human beings, and in so doing we come perilously close to Heidegger's notion regarding the fallen-ness of mankind, not that he would ascribe to or assent to any of my comments regarding sin per se. The chain of reasoning and argument here quite simply concerns human beings. The notion of desire is excluded from inanimate objects—the stone desiring the center of the earth—as is also the culpability of animals and non-rational beings.

A possible distinction in English between coveting and concupiscence is of little help in discerning the meaning of Paul and Augustine since in almost every case the Greek is some form of ἐπιθυμία and the Latin some form of *concupiscentia*. One might think of the state of coveting as an internal imbalance, not explicitly connected to sensation. Nonetheless, the state is one of desire, one of wanting to replace a current condition with a successive condition, and in that case, a temporally successive condition.

By introducing justice, Anselm has broadened the state to one that is not directly physical. Human nature in its entirety was created with original justice, and it is this justice—balance—that has been lost. Aquinas further elucidates the state in his conjunction of concupiscence with lack of justice by referring to the powers of the soul that have become inordinate. Here the disorder is explicitly noted to be one of the soul, a location already identified by Augustine in *The Literal Meaning of Genesis*. Luther and Calvin, however, are the authors who provide the final expanded description of the fallen state, and a description that may accord most fully with my notion of time and sin.

For Luther, fallen man has corrupted his reason and reason's offspring, which include concupiscence, wrath, impatience, pride. We are no longer concerned with fleshly lust only but rather "the whole kingdom of sin." As vicious as wrath may be, and as all-encompassing as the sin of pride may be, Luther's impatience speaks directly to our concern. Waiting is indeed the mark of the alien time, the time that we suffer. Impatience is our acknowledgment of the disorder and imbalance. Waiting is as close as we come to understanding the sinfulness of time.

With every stage of development of the notion of desire as expressed as ἐπιθυμία, that is *concupiscentia*, loss of original justice, disorder of the powers of the soul, and Calvin's culminating "the whole man is nothing else than concupiscence," I agree and find these interpretations to support my claim about time. But none of them goes far enough. The entire discussion among the theologians outlined here is concerned with human nature and its transformation. My claim extends beyond "human nature."

The various authors seem to agree regarding personal guilt: it belongs only to Adam and Eve; the debt or sin that is inherited is one where the guilt, if there be any, is absolved by baptism and furthermore expiated by the salvation of Jesus Christ. Accordingly original sin, the inclination or the sin itself, is our fault only because it is a part of our nature, it is who we are, but in a way it is not our fault by personal choice. This seems to be the claim of all considered here.

If I am correct, however, in assuming that sin always and at all times carries with it culpability, then there is no exoneration for the human being, at least not on the basis of some notion of innocence. Time might well be considered a part of "human nature," perhaps phase time. But succession time is the alien, apparently not natural, or at least not natural to the human being. And if all time be sin, both inner organization and externals suffered, and if all sin be blameworthy, then each and every one of us bears responsibility for our own transgressions, but also, like Zosima's brother Markel, for those of everyone else. Furthermore, we bear the burden of so-called natural disasters. But these are considerations for another part of this study. Here the aim has been to show the contribution to the argument made by the particular part of original sin identified as concupiscence.

5

Perseverance

THE VIRTUE OF PERSEVERANCE by its very nature entails time. If sin is time, or at least if sin and an aspect of time have the same origin, then the maintenance of an action through time or in the course of time pertains directly to sinfulness. Perseverance in virtuous action becomes an engagement with time, a confrontation with sin. Perseverance is explicit acknowledgment of sin.

As a virtue, perseverance has often been treated as secondary or subsidiary. One might even ask, and Aquinas does, if perseverance is a virtue at all, or perhaps only a part of every other virtue. A question that immediately comes to mind regarding perseverance is "For how long must one persevere?" It takes little effort to ridicule the notion of perseverance with concocted examples, especially if we combine perseverance with some other Christian virtue. Consider intermittent chastity, or even momentary chastity. Is it chastity? Or consider the ubiquitous religious practice of fasting. How about fasting between eating? No, that is not fasting. Perhaps fasting between meals, or fasting all night, or fasting for twenty-four hours?

These examples are admittedly narrow, contrived, and skewed. These examples entail virtues of abstinence, and at least with the case of fasting, abstinence from a necessity of life, food. Surely there are more active or positive expressions of perseverance, for example in generosity or courage, and in a theological sense, in charity or in hope. We shall consider more carefully the question of "For how long?" below, but first let us trace out the use of the word in its theological sense. The procedure will be the same as that used with the notion of concupiscence in the previous chapter. We shall provide a brief summary of the occurrences of the relevant words in some Christian writings, especially in the New Testament. There is also a rather extensive treatise on perseverance by Augustine along with comments by Aquinas in his *Summa theologica* and by Anselm in his *On the Fall of the Devil*.

Cicero deems *perseverantia* to be a part of courage or fortitude, other parts being magnificence, confidence, and patience.[1] Fortitude is the principal or cardinal virtue. Accordingly, one reads in *The Catholic Encyclopædic Dictionary* the following definition of perseverance: "A moral virtue annexed to fortitude, disposing one to continue in any good work, whether spiritual or corporal, sacred or secular, without being daunted by besetting difficulties and discouragement." The dictionary gives a second definition for "final perseverance." "The grace of persevering to the end in a state of grace not necessarily from the beginning, but for a time from the last conversion to death; or, in the extreme case of a death-bed conversion, the grace of dying in a state of grace."[2] The second definition is treated at length by Augustine in his treatise on the subject of perseverance. The first definition is connected to remarks by Aquinas, who is familiar with the definition given by Cicero. In turn, Cicero may be relying on the Aristotelian notion of the courageous man who endures suffering.

We read in the *Nicomachean Ethics*, "But the courageous person is as undaunted as a human being can be, and while such a person will be frightened even of such things as vary in magnitude, he will endure them in the way one ought and keeping them in proportion, for the sake of the beautiful, since this is the end that belongs to virtue."[3] The courageous person "endures or fears what one ought, for the reason one ought, as one ought, when one ought."[4] He does these things, he acts this way "for the sake of the beautiful."[5] Aristotle concludes, "So it is for enduring painful things, as was said, that people are called courageous. Hence courage too is painful, and it is justly praised, since it is more difficult to endure

---

1. Cicero, *De inventione* II.54.
2. Attwater, *Catholic Encyclopædic Dictionary*, s.v. "perseverance."
3. Aristotle, *Nicomachean Ethics* III.7.1115b.
4. Aristotle, *Nicomachean Ethics* III.7.1115b.
5. Aristotle, *Nicomachean Ethics* III.7.1115b.

painful things than to refrain from pleasant ones."⁶ Here we have the active manifestation of virtue favored in comparison with the negative examples such as abstinence.

The Greek verb used by Aristotle here is ὑπομένω, "to endure." We shall consider the etymological line connecting Aristotle's endurance with the medieval, Christian virtue of perseverance. But first let us note that one may question whether or not perseverance per se is truly a virtue, or perhaps merely a characteristic of all virtue. Thus it may seem odd to choose to devote an entire chapter to the virtue of perseverance. The reasoning is that by means of or through that which we normally call perseverance, we directly encounter original sin as time. Perseverance is about time and its passage. In other words, perseverance is usually classified among the virtues, which in turn have their contrary vices. Neither virtue nor vice is sin, as Aquinas argues, above. If there be a contrary to sin, it is grace, although Kierkegaard claims the opposite of sin to be faith.⁷ Faith however is the result of grace. Perseverance forms a bridge from the vice-virtue category to the sin-grace category.

The Greek verb means "to stay behind, survive; to await; to be patient, abide; to stand one's ground, to submit." The verb stem μενῶ means "to stay, stand fast, abide, to await." The most common meaning of the prefix ὑπο- is "under." Some form of ὑπομένω occurs seventeen times in the Greek Bible, excluding the Apocrypha (Strong #5278). The Latin adjective *severus* means "severe, serious." Combined with the prefix *per-* ("through, throughout") we have "through severity." Perhaps more colloquially we might render the notion as "staying strong." *Perseverare* is only one of several Latin words used in the Vulgate to translate ὑπομένω. One finds also most commonly *sustinere*, but also *permanere, sufferre*, and the noun *instantia*.

The Christian virtue of perseverance seems to derive primarily from exhortation given by Jesus to his disciples as he is sending them out to preach to the lost sheep of the house of Israel. Jesus warns his followers that he is sending them out as sheep amid wolves, and that they will be persecuted for delivering his message. But "it is not you who speak, but the Spirit of your Father speaking through you. Brother will deliver up brother to death, and the father his child, and children will rise against parents and have them put to death; and you will be hated by all

---

6. Aristotle, *Nicomachean Ethics* III.9.1117a.
7. Kierkegaard, *Sickness unto Death*, 82.

for my name's sake. But he who endures to the end will be saved" (Matt 10:20–22).

Here the Vulgate translates ὑπομένω with *perseverare*. But later, on the Mount of Olives, Jesus makes a nearly identical claim about salvation as the reward for the one who endures until the end (ὁ δὲ ὑπομείνας εἰς τέλος, Matt 24:13; Mark 13:13). The Vulgate has *permanere* in Matthew and *sustinere* in Mark.

In his letters, Paul often preaches endurance and persistence, especially in prayer and in suffering. "If we persevere, then we shall reign with him" (εἰ ὑπομένομεν, καὶ συμβασιλεύσομεν· 2 Tim 2:12). The Vulgate uses *sustinere*. The Letter of James also makes explicit the reward of salvation for perseverance. "Blessed is the man who endures trial, for when he has stood the test he will receive the crown of life which God has promised to those who love him" (Jas 1:12). The Vulgate uses *sufferre*.

Augustine devotes the entire second book of his *On the Predestination of the Saints* to the subject of perseverance. He wrote these books in response to questions put forth to him on a variety of matters concerning original sin, and especially regarding the Pelagian hypothesis that the human being possessed some power or capability to assist in his own salvation. In style, these books are stridently didactic, and in many instances Augustine is responding to very specific comments and criticisms of the doctrine of the church as formulated at the beginning of the fifth century. This second book is widely known as "On the Gift of Perseverance," and this title suits the work well, although it may not have been the original title. Specifically, Augustine treats perseverance as a gift from God. He also addresses the subject of perseverance at length in his letter addressed to Valentinus and the monks of Adrumetum, a letter now known as "On Rebuke and Grace."

Of special interest to Augustine is the notion of what is now called final perseverance, i.e., the second definition given by the *Catholic Dictionary* for perseverance in faith until death. At the beginning, Augustine groups perseverance with other virtues, e.g., chastity and patience, and asks if these qualities can be attributed to someone who does not maintain or persevere in the exercise of the virtue. "Therefore it is uncertain whether any one has received this gift [of perseverance] so long as he is still alive." Regarding the man who is acclaimed to possess one of these virtues, "he was continent, or he was righteous, or he was patient, or he was believing, as long as he was so; but when he ceased to be so, he no longer is what he was. But how should he who has not persevered have ever been persevering, since it is only by persevering that any one shows himself persevering." Accordingly, Augustine restricts the proper identification of perseverance in faith to one who, regardless of when he starts, believes to the end, i.e., to death. "And the believer of one year, or of a period as much shorter as may be conceived of, if he has lived faithfully until he died, has rather had this perseverance than the believer of many years' standing, if a little time before his death he has fallen away from the steadfastness of his faith."[8] Augustine's thinking seems to be remarkably delimited by time, specifically a lifetime, and it gives evidence of categorizing an activity that is temporally ongoing. Perseverance *is* a virtue in his mind, and virtue is largely or entirely a concern of human beings. Animals are not considered, even if we characterize traits of animals with names of virtues, such as the courage of the lion. Angels are a special case, considered elsewhere. But for Augustine, human beings live a life and at some specific point they die, thus ending a consideration of virtue or perseverance in the case of an individual. Perseverance pertains to life-time. Augustine does not tell us how we should think about or refer to the efforts of endurance by the person who fails to persist to the end. The failure cannot be deemed perseverance, and Augustine confidently asserts that the person in question did not receive the gift. Augustine's conception of the virtue has an aorist quality to it. The gift is a complete action or thing despite being a gift that is inextricably bound up with time, extended through time. The complete action, however, always has a finite duration, an elapsed interval of time. The individual who perseveres in a virtuous action receives a certificate of completion. The entire matter is considered after the fact.

From the very beginning it is evident that time and duration are central for an understanding of perseverance and in fact for all virtue. Augustine proceeds by citing the passage from the Gospel of Matthew (10:22), "He that persevereth unto the end, the same shall be saved."[9] He then draws repeatedly on St. Cyprian's commentary on the Lord's Prayer, especially on the request to "lead us not into temptation." Critical to Augustine's understanding is that the perseverance to resist temptation is a gift from God, something for which one should offer prayerful petition. One who receives the gift of perseverance receives it from some starting point continuously to the end.

8. Augustine, *Gift of Perseverance* I.1.
9. Augustine, *Gift of Perseverance* II.2.

The entire treatise including *On the Predestination of the Saints* is a reply to Pelagian notions of the role played by human merit on the road to salvation. Augustine thus emphasizes what he understands to be central doctrine of the church regarding original sin. (1) "The grace of God is not given according to our merits." (2) "No one lives in this corruptible body, however righteous he may be, without sins of some kind." (3) "Man is born obnoxious to the first man's sin, and bound by the chain of condemnation, unless the guilt which is contracted by generation be loosed by regeneration."[10] These are the very tenets adopted and amplified by Luther and Calvin, especially in their dispute with the Roman Catholic Church. The regeneration of baptism and the ultimate salvation by Jesus Christ, of supreme importance, are not part of my investigation here, although the Council of Trent asserted that baptism and subsequent infusion of grace remedies the corrupted nature of man from its state of sin, while leaving behind the inclination of concupiscence.

The first tenet is critical to Augustine's argument regarding perseverance, and in fact regarding all virtue. The exercise of these virtues by an individual is owing strictly and solely to God's grace that has been bestowed upon the individual. The person who prays to God for the ability to remain chaste, or righteous, or pious, and who indeed does so remain, assuredly has received "perseverance itself, the great gift of God, whereby His other gifts are preserved."[11] One stays the course only with continuous divine assistance.

Most important for Augustine is perseverance to the end, that which the *Catholic Dictionary* termed "final perseverance." In this regard, Augustine is explicit about the temporal duration of perseverance, or of any virtue. The starting point in life is variable, but the ending point is death. "For we are speaking of that perseverance whereby one perseveres unto the end, and if this is given, one does persevere unto the end." The criterion for reception of this gift is the fact of having persevered until death. "But since no one has perseverance to the end except he who does persevere to the end, many people may have it, but none can lose it."[12] And none can lose it because, at least according to Augustine's calculation, the determination is made at death. Game over! Perseverance, then, has the character of historical record-keeping. It denotes an achievement extended in time, and by definition cannot be lost. It is a qualification.

10. Augustine, *Gift of Perseverance* II.4.
11. Augustine, *Gift of Perseverance* II.4.
12. Augustine, *Gift of Perseverance* VI.10.

Augustine's purpose in this treatise is didactic, but one cannot help but wonder about his understanding of time in these matters. This is succession time that he has in mind, the kind of time that one suffers, one endures. This time attacks us. In this regard, Augustine's score-keeping approach to Christian virtue makes sense. Persevere to the end! Hold on to the finish line, i.e., death. And it is exactly in this regard that we discover the sinfulness of time and also our inherent sinfulness, because perseverance is in a way nothing but the beholding of sin.

In the request "Lead us not into temptation," Augustine is able to combine his understanding of the fallen nature of man, man's "corruption" in the terms of the Reformers, with the need for grace in all things.

> If, then, there were no other proofs, this Lord's Prayer alone would be sufficient for us on behalf of the grace which I am defending; because it leaves us nothing wherein we may, as it were, glory as in our own, since it shows that our not departing from God is not given except by God, when it shows that it must be asked for from God. For he who is not led into temptation does not depart from God. This is absolutely not in the strength of free will, such as it now is; but it had been in man before he fell.[13]

In Augustine's thinking, it seems doubtful, perhaps utterly impossible, that the corrupt human being would have the capacity on his own to resist temptation even for a moment. Were an individual able to resist temptation, to persevere in virtuous activity for a moment without the grace of God, then the individual would have done so entirely because of his own effort, which in turn would be accounted as meritorious. To Augustine, such a hypothetical scenario would scream of Pelagianism.

Augustine treats the matter of predestination at some length in his treatise on perseverance, and necessarily so since the very will to remain faithful, to be patient, to persevere is a gift, and apparently it is a gift not given to all.[14] One naturally inquires why this person may receive the gift and another may not. This is a subject that shall be dealt with later in the discussion of divine foreknowledge and freedom. Augustine grounds his arguments primarily in the letters of Paul, where the subject of predestination is frequently broached. For example, Augustine cites a passage in the Letter to the Ephesians where Paul describes God's plan, which

---

13. Augustine, *Gift of Perseverance* VII.13.

14. Augustine claims that more souls will be stricken with the second death than those who will die but once. In other words, the damned outnumber the saved. *City of God* XIII.23 and XXI.12.

included sending for Christ in the fullness of time. "In him, according to the purpose of him who accomplishes all things according to the counsel of his will" (Eph 1:11).[15] The Vulgate has here *"praedestinati secundum propositum eius"*; literally, "predestined according to his purpose."

In brief, Augustine argues that all men are justly condemned, and some are the fortunate recipients of God's mercy. Anticipating objections on the basis of fairness or justice, Augustine also refers to the famous passage in Matthew regarding the laborers called to work at various hours in the day, each of whom received one day's wages (Matt 20:1–16). When we inquire why this person rather than that one is fortunate, effectively we put him to whom God shows mercy in the place of the one justly condemned. In this comparison, Augustine seems oblivious to the obvious discrepancy between the two cases. In one case, everyone receives exactly the same wage, something good and desirable, for varying amounts of effort. In the other case, the group is divided exclusively into two, those who are rewarded and those who are condemned, apparently irrespective of individual effort. Perhaps Augustine would respond that "individual effort" is in fact a gift from God.

Especially problematic for Augustine's interpretation are the remarks of Jesus about the cities of Chorazin and Bethsaida, not because of his claims about these two cities but rather concerning the comparison made to Tyre and Sidon. "Woe to you, Chorazin! woe to you, Bethsaida! for if the mighty works done in you had been done in Tyre and Sidon, they would have repented long ago, sitting in sackcloth and ashes. But it shall be more tolerable in the judgment for Tyre and Sidon than for you" (Luke 10:13–14; Matt 11:20–22). Several hundred years earlier, both Tyre and Sidon were conquered and destroyed, perhaps because of their wickedness and unbelief.

With Tyre and Sidon we have a clear joining of Augustine's notion of final perseverance with the question of divine foreknowledge or predestination. The Tyrians and Sidonians were, according to Augustine, predestined to fall because of their wickedness and unbelief, and accordingly to be punished. Jesus, however, seems to imply that things might have turned out differently, for he claims that had the Tyrians and Sidonians been witness to the miracles shown to Chorazin and Bethsaida, they would have believed or at least repented, and presumably persevered in their belief and repentance.

---

15. Augustine, *City of God* VII.15.

Augustine uses this example to argue that death is sort of a statute of limitation for merit and culpability. In short, what one might have done if one had lived longer does not count. "Because no dead man is judged by the good or evil things which he would have done if he had not died, otherwise the Tyrians and Sidonians would not have suffered the penalties according to what they did; but rather according to those things that they would have done, if those evangelical mighty works had been done in them, they would have obtained salvation by great repentance, and by the faith of Christ."[16]

In another place, Augustine provides a more sanguine interpretation of this very limit. He argues that an individual's merit or blame depends solely on what actually happens and not on what might have happened. "I mean, if God takes account of what we deserve for future as well as past crimes and misdemeanors, then death will not deliver us from liability for them if it overtakes us before we have committed them, nor has any benefit been conferred on the one who was snatched away lest viciousness should change his understanding."[17] In Augustine's mind, the alternative would be that the individual would be responsible for his actions over the expanse of all time, actions both real and potential. This thought experiment, if it is that, has a terrifying quality to it. Each of us, and Augustine too, might speculate about the circumstances and temptations under which one might persevere or fail to do so. "Lead us not into temptation." The goal posts would be moved farther away, endlessly. It seems that some simple mathematical calculating would then render each and every individual as condemned.

Returning to the matter of the Tyrians and Sidonians, the rhetoric of Jesus is clear, and we use this kind of argument frequently. The comparison is one of relative gratitude, or ingratitude, often used by parents to admonish their children and urge them into action. Augustine also wants to argue against the notion that those infants who die before being baptized were the very persons who were not going to persevere in faith to Jesus Christ in any event. The unexpected death of infants would then be a slow-acting but natural way for God to reveal his foreknowledge regarding the saved and the damned. The children would die without the replenishment of baptism because they were going to stray from the true path at a later time, a macabre example of divine efficiency.

16. Augustine, *City of God* IX.23.
17. Augustine, *Literal Meaning of Genesis* X.16.28.

We must inquire, however, what exactly is being asserted by Jesus, or Augustine, regarding time, the future, and culpability. It seems to me that here Jesus is confusing time and eternity. For even in this hypothetical case, there is not a single individual, not one real person, who lived in Tyre or Sidon and who would have believed having witnessed the miracles, but in fact did not witness the miracles. For what does it mean to say he would have believed? Signs are necessary for belief, but belief is not a function of miraculous degree. As we all know, signs, no matter how extraordinary, are insufficient to impart belief. Is not faith a gift?

As he elaborates his notion of predestination, Augustine returns to the Tyrians and Sidonians when he asks about those whom God did not predestine to be saints. "But where are the rest left by the righteous divine judgment except in the mass of ruin, where the Tyrians and the Sidonians were left?" Augustine, however, again concludes that "therefore the eyes of the Tyrians and Sidonians were not so blinded nor was their heart so hardened, since they would have believed if they had seen such mighty works, as the Jews saw."[18] Augustine, in his zeal to defend the church against Pelagian heresy, seems to have forgotten arguments that he had made elsewhere. The Tyrians and Sidonians saw other things and did not believe. The *miracle* of the work is that because of it someone who "sees" it believes. Earlier, in *On the Predestination of the Saints*, Augustine gives an explanation that better fits the case of Tyre and Sidon. "When, therefore, the gospel is preached, some believe, some believe not; but they who believe at the voice of the preacher from without, hear of the Father from within, and learn; while they who do not believe, hear outwardly, but inwardly do not hear nor learn—that is to say, to the former it is given to believe; to the latter it is not given."[19] "Blessed are you, Simon Bar-Jona! For flesh and blood has not revealed this to you, but my Father who is in heaven" (Matt 16:17). On this account, it was not given to the Tyrians and Sidonians to believe. The marvel of the miracles performed at Chorazin and Bethsaida was, for some present, just so many words of the preacher. They heard but they did not learn. They saw but did not believe.

Another matter related to predestination that Augustine feels the need to address is the activity of preaching or exhortation. It is evident from the treatise that the Pelagians had questioned the efficacy of preaching in the face of predestination. Some of Augustine's response is quite

---

18. Augustine, *Gift of Perseverance* XIV.35.
19. Augustine, *Predestination of the Saints* VIII.15.

narrow and unpersuasive. He accuses the Pelagians of doing the same thing, i.e., preaching and exhorting followers about matters that they acknowledge are controlled solely and exclusively by God.

The problem facing the preacher, of course, is manifest. Why should one alter his behavior, especially in the ways of increased exertion, denial of pleasure, abstinence and perhaps even mortification of the flesh, if these efforts will have no effect on one's salvation? The problem is not restricted in any way to Christian virtues and the Christian notion of salvation. The pagan might also ask quite reasonably why one should strive to live a life of temperance if such achievement, a temperate life, is of no advantage whatsoever to the individual or to anyone else, in this or in any other life. Generosity and courage would fare no better than temperance under these conditions.

After many wrong turns, Augustine eventually hits on a response worthy of consideration. It amounts to shifting the focus away from the individual. Exhortations to do this and to abstain from that then become not for the benefit of the person being exhorted. In a chapter entitled "Predestination Must Be Preached," Augustine writes:

> For as piety must be preached, that, by him who has ears to hear, God may be rightly worshipped; modesty must be preached, that, by him who has ears to hear, no illicit act may be perpetrated by his fleshly nature; charity must be preached, that, by him who has ears to hear, God and his neighbours may be loved;—so also must be preached such a predestination of God's benefits that he who has ears to hear may glory, not in himself, but in the Lord.[20]

The purpose for preaching about predestination is that "God may be rightly worshipped" (*Deus recte colatur*). The rationale behind the preaching is not so much to persuade the hearer to change his ways regarding this particular virtue or vice, but rather to call forth praise of God. In this case, exhortation is merely a matter of style and expression. Human beings have reason and language. They also have mouths to speak, eyes to see and read, and ears to hear. In accordance then with divine justice, the truth should be proclaimed. It is the right thing to do. Doing otherwise would be a sign of ingratitude. Not to proclaim the truth would be violation of eternal law, and therefore sinful. The benefit and glory of the preaching, if there are any, redound to God. Praise the Lord!

---

20. Augustine, *Gift of Perseverance* XX.51.

Throughout the treatise on perseverance, Augustine seems to have in mind succession time. And yet he has an end-of-the-world approach to writing about it. Although perseverance requires will and dedication at every moment, the perseverance itself is not accomplished until the clock runs out. Above I have described this characterization as aorist. Furthermore, the accomplishment is not one of the individual about whom we would say that he persevered. The so-called accomplishment is in fact a gift of God. This is a gift that God may have knowledge about, but no living human being can know that he has received the gift, at least in the case of final perseverance. One would need to know what humanly cannot be known. This condition is the state of original sin. To know would be to overcome the sinful state, to be saved. To know would be to fulfill time by subsuming it. The individual, in true Pelagian fashion, would save himself. One might persevere through a time-limited trial, e.g., courage to the end of a single battle. But assuming that life continues, there will be future battles to fight and future challenges to the individual's perseverance.

Before developing further this line of inquiry, let us look to other writers to expand the notion of perseverance as a virtue. The question whether or not perseverance is a virtue separate from other virtues has already come up. For how long must one be courageous, pious, chaste? Aquinas addresses this question, arguing that a virtuous deed involves goodness in two ways, with respect to the objective of the act and with respect to the act's duration in the face of adversity. He concludes that persistence in a good deed is a separate virtue. "Accordingly just as temperance and fortitude are special virtues, for the reason that the one moderates pleasures of touch (which is of itself a difficult thing), while the other moderates fear and daring in connection with dangers of death (which also is something difficult in itself), so perseverance is a special virtue, since it consists in enduring delays in the above or other virtuous deeds, so far as necessity requires."[21] Immediately it is clear that the requirements of "necessity" may be more flexible that Augustine's notion of perseverance until death.

In the same article, Aquinas considers the case where one seems to persevere for a time in some virtuous deed, but who at some point fails to stick with it. In such case, perseverance is lacking from the virtuous deed, for perseverance indicates completion of the act. Aquinas gives the

---

21. Aquinas, *Summa theologica* II-II, Q.137, A.1.

example of soldierly courage that must last until the end of the battle. "There are, however, some virtues whose acts must endure throughout the whole of life, such as faith, hope, and charity, since they regard the last end of the entire life of man. Wherefore as regards these which are the principal virtues, the act of perseverance is not accomplished until the end of life. It is in this sense that Augustine speaks of perseverance as denoting the consummate act of perseverance."[22] Perseverance therefore varies according to the virtue. For temperance, generosity, and courage, one might persevere over a period of time—until the end of battle—and the act can be viewed as having been completed. One persevered to the end, but lived on nonetheless. Perhaps Aquinas thinks that there are *not* other battles to be fought. Other virtues, however, the theological virtues, are apparently continuous, lifetime virtues, with death as the only cessation of action and responsibility. In both cases, perseverance consists of facing succession time, but doing so only for a finite interval of time.

Aquinas goes on to locate perseverance as a secondary virtue to fortitude. Here Aquinas explicitly follows Cicero, who seems to be following Aristotle. Then Aquinas considers the kinds of grace needed in order to receive the gift of perseverance. He concludes that two kinds of grace are necessary. The first is of a momentary sort. At each moment, the individual who is attempting to persevere in some virtuous act receives "habitual grace" to persist in the habit of virtue. But since there is Augustine's notion of final perseverance, there must be another kind of grace needed. It is as if each moment were considered as an infinitesimal, each infinitesimal in need of assistance. But the act of virtue, when considered in completion, requires an integration of the infinitesimals, a summing up. Aquinas writes:

> In this sense [perseverance] needs not only habitual grace, but also the gratuitous help of God sustaining man in good until the end of life, as stated above [I-II, Q.109, A.10], when we were treating of grace. Because, since the free-will is changeable by its very nature, which changeableness is not taken away from it by the habitual grace bestowed in the present life, it is not in the power of the free-will, albeit repaired by grace, to abide unchangeably in good, though it is in its power to choose this: for it is often in our power to choose yet not to accomplish.[23]

---

22. Aquinas, *Summa theologica* II-II, Q.137, A.1.
23. Aquinas, *Summa theologica* II-II, Q.137, A.4.

The individual is in need not only of habitual grace at each moment but also of God's sustaining grace in order to connect the moments.

Aquinas makes a similar point in answering the question whether fallen man can avoid sin without grace.

> But in the state of corrupt nature man needs grace to heal his nature in order that he may entirely abstain from sin. . . . And in this state man can abstain from all mortal sin, which takes its stand in his reason, as stated above [I-II, Q.74, A.5]; but man cannot abstain from all venial sin on account of the corruption of his lower appetite of sensuality. For man can, indeed, repress each of its movements (and hence they are sinful and voluntary), but not all, because whilst he is resisting one, another may arise, and also because the reason is always alert to avoid these movements, as was said above [I-II, Q.74, A.3].[24]

Clearly the enemy here is time, for according to Aquinas, even fallen man can abstain from every mortal sin and from *each* venial sin. But man cannot abstain from all venial sins. Man is not in the same position as were the angels when they were faced with their test of loyalty to God. Man resists over time, while there are movements over time. The accumulation of these movements, these moments, overwhelms man's resolve in his fallen state. Succession time attacks the individual continuously and sooner or later breaks through the defenses. It is as if man attempts to sum up the infinitesimal moments one at a time, finitely.

Aquinas accepts Augustine's notion that perseverance is a virtue per se, although secondary, and also that it is a gift from God. Furthermore, Aquinas seems to adopt Augustine's notion, at least in part, that one perseveres only if a temporal goal is established and achieved. But Aquinas also wants to consider the momentary aspect of virtuous action. This act too, this habit requires an infusion of grace according to Aquinas. What is absent in this treatment of perseverance, at least at this point in the *Summa*, is a consideration of predestination and foreknowledge, a concern that appears at every turn in Augustine's treatise.

I turn now to Anselm's discussion of perseverance in *On the Fall of the Devil*. I have inverted the chronology, considering Aquinas first, because Anselm's treatment will carry us the furthest in the principal aim of this section: to see how perseverance serves as a window into the connection of original sin and time. The very subject, the fall of the devil,

---

24. Aquinas, *Summa theologica* I-II, Q.109, A.8.

may strike us as an arcane topic of Christian theology, largely irrelevant to our daily lives. Thus the fall of the devil owing to his lack of perseverance may seem all the more arcane and irrelevant. One might even view Anselm's inquiry to be a narrow, scholastic study, more concerned with the proper grammatical and syntactical expression of the devil's fall than with anything that might be of practical concern to us. For a graphic and dazzling display of this fall, we have recourse to Milton's treatment in *Paradise Lost*.

Several aspects of this occurrence—the fall of the devil is not an event, at least not yet—pertain to this investigation. One aspect is the irrevocable nature of the decision, i.e., the decision to remain faithful to God or to rebel. Christian doctrine has it, at least by the time of Augustine, that upon deciding on the matter of loyalty, the angels, both good and bad, were fixed in that decision. The knowledge resultant upon or granted by the decision made a change of will or heart impossible. This state is in marked contrast with that of living human beings whose will is constantly capable of changing. This is the very point made by Aquinas, above. (The general matter of the fallen angels is taken up in more detail at the end of the next chapter.)

Before commenting directly on Anselm's treatise, we must first provide the common interpretation of the fallen angels as given by Augustine. In an attempt to answer the question whether or not Adam received the gift of perseverance, Augustine concludes that he did not, and then proceeds to distinguish our inherited position from that of the angels.

> Finally, certain angels, of whom the chief is he who is called the devil, became by free will outcasts from the Lord God. Yet although they fled from His goodness, wherein they had been blessed, they could not flee from His judgment, by which they were made most wretched. Others, however, by the same free will stood fast in the truth, and merited the knowledge of that most certain truth that they should never fall. For if from the Holy Scriptures we have been able to attain the knowledge that none of the holy angels shall fall evermore, how much more have they themselves attained this knowledge by the truth more sublimely revealed to them! Because to us is promised a blessed life without end, and equality with the angels [Matt 22:30] from which promise we are certified that when after judgment we shall have come to that life, we shall not fall from it; but if the angels are ignorant of this truth concerning themselves, we shall not be their equals, but more blessed than they. But the Truth

> has promised us equality with them. It is certain, then, that they have known this by sight, which we have known by faith, to wit, that there shall be now no more any fall of any holy angel.[25]

The "sight" reference is to Paul's Second Letter to the Corinthians, where the followers of Jesus Christ "walk by faith, not by sight" (5:7). The loyal angels have no need of faith because they can see and understand their loyalty.

In this passage, Augustine is arguing, in brief, that the statute of limitation for responsible deeds, actions for which we are held accountable, is death. But for angels a single act or choice determined their eternal state. Time as sin for the loyal angels has no meaning. In a way, it does not exist. For the rebellious angels, their punishment is eternal time, never-ending waiting. In this respect, time is sin entirely, all of which falls upon the disloyal angels.

Elsewhere in this study, we shall explore the similarity between the test of loyalty administered to the angels and the command of obedience issued to Adam and Eve in the garden. At this point, however, we are setting the scene for Anselm's remarks about the devil and perseverance. Let us begin with Anselm's conclusion. "So although the good angel received perseverance because God gave it, it's not the case that the evil angel did not receive it because God didn't give it; rather, God didn't give it because he didn't receive it, and he didn't receive it because he didn't will to receive it."[26] At this point I simply note the addition of the angel's will in Anselm's account.

Anselm's treatise is in the form of a dialogue between teacher and student. The intent behind the student's persistent questions is clear and the thinking must go thus. The good angel persevered and the bad angel did not persevere. Perseverance is a gift of God. The good angel, by his perseverance, gives evidence of having received the gift. The bad angel conversely gives evidence of not having received the gift. The student infers that the gift of perseverance is instrumental to remaining loyal to God. Therefore, the good angel persevered in loyalty because God had given and the angel had received the gift. The bad angel did not persevere because God had not given and the angel had not received the gift. In effect, the student mistakes the certificate of completion for an instrument, credentials for skill.

---

25. Augustine, *On Rebuke and Grace* X.27.
26. Anselm, *On the Fall*, 179.

Anselm objects strenuously to this line of reasoning, in particular to the last part where giving and receiving of the gift are considered as a single act. The teacher rebuts the student's argument. Creatures have all that they have from the creator.[27] All that is, is caused by God, and all that is, *is* only because God preserves it. If God were to stop preserving something, it would cease to be, but not because God caused it not to be. Nothing and non-being are not from God because God is solely supreme being.[28] If God gives and an angel receives, the angel receives the gift because God gave it. But if God gives and an angel refuses, it is not the case that the angel *does not* receive the "gift" because God did not give it.[29] God did not give perseverance to the bad angel *because* the bad angel did not receive it. God gave the bad angel the will and power to receive perseverance. God did not give the receiving of perseverance.[30] To persevere is to finish doing something. (This is Augustine's understanding.) To persevere in willing is to finish willing. Here, Anselm makes up a word combining *per* with *velle* (will). He has followed a Latin pattern of adding *per* to the infinitive to produce a verb indicating that the action is brought to completion. Adding *per* to *facere* (to do) produces *perficere* (to finish or complete).[31]

Anselm then arrives at the crucial step in his argument. The devil "spontaneously forsook the will he had." (*Sponte dimisit voluntatem quam habebat.*) The devil had the will to persevere, but the devil forsook (*dimisit*) that will, and did so freely (*sponte*). "Now as long as he possessed what he later abandoned, he received his possessing it; and in the same way he could have received his always retaining what he abandoned" (*ita potuit accipere semper tenere quod deseruit*). One manuscript has "*accepit posse*" instead of "*potuit accipere.*" "But since he abandoned it, he did not receive his always retaining it" (*sed quia deseruit non accepit*). "Therefore, it was because he abandoned it that he did not receive his retaining it" (*Quod ergo ideo non accepit tenere quia deseruit*).[32] I have followed the translation of Thomas Williams, and now propose to look even more closely at this portion of the argument.

27. Anselm, *On the Fall*, 169.
28. Anselm, *On the Fall*, 170.
29. Anselm, *On the Fall*, 172.
30. Anselm, *On the Fall*, 173.
31. Anselm, *On the Fall*, 174.
32. Anselm, *On the Fall*, 175.

First let us note that in Anselm's description of the devil's fall, time seems to be passing. We must pay attention to tenses, although we must also attempt to distinguish between logical entailment or strict succession on the one hand and temporal succession on the other. In this regard, verb tenses can be ambiguous.

We have that the devil "could have received his always retaining what he abandoned." This translation seems to capture the sense intended by Anselm with "*semper tenere.*" The infinitive, here rendered as a gerund, indicates the a-temporal or perhaps trans-temporal condition or state that Anselm is writing about. (On the basis of these words, it seems to me that Thomas Williams assumes license to include infinitude in the rest of the paragraph.) It is natural to imagine a stretch of time passing during which the devil *always* could have received perseverance. We think of moment to moment, each with the devil *existing*, in each moment being able to will to persevere in his loyalty to God. This is a natural and reasonable depiction of the state because we put ourselves in the devil's shoes. We go from moment to moment, and at each one, as Aquinas pointed out, even in our fallen state we have the capacity to persevere. What we do not have, however, is the capacity to persevere through all the moments. This is our very sin, our original sin.

Anselm has written, literally, "but since he abandoned he did not receive." Abandon and receive what? Williams fills this out with "His always retaining [perseverance]." If we ignore the "perseverance" momentarily and stick with Anselm's sentence, we can derive a strictly logical interpretation. Let us substitute the variable x for the object abandoned and therefore not received. Logically this is not a temporal sequence of events, it is a necessary sequence. But the addition by Williams, which may not at all be out of place, turns x doubly or triply into a temporal object. First, the x of the object is perseverance, a concept necessarily temporal. Second, Williams repeats the "always" from the previous phrase. The word is not necessarily temporal if by "always" one means to say by "all ways."[33] But normally, the word has a temporal connotation. Third, Williams has repeated the gerund "retaining," the infinitive *tenere* that had appeared in the earlier phrase.

The effect of these repetitions or interpolations is to cement the temporal aspect of the devil's fall. (We shall see elsewhere that a strictly logical, non-temporal rendition of the fall of the devil is the correct

---

33. Plotinus makes a similar distinction between "always" and "all ways." *Enneads* V.3.7.2.

understanding of the fall of mankind.) And thus Anselm can conclude that because the devil abandoned perseverance, he did not receive retaining perseverance. One cannot help but wonder at this point if we have before us an exquisitely subtle argument or perhaps simply the product of a scholastic theologian pushing words together. At the end of the quoted passage, for a second time we have the infinitive *tenere*.

Is perseverance a thing? Is any virtue a thing? Let us grant reality, thing-hood, to some virtues such as courage. Is perseverance anything other than the score at the end of the battle, at the end of life? The soldier was courageous throughout the battle until it was over. He persevered. The Christian was faithful and charitable through his life, i.e., until and through death. He persevered. Does it matter when the Christian embarked upon his faithful and charitable life? What about the deathbed conversion? The individual who has denied that Jesus is the Christ, who by all accounts including his own has lived a life devoid of charity, moments before his death accepts Jesus to be his savior and all that such acceptance might entail. Has our late convert persevered? Score-keeping of this sort would make a mockery out of the *per-* in perseverance. Through what did the individual remain loyal, steadfast, true? A moment? And yet this seems to be a possibility according to the definition of final perseverance in the *Catholic Dictionary*. Under the heading of "chastity," there is no similar description of final or momentary chastity.

This fanciful acceptance of our late convert is not perseverance and in no way does it convey what we mean when we use the word. Nor is this the intention of Jesus in the Gospel of Matthew, nor Aristotle nor Cicero nor Augustine nor Aquinas nor Anselm, the *Catholic Dictionary* notwithstanding. What is missing in our last-minute conversion is the minute itself. Time is absent. But perseverance is about time, and in a way only about time. Perseverance requires the use of an infinitive not because it is a-temporal. It was wrong to entertain that description of Anselm's remarks, but not wrong in purposing "trans-temporal."

Perseverance embraces time, and it does so as an enemy. Perseverance looks directly at time, succession time, and in so doing it sees not merely an alien but a treacherous one at that. For this alien time, succession time, is the same as our inner organization, so-called phase time. We are the alien to ourselves, reflected outward. In this way we come to know ourselves. We betray ourselves, and we do so because we bear the burden of original sin.

Both Anselm and Aquinas acknowledge a role for the will. Anselm does so explicitly with the development of his notion of perfection of willing or finishing willing. Aquinas is less direct, but his treatment of habitual grace indicates that part of perseverance consists in momentary action, enduring for a moment. Augustine no doubt would at least emphasize the need for grace in order to carry out each of these momentary acts. For him, the capacity to will a virtuous act is a gift from God. No merit, it seems, is attributable solely to human effort. Pelagianism must be repelled at every turn.

This is not the place to comment further on foreknowledge, freedom, and predestination. It is sufficient to have shown that perseverance is an encounter with time, a temporal act. Whether or not it is a gift and whether or not it is a virtue do not alter this fundamental aspect of perseverance. In one sense, perseverance is similar to concupiscence, and accordingly the two notions have been dealt with in similar fashion. Concupiscence of any sort, carnal, intellectual, spiritual, is a longing, a nisus. One suffers concupiscence, just as one perseveres in virtue. The individual, in his intent, is challenged by his alien self, by his original sin of time.

6

The Fall (The Choice or The Event)

THE PRECEDING CHAPTERS HAVE mapped out the territory that surrounds sin, original sin, time, and the eternal. We have seen that we human beings have access to both the temporal and the eternal, that in a way we stand at the intersection of the temporal and the eternal. In one respect, it may not seem remarkable to claim that the human being is temporal. But as soon as we are required to state what it is that makes the temporal as such, as soon as we are called upon to specify what we mean by time, we founder. At the very least, we know the difference between the mutable and the immutable, a difference that we encounter superficially but understand deeply. The mutable and the immutable are seemingly a single thought that serves generally for an investigation of the temporal and the eternal. These notions have led me to posit the eternal act as a sure sign of the eternal and, we might even say, of the eternal in our lives. Of course, the expression "eternal act" seems to be inherently contradictory because we attribute time, at least tacitly, to action. In the chapter on the temporal and the eternal we saw that we have a perfectly good understanding of eternal action, and that we understand this action to be entirely independent of temporal underpinning. In a sense, we have found an alignment of eternal with mutable. By establishing the eternal we are able to assert the temporal. For just as immutable and mutable are a single thought, so are eternal and temporal. The thought, of course, seems to be complex, and all such pairings reflect an apparent paradox of immutable and mutable, i.e., that each member of the pair presupposes the other. This is a matter then we encountered above (chapter 2) in the context of flux. There we acknowledged that most deeply we were adopting the Kantian substrate as first. In other words, we presuppose permanence. Accordingly we are certain about the eternal. Were we unable to be certain about the eternal, that uncertainty would then pertain to time. We would soon find ourselves in the difficult position not only of being unable to say what time is but also of being unable to assert that there is time at all. The comment here is not that time *exists* but simply that it *is*. Those authors who argue that there is no time presuppose time in order to deny it, but as we noted, to presuppose permanence does not require the additional presupposition of impermanence.

The mapping undertaken has been achieved with broad strokes with respect to both time and sin. With the latter it was necessary to reveal the presence of the former. Time and sin are inextricably linked. When it comes to sins themselves, this connection is a matter of fact. Sins are events. That the sins are in fact sinful, however, depends at least in part upon revelation. These events are sinful in our relationship to the God who reveals himself in Jesus Christ. The sinner assumes a position with respect to God. With regard to the origin of sin, still to be developed in a rigorous way in the next chapter, time is both present in the meaning of the sin but also absent in a factual way. Original sin is not one event among many, but rather it is *the* qualifying event. Along with the event-like status of sins, I have also tried to characterize all sin as disorder, to address the necessary consequence of blame and culpability, and to distinguish sin from evil.

With the landscape limned, finer instruments were employed to fill out the picture. In particular, the notions of concupiscence, original justice, and perseverance revealed characteristic features of the interconnection between time and the origin of sin. These are some of the terms that theologians have used in the past in their efforts to understand human nature, and particularly in a Christian sense, to understand man as a sinner. These notions point to desire, a notion which will also be developed in the next chapter.

We arrive now at a particular characterization of sin and original sin, i.e., as a fall. The verb and noun, *to fall*, *fall*, indicate a change, and especially a change for the worse. The fall is downward, and in most cases up is preferable to down. The fall necessarily is characterized as a change, an event. Furthermore, it is traditionally conceived as a willful change, one brought about freely and with intent. It entails responsibility and presupposes freedom.

The story of Adam and Eve in the Garden of Eden presents an account of disobedience that serves as foundation for thinking about and inquiring into the state of mankind.[1] Their violation of God's prohibition is traditionally referred to in Christian writings as the fall of man and the origin of sin, although some Christian traditions and writers reject the very notion of original sin. I shall treat the mythological account of Adam and Eve in a variety of ways. My intent is to show that collectively these treatments will disclose the meaning of this entire endeavor, this attempt to understand sin in the context of time and time in the context of sin. Although these treatments will not be presented in strictly deductive fashion in this chapter, they cover all or nearly all aspects of the connection between sin and time. This chapter then constitutes circumstantial evidence. In the next chapter, the central matter will be taken up deductively. Here I address the connection in the following six ways.

A. The Temporal Garden
B. Orientation to the Task at Hand
C. The Prohibition
D. Original Sin and the Bible
E. The Meaning of the Myth
F. The Fallen Angels

Surely one does not need to read these comments to appreciate the significance and the importance of the fall of mankind. Even the most obdurate of investigators will glean from this story the characteristic elements of human being, those very elements that render us fallible, inconstant, timorous, and diffident. My aim, however, is to show the special significance that the myth has for my conception of time and sin.

A. THE TEMPORAL GARDEN

A.   Sun's up, hon.

E.   Hunh?

---

1. According to Nightingale, "In Augustine's view, when Adam and Eve 'fell' into earthly bodies, they also 'fell' into time." *Once out of Nature*, 7. Cf. Augustine, *Enarrationes* 74.5, regarding Jesus: "Just as he accepted slavery, so he accepted time."

A. It's morning. A new day. Time to get up.

[Pause]

E. Why?

A. What do you mean, "Why?"

E. What do I mean? Why get up?

A. Because it's morning. We get up every morning.

[Long pause]

E. Yes, we get up every morning. I suppose it's still there.

A. It? What do you mean by "it"?

E. You know what I mean.

A. What?

E. The tree.

A. There are a lot of trees.

E. *The* tree. You know. *The* tree!

A. Well, to tell the truth, I haven't looked.

E. You don't have to look.

A. Okay, I suppose the same trees that were in the garden yesterday are still in the garden today. No changes overnight.

E. You suppose so?

A. Yes, and each bearing fruit that is good for food and a delight to the eyes.

E. Yes, same trees, same fruit, same garden. Same every day. Except . . .

[Pause]

A. Except what?

E. Except that one tree is not the same as all the others.

A. Oh, *that* tree.

E. Yes, *that* tree.

A. Well, I suppose it's still there, just as it was yesterday.

E. And the day before that, and the day before the day before that. And just as it will be there tomorrow, and . . .

THE FALL (THE CHOICE OR THE EVENT)

[Pause]

A.   I don't think I like where this conversation is going.

E.   We've had it before.

A.   Yes, we've had it before, and each time that we have it we come to the same resolution.

E.   *We?*

A.   Yes, *we*. We resolve to keep on, to persevere. This is no great burden. Plenty of trees, plenty of fruit. Lots of free time.

E.   Yes, lots of free time. Too much free time.

A.   Don't say that. One can never have too much time.

[Long pause]

E.   Did you speak to him?

A.   Speak to . . . about what?

E.   You know!

A.   You mean about what we were talking about, the tree?

E.   I mean about what we always talk about, the only thing we talk about.

A.   He's not going to change his mind.

E.   Did you speak to him?

A.   Yes.

E.   What did you say?

A.   I asked about the trees in the garden.

E.   What about the trees in the garden?

A.   I asked if all the trees in the garden were the same.

E.   And what did he say?

A.   He said that he knew they all looked the same.

[Pause]

E.   That's it? *He* knows that they all look the same. Of course he knows they all look the same because he made them that way.

A.   Yeah.

E.   Did you or did you not ask him about *the* tree?

A. Believe me, he is adamant about the prohibition.

E. It seems to me the least you could do is ask him point blank about *the* tree.

A. What would be gained by that? We know already that he said on the day we eat of the fruit of that tree we shall die. Either the tree is like all the others, or it is imperceptibly different. Either way, what good would the knowledge be to us?

E. So that's it. We don't know. He won't tell, or at least we don't have the courage to find out one way or the other.

A. What does it matter? I think that you are overly concerned about cause and effect. Besides, we have all the other trees with their good fruit.

E. We don't have *that* tree.

A. We don't *need* that tree.

E. No, you don't seem to understand, do you? Why don't you admit that, as far as we are concerned, there is not a garden full of trees. There is a garden with one, *just one* tree in it.

[Pause]

A. I know.

[Pause]

E. Do you think, just for one day, he could designate a different tree?

A. I doubt it.

E. We could ask.

A. I suppose so.

[Pause]

E. Can we kill ourselves?

A. No, we can't.

E. That's what I'm afraid of.

A. Killing yourself?

E. Not being able to kill yourself.

[Pause]

A. It looks like it's going to be a nice day. Perhaps this afternoon, after the tilling and keeping, we could play bocce.

E. I've got a better idea. Why don't you go piss on the tree?

A. Me? . . . Why don't *we* go piss on the tree?

E. We? . . . I suppose I could climb into the tree and squat.

A. Yeah. Let me know when you're done and then I'll come over and work on the base and roots.

E. Okay.

A. What good do you think this will do?

E. Pissing on the tree?

A. Yeah, pissing on the tree.

E. Perhaps it will kill the tree.

A. Unlikely.

E. Maybe the fruit will wither.

A. Equally unlikely. He won't let that happen.

E. Well at the very least, we would be expressing our feelings.

A. About the tree?

E. Yes. And to the tree?

A. Don't you think he'll get angry?

E. What of it? Besides, he gave us but one command, one prohibition. Don't eat! He didn't say, "Don't piss!"

A. I don't know, hon. I don't think I like this.

E. What else are we going to do? And don't mention bocce.

[Pause]

A. We could wait.

B. ORIENTATION TO THE TASK AT HAND

The interpretation of the myth of Adam and Eve that is being developed here is absolutely antithetical to what has been described in the previous section, "The Temporal Garden." There is truth contained in the Temporal Garden, and it is truth that has occurred, that occurs every day, and that will occur in the future. In this respect, it is similar to Milton's *Paradise Lost*, which describes a place where the fallen suffer the consequences of the fall before they in fact fall. But the Temporal Garden is decidedly not the truth of original sin, Milton and the traditional Christian interpretations notwithstanding. Quite the opposite is the case. Original sin is the qualification that makes the Temporal Garden possible. The Temporal Garden is the result of original sin, the effect that is caused by the disobedience of Adam and Eve. The Temporal Garden is a historical account, even though it is rendered mythically. In the garden we encounter Adam and Eve as real persons, our original parents, not utterly different from our biological parents. To them we attribute the material cause of all mankind. We are their effects in the same way that physicists attribute the universe as effect to the Big Bang as cause. In other words, like the Big Bang, Adam and Eve are presuppositions that must be freely supposed. Thus according to most common interpretations of the account in Genesis, the world unfolds naturally and materially, even when the interpretation includes the degradation of human nature. Even when interpreted as a mythical, coming-of-age story, the account in Genesis entails a series of events. The events of the Temporal Garden occurred, occur, and will occur, unlike original sin, which makes occurrences possible. The subject of the Temporal Garden is waiting. It is time as the alien, time that one suffers.

What do we see in the Temporal Garden? In the beginning, God creates the heavens and the earth. God says, "Let the earth put forth vegetation and fruit trees bearing fruit." And God says, "Let the earth bring forth living creatures: cattle and creeping things and beasts." Then God says, "Let us make man in our image, after our likeness." So God creates man and woman.

In the beginning, everything is but everything changes. First there is light, then cattle, and finally human beings. There are, of course, two creation accounts at the beginning of Genesis.

The LORD God plants a garden in Eden, in the east; and there he puts the man and the woman. Out of the ground the LORD God makes to grow every tree that is pleasant to the sight and good for food, the tree of life in the midst of the garden and the tree of the knowledge of good and evil. And the LORD God commands the man, saying, "You may freely eat of every tree of the garden; but of the tree of the knowledge of good and evil you shall not eat."

The fruit of the tree of the knowledge of good and evil looks exactly like the fruit of all the other trees in the garden, but the man and the

THE FALL (THE CHOICE OR THE EVENT)

woman know which tree is which. God is malicious. God hates the man and the woman.

The story, as told in Genesis, is not entirely in the present tense. There is, also, no direct attribution of malice to the Lord God in that rendition. That characterization is left for us to infer. Furthermore, the story contains interesting aspects that are entirely extraneous to the principal aim of this interpretation. For one, there is punishment for disobedience, specifically death. Although the scriptural account provides no evidence that Adam and Eve know what death is, at the very least Adam knows that death will be a consequence of his failure, should he fail, to adhere to the prohibition. He is told this much directly by God. But the story is told to listeners and readers who do know about death, at least to the extent that it is inevitable, mysterious, and apparently to be feared. Punishment per se is not extraneous to our study, but this particular punishment is simply one among many possible punishments. Some Christian writers have even described death not as punishment but as merciful release from our sinful human nature, the alternative being an endless life of sin.

Sexuality is another prominent aspect of the story that is not entirely germane to this interpretation. Nonetheless, the presence of sex is quite obvious, from explicit mention of the nakedness of Adam and Eve, both before they ate, when they did not know that they were naked, and after they ate at which time they did know they were naked. If we are to take seriously the claims about their prelapsarian self-awareness, then Adam and Eve not only did not know that they were naked, they also did not know that they were without clothes. *We* know that they were not wearing clothes, and we transfer to them our psychological understanding of nakedness. The story of the fall is told to and for the fallen, the clothed.

The sexual nature of the story is enhanced by the appearance of the serpent, fearsome and repellent for various reasons, not the least of which is its symbol as a phallus. One need not look far or wide to find a female stripper who includes a python or a boa constrictor in her performance.[2] We, the readers, are to see the naked woman tempted by the phallic serpent, not by some other creature such as a goat, or even a fearsome crocodile. Thus the account in Genesis is full of aspects that we find intriguing, that to varying degrees may pertain to our principal inquiry, and which have been the subject of nearly boundless commentary. These intriguing qualities and occurrences lend a literary quality to the

---

2. In this regard, the cover design by Jo Anne Metsch of Elise Loehnen's *On Our Best Behavior* is a good example.

story, one that inevitably degrades the word of God through obfuscation. These intriguing qualities and occurrences interest us as anthropologists, as psychologists, and as students of the human history of learning and self-consciousness. But all these aspects are ultimately extraneous to the central point being developed here. They serve merely as decoration, seductive and insidious. These aspects of the story elicit an eagerness of those who pursue them to change the subject from the central theme of disobedience. They are diversionary. In retrospect, they are the trappings of sin, its near occasion.

We do not need the snake, or the naked human beings, or even death to see and understand the malice with which the story has been concocted. In fact, we do not even need Eve (or Adam) for this consideration, i.e., not both of them, although the couple provides for yet other aspects of the story: the intimacy of spouses; the unreliability of secondary sources; the attempt to shift responsibility and blame from one to another. But for this interpretation, one person will do, the second person adding a literary or perhaps merely ornamental quality to the story. There need be but one command: FORBIDDEN! What more incentive could anyone want? The command itself, however, becomes truly and unbearably malicious when time is introduced. In the section below on prohibition, we shall return to the command itself.

What more is needed? A rational creature; the garden with the tree of the knowledge of good and evil; sufficiently many other trees to provide fruit, sustenance for the creature; and most important, time.

> The LORD God took the man and put him in the garden of Eden to till it and keep it. And the LORD God commanded the man, saying, "you may freely eat of every tree of the garden; but of the tree of the knowledge of good and evil you shall not eat, for in the day that you eat of it you shall die." (Gen 2:15–17)

We need know nothing more about the command, about the fruit, about the garden, although one might well admire the clever distinction in English translation between the imperative and the future tense: "you shall not eat" and "you shall die." We presume that the garden would provide amply for the sustenance of Adam and Eve. We do not even need to know that "the tree was good for food, and that it was a delight to the eyes" (3:6). In the Temporal Garden, it was assumed that the fruit of the forbidden tree looked just like all the other fruit hanging on trees in the garden. Nor do we need to know that particular name of the tree, as

THE FALL (THE CHOICE OR THE EVENT)

intriguing as the name may be. Knowledge of good and evil seems to be of extraordinary significance. The mind can run riot making connections between this kind of knowledge and divine knowledge, as does the text itself (Gen 3:22). The mind can connect having been made in the image of God with this great knowledge. Just as the mind can dwell nearly endlessly on the sexual connotation of the story and on the interpersonal relationships of the story, one can dwell on the ability to know the difference between good and evil. All this is interesting in its own way, and all this is superfluous to the fundamental nature of sin. All this—wisdom, interpersonal relationships, sex—is nothing but decorative noise—worse than baroque, it is positively rococo—when it comes to what really happens, for what really happens, in a conventional sense, is made possible by the disobedience of Adam and Eve. What really happens are events.

The Temporal Garden treats a day in the lives of Adam and Eve, but really it treats many days. What were these days like? Did Adam and Eve spend much of their time tilling and keeping the garden? By the point where we meet up with them, they have developed some activities for amusement and to pass the time away: bocce, and perhaps chess for rainy days. Note that this is not the quick, six-hour fall that is presented by Dante in his *Comedia*. Dante's version with its brief time span may be dispiriting, but in fact the quantity of duration of time matters little if at all. Six hours, six days, six years are all the same with regard to the time that we suffer, in the case of Adam and Eve with regard to the passage from truly indigenous people to refugees.

What does matter is that every day the sun comes up, even on rainy days, the day stretches out, and the sun goes down. By and large, every day is the same. Adam and Eve go about their business, tilling, playing, eating fruit. This they do, and one might say they do these things both naturally and gladly. We need not concern ourselves with whatever else they may do every day, or most days, or only on rare occasion. But what they must not do is eat of the fruit of the tree of the knowledge of good and evil. They must not eat of the fruit each and every day, *and* they must not eat for every moment of each and every day. Every day is exactly the same. Every moment is exactly the same. Don't eat!

How horrible! Not the living, the sunrise and sunset, the good food, the work and the play. No, that is not horrible. The prohibition is horrible. It could have been issued only by a cruel and malevolent creator, one who must have delighted in the torture of his creatures. This is the being who added the serpent, the name of the tree, and for that matter, Eve, merely to clothe his malicious intent, to provide some frivolous amusement for all concerned while torturing the human beings. In short, this creator has done his best to confuse us the readers along with Adam and Eve in order to disguise his malice.

By telling this story I attempt to arouse sympathy for Adam and Eve. Well, and perhaps a bit more: I tell this story this way to exonerate them, but only in the sense that we always make excuses for ourselves by appealing to extenuating circumstances. In this case, we have the greatest, the most comprehensive extenuating circumstance of all time: time itself. And I tell this story to condemn the creator, he who is so evil as to place such a prohibition on our first parents and then condemn them to perpetual obedience. What perseverance it would take! Supernatural.

Or, perhaps, time was not a factor in the origination of human sin.

C. THE PROHIBITION

There are many aspects of the story of Adam and Eve in the garden that are worthy of comment, and the commentary on this story is enormous. Not all commentary concerns the origin of sin, and some writers do not accept the very premise or assertion that sin per se arises from the disobedience of Adam and Eve. Augustine has shaped much of the discussion ensuing over the ages by describing the transgression as original sin. In a way my entire study accepts this description, although I certainly do not attribute to him the notion that time is sinful. In Augustine's famous meditation on time in chapter 11 of *Confessions*, the creation of time is attributed to the creator, and for Augustine, all creation is good. Here, however, our concern is strictly with the prohibition issued by the LORD God. Furthermore, the concern is with the prohibition per se as prohibition. In other words, we shall not delve here into the punishment for disobedience, which in the case of Adam and Eve is apparently death: "for in the day that you eat of it you shall die." This certainly is the interpretation of the apostle Paul. And I say "apparently" only because one might claim that Adam and Eve did not die *on* the same day that they ate the forbidden fruit.[3] Nor am I especially interested, here, in the attractiveness of the

---

3. An observation, perhaps too subtle, concerns the tense, the timing of the punishment. The Hebrew text has the second person, singular, Qal imperfect of the verb "to die," *muth* (Strong #4191), which is often translated with the English future tense. The Septuagint and the Vulgate also have the future tense. Thus the punishment would be rendered: "you will die." In the RSV translation (and in other English translations

name of the forbidden tree. My sole concern is: forbidden. The pertinent passages are Gen 2:9 and 2:16–17.

> And out of the ground the LORD God made to grow every tree that is pleasant to the sight and good for food, the tree of life also in the midst of the garden, and the tree of the knowledge of good and evil. (Gen 2:9)

> And the LORD God commanded the man, saying: "You may freely eat of every tree of the garden"; (Gen 2:16)

> "but of the tree of the knowledge of good and evil, you shall not eat, for in the day that you eat of it you shall die." (Gen 2:17)

Let us begin with the creation of trees and their purpose, i.e., to produce fruit that both looks good and is suitable as food for Adam and Eve.

> And out of the ground the LORD God made to grow *every tree that is pleasant to the sight and good for food.*

Most especially consider the expression *kal ets*—"every tree." The verb *kalal* (Strong #3634) means "to complete, to perfect." Associated with the verb is the noun (and adjective) *kol* (Strong #3605), "the whole, all." In the construct chain or genitive relationship such as we have here with "tree" (*ets*, Strong #6086), with the singular noun understood collectively, the expression becomes "the whole of trees or every kind of tree."[4]

The LORD God has placed many trees in the garden, and it is not presumptuous to conclude that each and every tree is desirable and good for food, each in its own way. Among the many trees, two are identified by name or description, the tree of life and the tree of knowledge of good and evil. The tree of life is in the midst of the garden, but the text is silent about how these trees may differ, at least visually, from the many other trees as well as regarding the exact location of the tree of knowledge of good and evil. Eve confirms in the next chapter that the tree of knowledge of good and evil is also in the midst of the garden (Gen 3:3). I presume that *all* the trees are the same with respect to their desirability and goodness for food. The fruit of one tree may differ from the fruit of another.

---

including the King James), however, we find the imperative: "you shall die." Accordingly, the temporal aspect of succession, represented by the future tense, is replaced with the non-temporal, more strictly cause-and-effect aspect of succession. Therefore, one might elaborate the punishment: "for in the day that you eat of it I command that you die."

4. Brown et al., *Brown-Driver-Briggs*, 480–81.

This was indicated in the first creation story in which God caused to grow from the earth trees each producing fruit according to its own kind or species (Gen 1:11–12; *min*, Strong #4327). God saw these trees as good and gave them to man for food (1:29). Therefore, from the fruit of the apple tree, or more precisely from the seeds contained in the fruit of the apple tree grow trees bearing apples. Pear trees, however, produce pears.

I have engaged in this little bit of close textual reading to make a simple point. Adam and Eve were placed in a setting, a garden filled with trees, each and every one of which was desirable to look at and with its fruit desirable to eat. Other than names and location, the trees in their desirability are identical. Apples and pears are not identical in the shape, color, fragrance, and flavor. They are nonetheless identical in so far as they are fruit, and they may even be identical in their desirability, perhaps not at the same time. Today Adam might desire apples whereas Eve desires pears. *But* one tree, the tree of the knowledge of good and evil, has been singled out from all the other trees by God's prohibition. Has not the Lord God, by issuing this prohibition, made the tree of the knowledge of good and evil the most interesting tree in the entire garden? This is a tree that has been identified. We presume that there are apple trees and pear trees, but these trees are not explicitly identified. The tree of knowledge of good and evil too is in the midst of the garden along with the tree of life. But other than the prohibition, this tree is similar to every other tree, indeed *identical* to every other tree in its desirability. The subject of good and evil itself elicits interest from all of us, but the intrinsic interest of the subject is secondary to our immediate response to the prohibition. We might even reasonably ask what the words "good" and "evil" mean, if anything, to Adam and Eve. Presumably they are meaningless, but Genesis was not written for Adam and Eve.

Let the tree of the knowledge of good and evil be an apple tree, and further let there be other apple trees in the garden. All the apple trees of the garden produce apples, unlike the pear trees which produce pears. The individual fruits of the apple trees are individual, discernible, countable, desirable to look at, and edible. Each apple is distinct in its individuality, in that it can be counted among the many apples. But each apple is identifiable as an apple, because each has been produced according to its own species or kind, from its own seed. Therefore, given two apples, one from the tree of the knowledge of good and evil and one from another apple tree in the garden, the two apples are distinct from one another in that and only because each apple is an individual apple. Upon viewing the two apples, Adam and Eve would see that one is to the left of the other, or perhaps behind the other. But Adam and Eve would also note the extreme similarity of the two apples, because from among the many objects identifiable in the garden, these two are apples. Augustine claims as much. "We must assume, I imagine, that the apple on that tree was the same kind as the apples they had already found to be harmless on other trees."[5] With this remark, Augustine touches on an aspect of psychological torture that might be attributed to the creator of the Temporal Garden. For now the reader thinks of Adam and Eve having had experience with eating apples.

For all practical purposes such as viewing or eating, therefore, we might say that the two apples are indistinguishable. But they are entirely and absolutely distinct not merely perceptually, i.e., one in spatial location with respect to the other. The two apples are distinct because God has forbidden Adam and Eve from eating one of them while inviting Adam and Eve to enjoy eating the other apple. Surely it is inconceivable that any rational, sentient being, any human being would not want to know more about the forbidden fruit. What is the make-up of one apple such that it is radically distinguished from another apple? Perhaps nothing. With this suggestion, we even go beyond the serpent, for now we are proposing that the only difference between the two pieces of fruit is the prohibition. Absolutely nothing is at stake except for obedience.

Readers of Genesis no doubt will recall the incentives provided by the serpent as well as the punishment of death threatened by God. The serpent offers Eve the opportunity to be God-like and immortal. These incentives, although appealing in a pragmatic—i.e., in a temporal, actual—sense, along with the punishment of death are entirely extraneous to the central challenge of the prohibition. They too amount to noise surrounding the signal of obedience, the real message of the myth.

Other readers of Genesis may accept provisionally this argument regarding the similarity of the two fruits, the two apples, only then to try to connect the seeming indistinguishable state with the innocence of Adam and Eve regarding good and evil, something they had no knowledge of. Although this suggestion has some merit, it is superficial merit that directs our attention away from the centrality of the prohibition. Innocence, evil, and knowledge all amount to extenuating circumstances in the form of context. These are the terms of ethics, morality, and philosophy. The

---

5. Augustine, *Literal Meaning of Genesis* XI.31.41.

prohibition, on our reading however, is above contextual considerations, or perhaps we should say below, as in being absolutely fundamental.

All of the trees are pleasant to the sight and good for food. Admittedly, when the serpent comes on the scene, it has a way of obscuring that fact while focusing attention on another fact. An unsympathetic reading of the account might even attribute to the creator the intent to disguise his real purpose by misdirecting attention and sowing confusion. The serpent said to the woman, "Did God say, 'You shall not eat of any tree of the garden'?" This is surely a clever maneuver, insidious as it may be. The serpent is directing Eve's mind toward categories while appealing, perhaps, to Eve's ability to choose from which trees to eat. They are all okay except for one. Several times each day, Eve chooses fruit from the trees of the garden to eat. A pear for breakfast, an apple for lunch. And the serpent continues that if you eat from the forbidden tree "you will be like God." Barth notes, "What the serpent has in mind is the establishment of ethics."[6]

Regardless of how poorly defined or understood is the notion of the will, the signal speaks directly to it. On the assumption of pure choice, this or that, eat or do not eat, we find in Eve and Adam, *on my interpretation*, an unencumbered will. The choice is to obey or not to obey. It is not to live forever. It is not to be like God. It is not to suffer death. There are no extenuating circumstances that entice or frighten. There is no waiting, because there is no time. In other words, the most fundamental of all extenuating circumstances is absent. Adam and Eve, each an "I," each choose: obey or disobey. In section E, "The Meaning of the Myth," I shall consider more closely how we might understand this choice.

The rendition of the command into English in some translations emphasizes the difficulty that Adam and Eve face in abiding by the prohibition. At Gen 2:17 the Revised Standard Version of the command is "thou shalt not eat of it" or "you shall not eat." This is indeed a standard English rendition, but one can find "do not eat" in the New Life Version, and "don't eat" in the Common English Version. The auxiliary English verb "to do" points to the problem.

The Hebrew command is straightforward: *lo ṭo 'ḵal*. The negative *lo* (Strong #3808) is followed by the second person, singular, Qal imperfect of the verb "to eat" (*aḵal* Strong #398), which is commonly interpreted to be imperative. The Greek of the Septuagint is also straightforward and

---

6. Barth, *Church Dogmatics*, 4/1:448.

THE FALL (THE CHOICE OR THE EVENT) 135

constructed in the same way as the Hebrew: οὐ φάγεσθε. The same holds true for the Latin of the Vulgate: *ne comedas*. As we move to some modern languages where the mood and the person are not necessarily contained in the single word of the verb, we see an increase in the number of words.

German	sollst du nicht essen
French	tu ne mangeras pas
English	you shall not eat!

Some Romance languages retain the economy of the Hebrew, Greek, and Latin.

| Spanish | ¡no comerás! |

We can even appeal to simplified negative commands in some Romance languages where the negative simply precedes the infinitive.

| Italian | non mangiare |

The simple construction is rarely encountered in English and has a slang or hip quality to it, such as in "not to worry."

The most common, modern version of the command in English is "Do not eat!" Even more direct and emphatic is the contraction, "Don't eat!" What appears to be a quirk of the English language indicates the real problem. The auxiliary verb "to do" is used in negative commands in English but not in their corresponding positive commands. "Eat!" suffices for the positive imperative, but for the negative, English enlists "to do" as in "Do not eat!" There is the alternative of "Eat not!" which is economical in length but suitable only in the most rhetorically self-conscious English. Equally self-conscious and pompous is the positive command "Do eat!"

In those cases where the command is given with urgency, the English use of the auxiliary verb is the norm. One can hardly imagine that a parent, upon seeing a small child approaching a hot stove, would say, "Thou shall not touch!" It is much more likely that the parent would say, "Don't touch!" The insertion of the auxiliary verb might even present a complication in the face of the imagined emergency. Thus, the parent might sacrifice grammar for exigency and say, "No touch!"

The prohibition itself, perhaps expressed as "Forbidden," is sufficient to elicit interest on the part of those to whom the command is issued, but of course not mere interest to obey. Quite the opposite sentiment occurs. Our interest is drawn to what is being forbidden and why. Surely one of the first reactions to the imperative "Don't eat!" is "Why not?" The *do* of "Do not eat!" underscores the difficulty. *To do* is to act, to engage the will. *To do* requires personal commitment, resolve. One *does* something. But here the action, the will, the commitment, the resolve are all enlisted negatively. Act not! Will not! Commit not! Resolve not! Were the command to be issued in the temporal garden, then Adam and Eve would be required to act, will, commit, resolve at every moment of their existence and forever. How burdensome and terrifying! Who could issue such a command? How malicious!

D. ORIGINAL SIN AND THE BIBLE

The doctrine of original sin, as developed by Christian writers, has its roots in the Bible, especially in the letters of the apostle Paul. Those Christian traditions that deny the reality of original sin must make some attempt to explain away these passages or at least to explain why they do not point to the origin of sin. Other traditions, such as Judaic, must account for the evil inclination of mankind as well as the proliferation of sins throughout the Hebrew Bible. At no place in the Bible is the transgression of Adam and Eve referred to as the "original sin." Augustine, perhaps relying on Irenaeus, seems to be the first writer to develop the transgression as such. The expression "original" is open to at least two interpretations. The first is chronologically, and perhaps it is strictly and solely chronological. This is the most common interpretation, the one that presupposes time. The second interpretation of "original" views the sin as the source of sin, the ur-sin. This second interpretation is the one that is pursued throughout this study.

In this section, however, my intent is to present those biblical passages that are commonly identified as revealing the truth about the origin of sin in mankind, whether that origin be construed as an occasion or strictly, fundamentally, and merely as the source. These passages traditionally are interpreted as indicating a sinfulness of mankind. They point to sinfulness in the nature of man. Writers claim to varying degrees that this sinfulness inheres in man, to varying degrees that his nature has been degraded, and to varying degrees that he is culpable for his sin. Many of these treatments amount to an attempt to acquit God and his creation from being inherently evil. It is unnecessary to respond to the various attempts to refute the Pauline-Augustinian interpretation. My entire study makes the reality of original sin manifest. The degree of culpability incurred by mankind which must necessarily attend any true notion of sin is another matter, but I shall speak directly to that in later sections.

> ¹² Therefore as sin came into the world through one man and death through sin, and so death spread to all men because all men sinned—¹³ sin indeed was in the world before the law was given, but sin is not counted [ἐλλογέω] where there is not law. ¹⁴ Yet death reigned from Adam to Moses, even over those whose sins were not like the transgression of Adam, who was a type of the one who was to come.
>
> ¹⁵ But the free gift is not like the trespass. For if many died through one man's trespass, much more have the grace of God and the free gift in the grace of that one man Jesus Christ abounded for many. ¹⁶ And the free gift is not like the effect of that one man's sin. For the judgment following one trespass brought condemnation, but the free gift following many trespasses brings justification. ¹⁷ If, because of one man's trespass, death reigned through that one man, much more will those who receive the abundance of grace and the free gift of righteousness reign in life through the one man Jesus Christ.
>
> ¹⁸ Then as one man's trespass led to condemnation for all men [πάντας ἀνθρώπους], so one man's act of righteousness leads to acquittal and life for all men. ¹⁹ For as by one man's disobedience many [οἱ πολλοί] were made sinners, so by one man's obedience many will be made righteous. ²⁰ Law came in, to increase the trespass; but where sin increased, grace abounded all the more, ²¹ so that, as sin reigned in death, grace also might reign through righteousness to eternal life through Jesus Christ our Lord. (Rom 5)

> ²¹ For as by a man came death, by a man has come also the resurrection of the dead. ²² For as in Adam all [πάντες] die, so also in Christ shall all [πάντες] be made alive. (1 Cor 15)

> ¹ And you he made alive, when you were dead through the trespasses and sins ² in which you once walked, following the course of this world, following the prince of the power of the air, the spirit that is now at work in the sons of disobedience. ³ Among these we all once lived in the passions of our flesh, following the

desires of body and mind, and so we were by nature children of wrath, like the rest of mankind. (Eph 2)

These excerpts from Paul's letters lay out the fundamental doctrine of original sin, and do so by developing the analogy between Adam and Jesus Christ. Christ is the new Adam, and just as Adam is seen to transform human nature by his transgression, so Christ is viewed as the true redeemer of man, the one who by his birth, life, death, and resurrection creates a new man. The old man, Adam and all of his progeny, is disordered with respect to God and to all of creation. Man is not entirely evil (almost entirely, according to Calvin), but his disposition is permanently impaired from its original state. Man suffers from concupiscence of the flesh. It is Jesus Christ who through his being, i.e., by means of living and dying, because of his temporality in conjunction with his eternal divinity, has justified man. Christ reorders the disordered nature of man. He straightens that which was bent.

We, the children of Adam, are the "children of wrath." This wrath, the wrath of God, is death, which is the wage of sin. Christ, by his resurrection, has conquered death and thereby given a visible sign that man has been justified, for the risen Christ is the Christ who died, i.e., the risen Christ retains his humanity.

Although most Jewish commentary on the disobedience of Adam and Eve does not interpret the transgression as "original sin," this commentary does acknowledge the evil inclination (*yetzer hara*) common to all mankind if not specifically to Adam and Eve.

> [5] The LORD saw that the wickedness of man was great in the earth and that every imagination of the thoughts of his heart was only evil continually. [6] And the LORD was sorry that he had made man on the earth, and it grieved him to his heart. (Gen 6)

> [21] And when the LORD smelled the pleasing odor, the LORD said in his heart, "I will never again curse the ground because of man, for the imagination of man's heart is evil from his youth; neither will I ever again destroy every living creature as I have done." (Gen 8)

A remarkable aspect of these very similar statements about the heart of man is that they enclose the account of the flood. The LORD God was so displeased with the state of man that he decided in effect to start over by cleansing the earth of these wicked creatures (Gen 6–8). Only Noah "found favor in the eyes of the Lord" (Gen 6:8). Upon disembarking, Noah built an altar to the Lord and sacrificed animals. The Lord found the odor pleasing and vowed not to curse the ground again because of man, although the imagination of man's heart remained evil (8:21). In other words, Noah's favorable status and the blotting out of man from the face of the ground (6:7) were insufficient to effect a change in the Lord's estimation of the heart of man. It remains evil from his youth.

Evil, of course, is not identical with sin. But if the disobedience of Adam and Eve be not sin, there nonetheless can be no dispute about the consequence of the disobedience. No, they did not die on the very day of their transgression, but die they surely did. And cursed they surely were, as well as being expelled from paradise. Calvin goes so far as to claim that the death penalty was an act of mercy on the part of God, thereby relieving mankind of the anguish of living forever in a corrupt state.

There are the often quoted verses from Pss 51 and 14 that are cited as evidence that man is evil from the point of conception, i.e., inherently evil, and persistently evil.

> [5] Behold, I was brought forth in iniquity,
> And in sin did my mother conceive me. (Ps 51)

> [1] The fool says in his heart,
>   "There is no God."
> They are corrupt, they do
>   abominable deeds,
>   there is none that does good.
> [2] The Lord looks down from heaven
>   upon the children of men
>   to see if there are any that act wisely,
>   that seek after God.
> [3] They have all gone astray, they are
>   all alike corrupt;
>   there is none that does good,
>   no, not one. (Ps 14)

The specific transmission of original sin was and is a subject of great interest to Christian writers, who have variously wondered if the inheritance of the fallen state was a biological fact, i.e., materially hereditary, and consequently strictly chronological. Some writers have gone to considerable trouble in an attempt to understand the transfer of sinfulness from the perspective of material cause and effect. This attempt seems to me and to some other Christian commentators as misguided in that it consists of an assault on the myth itself by de-mythologizing it. To see sinfulness as a result of biological procreation is to render the sinful state biological, specifically bio-chemical and material. To do so further presupposes time, and I argue that time is in a way a consequence and not a presupposition of sin. Contemporary versions might give a genetic account of sin. Human beings are indeed animals, and they consist of bio-chemical molecules, of cells and genes. Furthermore, these cells, genes, and molecules participate materially in the commission of sin, but their participation is strictly that, *material*. Molecules do not take a position before God. Sin is not in any way material, even though the individuals who commit sins consist in part of matter. Sin is disorder between the creator and his creatures. It concerns the soul. The strict materialist absolves mankind in effect of all culpability, along with all merit and glory. For the materialist there may be violations of cultural norms, but there is no sin.

I do not mean to deny that "creation was subjected to futility," that it is in need of being "set free from its bondage to decay," and that "the whole creation has been groaning in travail together until now" (Rom 8:20–22). In a way one might look to the so-called natural unfolding of the world for evidence of sin, for evidence of the fall. The subject of natural disasters and the extent to which human beings might be considered individually culpable for these disasters will be taken up later. But here my concern is to point to the biblical characterization of disorder as sin. Such characterization is a matter of the spirit and of freedom. Sin entails culpability and blame, and accordingly it transcends the biological and the material.

The remaining passages noted here come from the Apocrypha, according to the Protestant tradition. These books, with the exception of Second Esdras, appear in the Septuagint and were decreed to be canonical by the Council of Trent. Second Esdras is preserved in Latin, with only 15:57–59 surviving in a Greek papyrus.

> [23] for God created man for incorruption,
> And made him in the image of his own eternity,
> [24] but through the devil's envy death entered the world,
> And those who belong to his party experience it. (Wis 2)

> [24] From a woman sin had its beginning,
> And because of her we all die. (Sir 25)

THE FALL (THE CHOICE OR THE EVENT) 141

The passages from Wisdom and Sirach assert the presumed immortality of the newly created Adam and Eve, an immortality appropriate for a creature made in the image of God. But this immortality was lost with the act of disobedience, as the Lord God had threatened. This much seems to be indisputable according to all accounts and traditions. The passage from Wisdom connects the devil to the fall, presumably by means of the serpent. This connection pushes back the ultimate blame for the transgression by an order of magnitude. The Genesis account provides no rationale for the appearance of the serpent and comments simply that it was the most subtle of beasts. Christian commentary, however, has connected the serpent with the devil, who in turn is seen as a fallen angel, specifically an immortal creature of God who rebelled or disobeyed at an earlier time. This sort of reasoning constitutes indirect acknowledgment of the problem of time that tacitly pervades the Genesis account. In the canonical books, there are oblique references to this fall. In response to the wonder of the seventy newly appointed disciples who observe that even demons are subject to his name, Jesus claims, "I saw Satan fall like lightning from heaven. Behold, I have given you authority to tread upon serpents and scorpions, and over all the power of the enemy; and nothing shall hurt you" (Luke 10:18–19). The fifth of the seven angels seen by John as Revelation "blew his trumpet, and I saw a star fallen from heaven to earth, and he was given the key of the shaft of the bottomless pit" (9:1). Other references appear below in the discussion of the fallen angels.

The excerpt from Sirach explicitly connects the death penalty with sin and further draws the connection between the punishment inherited by all with the disobedience of our first parents. A passage from Second Esdras (3:7) reiterates the second connection, and another passage underscores the first connection (7:48).

> [7] And thou didst lay upon [Adam] one commandment of thine; but he transgressed it, and immediately thou didst appoint death for him and for his descendants. From him there sprang nations and tribes, peoples and clans, without number. (2 Esd 3)

> [19] And thy glory passed through the four gates of fire and earthquake and wind and ice, to give the law to the descendants of Jacob, and thy commandment to the posterity of Israel.
> [20] Yet thou didst not take away from them their evil heart [*cor malignum*], so that thy law might bring forth fruit in them.
> [21] For the first Adam, burdened with an evil heart, transgressed and was overcome, as were also all who were descended from

> him. [22] Thus the disease became permanent: the law was in the people's heart along with the evil root, but what was good departed, and the evil remained. (2 Esd 3)
>
> [30] For a grain of evil seed was sown in Adam's heart from the beginning, and how much ungodliness it has produced until now, and will produce until the time of threshing comes! (2 Esd 4)
>
> [48] O Adam, what have you done? For though it was you who sinned, the fall was not yours alone, but ours also who are your descendants. (2 Esd 7)

These excerpts also refer back to the evil heart of man that the LORD God had decried in Genesis (6 and 8). Esdras also makes explicit the degradation or deformation of the progeny of Adam and Eve. The fall is *our* fall, the glory of Jacob notwithstanding. These assertions harken back (or forward) to Paul's elucidation in Romans, where through one man's transgression we all transgress. With the transgression sin enters the world, even before the issuance of the law to Moses, and here sin reigns. Each and every one of us is condemned to suffer the wrath of God, death.

This much is the conventional interpretation of these biblical passages. Christian and a few Jewish writers have looked to these passages as scriptural confirmation of the origin of sin in the Garden of Eden. I turn now to an attempt to summarize my interpretation of the myth of Adam and Eve, an interpretation that has been presented piecemeal thus far in this section.

E. THE MEANING OF THE MYTH

Sooner or later, each and every rational being must ask: Who am I? How did I get here? Why am I here? What is "here" and why is it *here*? The first few chapters of Genesis quite obviously present a story or account that attempts to address these questions. The Greek title of the book itself, γένεσις, means "origin" or "source." The first Hebrew words of the book are *bereshit*, i.e., "in the beginning." It is well known that in Genesis there are two accounts of creation. The first runs to 2:4. It begins with the creation of the heavens and earth and culminates with the creation of man "in our image" on the sixth day, and God's survey, on the seventh day on which he rested, of the good work he had performed over the preceding six days. The second account runs from 2:5 to 2:24, the end of the chapter.

THE FALL (THE CHOICE OR THE EVENT)

It is here in the second account that we have the creation of the tree of life and the tree of the knowledge of good and evil. Here God prohibits Adam from eating from the latter tree. In contrast to the first account where God made man, male and female, in the second account God creates a helper, the woman who will be named Eve, for Adam. The first word of the third chapter is *nachash* (Strong #5175), "serpent."

An account of our origin, our being, and our purpose helps us to know and understand who we are. This is in response to the age-old commands to know thyself and to examine one's life. Regardless of our inadequate attempts to account for our being, we can be certain that in some sense *we are* and *we are this way*. By *this way* I mean that we have thought, language, and experience (Augustine's memory). We talk to ourselves and to others about ourselves. We know ourselves, no doubt imperfectly, by means of the stories that we tell to ourselves about ourselves. These "stories" include all explanations of our being, all deductions, all elucidations. These include material accounts that begin, quite lamely in my opinion, from the Big Bang, and proceed by means of cause and effect. These accounts enlist evolution as explanation, i.e., descent with modification. And of course, these accounts presuppose time as a background against which we are located. We also provide ourselves with spiritual and rational accounts of our being that attempt to reason back or up from that which is to that which must be or that which must have been. And sooner or later, we are faced with the problem of time and its relation to cause and effect. I have already commented on this latter problem in the section on the temporal and the eternal (chapter 2). There my remarks were general. Here I shall address my comments to the specific story or myth of Adam and Eve, that which Barth calls a "biblical saga."[7] We might wonder about the adequacy of the various accounts of our origins, specifically what it is about them that we find satisfying or unsatisfying. With all such storytelling we run the risk of merely supplying a succession of names for matters and relationships that we do not

---

7. Barth, *Church Dogmatics*, 4/1:508. Paul Ricoeur goes so far as to render all problems concerning time in terms of narrative. "We shall later show how important it is for a theory of narrative that both approaches to the problem of time remain open, by way of the mind as well as by way of the world. The aporia of temporality, to which the narrative operation replies in a variety of ways, lies precisely in the difficulty in holding on to both ends of this chain, the time of the soul and that of the world. This is why we must go to the very end of the impasse and admit that a psychological theory and a cosmological theory mutually occlude each other to the very extent they imply each other." *Time and Narrative*, 3:14.

understand, e.g., Big Bang, God, evolution, chance, love. Such characterization amounts to the Hobbesian denigration of reason as being merely the process by which we add and subtract names, a grand elucidation. In some cases, however, the naming and re-naming contribute to our understanding, even if they do so in a circuitous and serendipitous fashion. We *are* poets, conversational poets. The names that we use are not simply and solely names, but rather they have significance associated with them. In all these accounts, we speak to ourselves, and we do so in the words and contexts of our lives.

For Hegel, language contains the divine in the way that it expresses the truth even when the words do not say what the speaker intends. The words, so to speak, speak the truth despite the speaker's intention. My comments on the story of Adam and Eve, the language that I employ, will have the effect of something almost opposite to Hegel's assertion. These statements will, when taken together, indicate the truth and such *is* my intention. Nevertheless, every statement will be riddled with falsehood, equivocation, and inaccuracies. These true falsehoods include the following.

> With the disobedience of Adam and Eve, time begins.

> Adam and Eve create time by disobeying God. (Present tense)

> Adam and Eve choose freely to disobey God. The choice is a-temporal. It is not in the past. (Present tense)

> The original sin of Adam and Eve is inherited by us only in the most abstract sense of cause and effect, but not in the sense of material propagation. The inheritance is constituent to our being.

> Before the disobedience of Adam and Eve there is no time. It is not the case that before Adam and Eve there was no time. Rather, there *is* no time before Adam and Eve, and this is so because "before" does not mean "before."

Despite the many words that have led us thus far, original sin is the sin that needs no introduction. Nearly everyone can cite some evidence for it, although the evidence surely varies from person to person. Furthermore, the terms used to refer to original sin vary equally widely, with many people reluctant even to acknowledge that what they are talking about is sin. This reluctance is entirely understandable, since the very word "sin" entails some sort of blame, and presumably a just punishment meted out by a judge. Sin entails judgment. Therefore, the Genesis account, no matter how fantastic it may seem to some, appeals to our mind in its attempt to speak to the cause for this universal evidence.

The story about the garden is a myth, i.e., its truth extends far beyond the historical tale it purports to tell. Clear evidence of the mythical extent and power of the story is given by the presence of the serpent and the subsequent recognition of nakedness on the part of Adam and Eve. The veneer of sexuality is not to be overlooked in the telling, and in a sense it is not to be *understood* in the way one might understand the nakedness of children. The story of the fall is told by and for the fallen. The story is for those who associate nakedness with being unclothed and thereby a cause for shame. When we "understand" the nakedness as that of a two-year old running around without any clothes on, we turn Adam and Eve into children, thereby making them so innocent that they are unable to distinguish between good and evil. We seriously err in mistaking one development for another, and in so doing we excuse Adam and Eve. We locate Adam and Eve in this midst of life, our lives, very close to the beginning of human life. No longer are we concerned with origins, but rather with progress in context. We identify the extenuating circumstance of their state of being, tacitly acknowledge to ourselves its intrinsic sinfulness, and then bestow circumstantial absolution. (Augustine is right, I think, to question in *Confessions* the tolerance and quasi acceptance of certain behavior in children that in older persons would be considered cruel, malicious, and obnoxious.) Nonetheless, this important aspect of sexuality is not central to the association of time with sin except for circuitously connecting nakedness with concupiscence of the flesh, which in turn is fundamentally connected to desire and to time. This impetus or desire, then, would indicate an imbalance or lack of justice, which in turn could imply a temporal before and after. One might even think of a tripartite sequence: innocence, fallen-ness, and redemption. But the temporal interpretation of the myth is at best extraneous to the most basic truth expressed by the myth, and more likely this interpretation is misleading. In any true account of these matters, redemption comes first.

Adam and Eve did not persevere. (This is one of the many statements in this section that is true in the intent that motivates it and yet strictly false. It expresses truth by means of nonsense.) Adam and Eve, when they fell through disobedience, did not lack perseverance, contrary to the claims of Augustine and Calvin. Perseverance is not meaningful to them and their fall, and therefore for us perseverance confuses the issue. Adam and Eve fell freely. Their decision to disobey was not owing to a lack of steadfastness on their part. The fall of Adam and Eve was not a historical event in that it did not occur in a historical context. Rather than this, in Barth's words, "Adam is the truth concerning us as it is known to God and told to us." Our will is represented by the will of Adam and Eve.[8] Their fall was the beginning of history, the history of mankind, but the eternal judge is not a historian. Therefore, we must rephrase these remarks.

Adam and Eve do not persevere. Adam and Eve fall through disobedience, but they do not lack perseverance. There is no perseverance, just as there is no nakedness. Adam and Eve fall freely. Their decision to disobey is not owing to a lack of steadfastness on their part. God's prohibition may be *severus* but there is hardly any meaning to *per* that does not presuppose time. Augustine seems to come close to this observation, but not intentionally so. He wonders whether or not perseverance is a gift. He considers the case where someone continues along a path, let us say a path of virtue, for an extended period of time. How do we characterize that journey? We might well say that the person has persevered for the period of time indicated. Augustine's concern with perseverance, however, is about aligning one's being with the will of God, i.e., by having one's will and thoughts and deeds to be in accord with the will of God as expressed by eternal law. Augustine concludes ultimately that such alignment is a gift from God, that the accord between one's will and the will of God is truly a gift that the individual receives from God. The gift, although singular, is trans-temporal. For Augustine, the time period over which one may or may not persevere is a lifetime. The end of the period is marked by death. Perseverance then is intrinsically temporal.

The condition of fallen man, fallen-ness, is one of suffering, wherein man seeks to persevere endlessly. Man experiences fallen-ness, a passion. But owing to his sinful state, his corrupted nature, he is unable to concentrate sufficiently to persevere. "They are corrupt . . . there is none that does good, no, not one" (Ps 14:1, 3). This is the story of original sin as developed by Augustine and others. The account in Genesis, under my interpretation, is not one of suffering, at least not "until" Adam and Eve decide to disobey. Unlike Milton, I am determined not to have Adam and Eve suffer the consequences of their sin before they commit it. It is

---

8. Barth, *Church Dogmatics*, 4/1:510.

incorrect to speak of their condition before their fateful decision, if by *before* one implies temporal priority. Adam and Eve, at least with respect to the prohibition, were not temporal. Therefore, they did not persevere. In fact, we must say that they do not persevere. No period of time occurs before the act of disobedience. Here we are investigating the origin of sin, not its consequence. Sins occur as events; they are committed, but not sin.

It is not incorrect to speak of the state of Adam and Eve in which they were obedient, or at least not disobedient. And this state occurs before the state of disobedience, but only in so far as disobedience presupposes obedience. There is no loosening of whatever was never tightened. In every other regard concerning the prohibition, we must say that Adam and Eve do not persevere because there is no perseverance. Perseverance is nothing. Only "after" the decision to disobey does perseverance, to the extent that it is anything at all, come to be.

With this understanding of the state of Adam and Eve *before* the fall, let us return to several of the "true falsehoods" mentioned above, for they mark out the beginning of time.

> With the disobedience of Adam and Eve, time begins.
>
> Adam and Eve create time by disobeying God.
>
> Adam and Eve choose freely to disobey God.
>
> Before the disobedience of Adam and Eve there is no time.

All of these statements are in the present tense. The fourth statement might better be rendered: Without the disobedience of Adam and Eve there is no time. I render them so in an attempt to indicate that the statements are timeless, although the statements refer to time. Furthermore my readers and I are all largely temporal beings, not just in our being but also in our thought. We put time everywhere, even where it does not belong. With the single, truly free choice by Adam and Eve to disobey God's only commandment, time begins in the sense that time *is*, and this time *is* in a way that accords entirely with Aristotle's time that always was.[9] With this choice, Adam and Eve transform their inner organization of all thought into an alien. They commit the sin of apperception, which will

---

9. Augustine seems to agree also with this interpretation when he claims that time was created but always existed. *City of God* XII.12.

be presented in the next chapter. Adam and Eve make time double, both inner and outer, and as *outer*, time becomes something to be suffered. We might even say that Adam and Eve, with their choice, create the possibility of perseverance.

I use "create" in these passages not in its true sense of to make something from nothing. (If time truly is sin, then "un-create"—not annihilate—would be more suitable.) Although many people use the term freely to indicate the clever way human beings are able to put things together, I have attempted to be careful with the word. Human beings are poets, not creators, and this poetizing that we engage in is a sure sign of our fallen-ness. Nevertheless, we have some notion, albeit cloudy, of virtues like perseverance. And if perseverance be anything at all, a virtue at least secondarily, a gift from God, then its possibility stems from the decision of our first parents to disobey.

What about the serpent? What is the serpent doing when it speaks to Eve and entices her to eat of the forbidden fruit? The serpent can be seen as time in potency, an image. Snakes are not our friends, they are aliens. Here we have reverse atavism, a prophecy. We have the foretelling of the history of mankind. Barth writes:

> In this respect the speech of the serpent in Gen. 3 smacks throughout of true human development. It circles around the theme of the necessity open to and indeed laid upon man to judge and then to act in respect of that which is worthy of him and proper to him. First of all there is the general question which obviously creates the atmosphere with its tone of sincere sympathy (and it is worth noting that as opening the way to autonomous action it is addressed to the wife): whether God has really said that they are not to eat of any of the trees of the garden? (v. 1) whether poor man has actually to be content to live in paradise and to be deprived of its fruits?[10]

But by eating, you will become God-like. You will possess knowledge of right and wrong. "What the serpent has in mind is the establishment of ethics."[11]

Our subject is original sin, i.e., *sin*, which is a turning away from God, a turning away that is made possible—possible from our perspective—by pride, which in turn is made possible negatively by unbelief. The turning away is a willful act, a choice to move away from that which is,

---

10. Barth, *Church Dogmatics*, 4/1:434.
11. Barth, *Church Dogmatics*, 4/1:448.

THE FALL (THE CHOICE OR THE EVENT)

Being itself, God. It is a choice of self, but self that has no being lest it comes from Being, God. And therefore the act, sin, is one for which the actor bears responsibility. The creature that turns away from the creator is culpable, and he is culpable exactly to the extent that his turning away is sinful. After all extenuating circumstances have been considered and discredited, the creature's act is blameworthy. Barth, following Calvin, claims that all sin is a matter of disobedience, rooted in pride and unbelief.[12]

In this world, in the world of time, the culpability of the blameworthy act has temporal consequences. We die. Death is the wage of sin. With sin comes death. And with sin comes time. Thus time and death are linked, each in a way as a consequence of sin. The sin itself is a way of saying "I" which rejects God. I shall return to this notion presently and at the very end when I speak of salvation, a redemption according to which the individual can say "I" without sinning. But here we must simply connect death with the being of time that is alien, that timely-ness which renders consciousness as suffering. This is the two-fold time of inner organization and outer assault. This is the time of Adam and Eve. It is the time in which we live and we die.

One might like to think of our sinful nature, our fleshy concupiscence, or our three lusts (lust of the flesh and the lust of the eyes and the pride of life, 1 John 2:16), as merely a condition, a necessary state of being human. This sort of thinking would remove the blame associated with original sin, and it is a kind of thinking that can be found in both Catholic and Protestant accounts of original sin and our sinful nature. I believe that it also forms the foundation for Heidegger's *Being and Time*. Presumably we are not directly responsible for a condition into which we our born, into which we find ourselves having fallen. Following Augustine, Calvin comes close to the argument being offered here in that he determines that human nature is so degraded as to be abhorrent to God, and accordingly the guilt of Adam and Eve is imputed "naturally" to each and every one of us. But Calvin arrives at his conclusion by ways quite different from those developed here. Indeed, in a perverse way, one can associate Heidegger's understanding of mankind, *Dasein*, with that of Calvin by removing all the negative rhetoric from the writings of the latter.

Predestination, foreknowledge, and the question of freedom will be dealt with later, but here we note that apparent freedom with which Adam and Eve make (N.B. present tense) the choice to disobey. Their choice is

---

12. Barth, *Church Dogmatics*, 4/1:414.

truly the kind that Kant would like to attribute to reason alone, the choice completely devoid of extenuating circumstances, truly spontaneous, made out of respect for and loyalty to the principle of non-contradiction. The rendition of prelapsarian man by Milton in *Paradise Lost* is far off the mark. Milton depicts a garden full of tension, circumspection, diffidence, and fear. Milton's first couple suffers mightily "before" the choice. Adam and Eve suffer the consequences of their sin prior to committing it. There we encounter Anxious Adam: the man with a choice; Deliberative Eve: the prudent woman trying to foresee the future with hopes for advancement.

I reject that interpretation in favor of the a-temporal one presented here. Adam and Eve have a choice under my interpretation, and one might even claim that only under my interpretation do they have a free choice. For under this interpretation they have no need to persevere. They have no need for steadfast faith and resolute heart. They need only to obey. It is correct to say that they need to obey only once, for in the state of the time-less, once is all.

Adam and Eve, even before the fall, are individuals. I do not say that they were individuals, because before the fall was not in the past. Correspondingly, salvation is not in the future, but it differs from the state of man before the fall. Salvation is not a return to the paradise of the garden. Salvation absorbs all history, it does not preclude it. Salvation, although in all ways in the present, is not ignorant of life and its temporality. The life and times of all are saved.

Adam and Eve, however, are capable of saying "I." Indeed, Eve does so most notably when, apparently enticed by the serpent and the appeal of the fruit itself, she sees, takes, and eats. Genesis 3:6 has *wattiqqah mippiryow wattokal*. The phrase, with verbs in the consecutive imperfect tense, is commonly translated in the simple past tense: She "took of its fruit and ate." The choice of tense fits with the supposition that the beginning chapters of Genesis are providing a historical narrative. But the Hebrew verbs themselves do not require translation with the past tense. Accordingly, on my interpretation of the entire myth as an account of the beginning of time, the expression reads: She "takes of the fruit and eats."

In so doing, Eve says "I" in a way that separates her from God and perhaps from all creation. In the extravagant rendition of this passage in *Paradise Lost*, Milton even has Eve deliberate regarding whether or not to share the fruit with Adam. Presumably her newly achieved god-like status might be worth saving for herself. In the biblical account, however, immediately after eating of the fruit, Eve gives some to Adam, who eats.

THE FALL (THE CHOICE OR THE EVENT) 151

Therefore, we can take their transgression of God's command as being mutual. The culpability assigned to one may be assigned to the other, even though Adam and Eve are quick in their attempts to shift the blame: from Adam to Eve, and from Eve to the serpent.

In this truly free act we find the origin of separation. It is here that the experience of alienation begins, for it is here that time begins. The sinful individual begins to disintegrate, to separate self from self, and self from God. The sinful individual begins to *not be*. This is the original sin that is committed by each and every one of us every day, and it truly is the origin of blameworthy-ness. This sin is the very qualification for being blameworthy.

Paul Tillich comes close to capturing the true meaning of the myth of the fall. In his terms, *the* event is rendered as a movement from essence to existence. "Mythologically speaking, Adam before the fall was in an essential, though untested and undecided, unity with God. But this is not man's situation, nor is it the situation of anything that exists. Man must ask about the infinite from which he is estranged, although it belongs to him; he must ask about that which gives him the courage to take his anxiety upon himself."[13] Although the terminology—essence, existence—seems abstract, we can see the correlation by keeping in mind the inextricably temporal nature of existence in contrast to essence. My comments above on the temporal and the eternal developed a kind of action, cause and effect, that is a-temporal. The subjects and objects of this action, primarily mathematical principles, are correctly viewed as being, i.e., as "having" essence. But of course, they do not "have" essence as a characteristic or an aspect or a quality of what they are. These principles simply *are*. In the realm of existence, however, time becomes an aspect of being. Being acquires circumstance; it is located and obtains context, circumstances.

Tillich makes explicit the distinction between essence and the temporal. "Therefore, it is inadequate to ask questions concerning Adam's actual state before the fall; for example, if he was mortal or immortal, whether or not he was in communion with God, whether or not he was in a state of righteousness. The verb 'was' presupposes actualization in time. But this is exactly what cannot be asserted of the state which transcends potentiality and actuality."[14] It is possible to render these accounts into traditional philosophical categories such as being and becoming. My

---

13. Tillich, *Systematic Theology*, 1:206.
14. Tillich, *Systematic Theology*, 1:259.

emphasis on the dual nature of time as inner organization and outer alien subsumes these other philosophical interpretations and allows further for the development of sin and culpability. Furthermore, the philosophical accounts and rendition are also subsumed not necessarily by my account but by the revelation of Jesus as the Christ.

The various Abrahamic religious traditions have given respectively various accounts of the meaning of the event of the garden. It is not nor has it been at any time my intent to provide a comprehensive and balanced presentation of these other opinions, although I have learned much from studying them. These remarks run the danger of oversimplifying. Among the traditional accounts, those given by Augustine and especially by the reformers Luther and Calvin strike most readers as being the most severe in their judgment of the human condition. For their interpretations see a radically degraded nature that is utterly incapable of even the slightest repair without the assistance of grace from God. Following Anselm's notion of original justice, Roman Catholicism has adopted a somewhat less severe evaluation of the human being, one which regards man as essentially good but now lacking a kind of balance or governor that he had before the fall. Much of the disagreement surrounds the meaning of "natural" as applied to the human being, the being created by God and the being which each one of us is. Indeed, much of the disagreement surrounds being itself. Augustine's fleshly concupiscence is a remnant of the fall, a scar on the nature of man, and the dispute is over whether the scar is permanently transformational or merely a permanent encumbrance. The Orthodox churches offer an even milder interpretation, one that focuses less on the fleshly concupiscence of Paul and Augustine, without denying the fateful consequences of the decision by Adam and Eve to disobey God's command. Jewish theologians by and large reject the terminology of original sin, although they acknowledge the evil inclination of man's heart mentioned in Genesis (6:5 and 8:21). All traditions recognize the explicit punishment of death in consequence of the disobedience, although often not with the rhetorical flair of the apostle Paul. "For the wages of sin is death" (Rom 6:23). The Jewish rejection of original sin, in my mind, conforms with the denial of Jesus of Nazareth as the Christ, for the meaning of the Christian redemption, the Christian messiah entails original sin.

In a way, my interpretation may appear to be the most severe of all. The deformation of human nature is time itself, both as it is and as it is understood by us. Thus far I have merely mentioned the prospect of correction, justification to be theologically explicit, without developing the notion or offering any prospect of grace. Those considerations are postponed for the end of this study, although they are necessarily presupposed. Sin presupposes grace. My account, however, might seem to be especially dispiriting because it renders our most fundamental ability to think at all as duplicitous, as that by which we organize all thought while being "at the same time" that by which we suffer. Things happen to us.

It is not my intent here to despair over our condition. Indeed, this inquiry seeks at every turn to find the cause of our culpability. How are we able to blame others and ourselves? How are we to understand that things might have been different? How can we possibly understand the word "ought"? And what are the stories and conversations that we must tell to ourselves and have with ourselves in order to *be* with ourselves, to examine our life so that it is worth living. There is a way of reconciling my interpretation with that of Roman Catholicism, although I am not familiar with any Catholic doctrine that attempts to do so. If the original justice of Anselm can be seen as the a-temporal state of Adam and Eve before the fall, i.e., as the unique position of being able to make a truly free choice, then there may be a way of viewing the two interpretations in concordance.

F. THE FALLEN ANGELS

By way of addendum to these comments on the fall of mankind, let us turn to the topic of the so-called fallen angels, and in particular to the fall of the devil, also known as Satan and as Lucifer. I shall not review the history or literature of fallen angels. Furthermore, I do not have an interpretation or an opinion of the fall of angels in particular, at least not in a way that is reserved exclusively for angels. The account given here, however, of the story of Adam and Eve might be considered by some to be more appropriate for the fall of Lucifer, the devil, Satan, or the angels. Aspects of the angelic fall have been incorporated into my interpretation of original sin, for these aspects truly pertain to the origin of sin. There may be some value in reserving certain understandings of culpability and its related notion of freedom for creatures unencumbered with bodies. Our bodies and material itself can at times seem to be impediments to our lofty aspirations. Concupiscence of the flesh. Paul goes so far as to claim "I know that nothing good dwells within me, that is, in my flesh.

I can will what is right, but I cannot do it" (Rom 7:18). But the pure or blank tableau that one might associate with rational beings who are not necessarily sentient, angels for example, is entirely pertinent and even necessary for an attempt to understand the responsibility of sentient rational beings. Kant's *Critique of Pure Reason* and *Grounding for the Metaphysics of Morals* are in a way attempts to understand how the purely rational part of human beings operates in a world of sensation.

I do not mean to suggest by these remarks that the human being can be reduced solely to animal and reason, although both are constitutive of our humanity. Nor do I claim that angels are solely rational beings. Along with reason and living body, human beings are creatures of faith, hope, and charity. Perhaps so too are angels. My purpose here is to present an interpretation of creatures like us but incorporeal, creatures that are free from sensory stimulus and inclination. Hence the concern with fallen angels.

The appearance of the serpent in the garden, for example, is often considered to be the work of the devil. It is seen as the work of a tempter who is evil in himself or at least whose intent is evil. This sort of consideration is extraneous to our principal interpretation, and in fact it diverts or subverts genuine consideration of the first appearance of sin by introducing circumstance and incentive. Of great significance, however, is the element of choice that is accorded to Adam and Eve in their disobedience. Their choice to disobey is absolutely free. A contextual interpretation of the garden, with food good to eat and apparently deceptive advice from the serpent, abolishes the absolute freedom necessary for my interpretation. This sort of contextual interpretation is one that fits our daily lives, our temporal and corporeal stimuli and temptations. It starts after things are already under way. This is the kind of interpretation, although necessarily for all who live, that obscures guilt while at the same time intending to give an account of guilt. This is the kind of interpretation that shifts blame. This is the kind of interpretation that always has an eye out for extenuating circumstances, and in so doing lacks the single-minded purpose needed to dive deeply into the original prohibition and its violation.

The absolute freedom of the choice here attributed to Adam and Eve is assigned to the fallen angels by those who treat the matter, and these treatments are at least as old as Augustine's writings. I shall address the critical matter of choice in a following section that deals with freedom and foreknowledge. The intent here is to bring forward the case of the fallen angels along with its traditional interpretation as addendum to my treatment of the fall of mankind.

The Book of Enoch is an ancient Hebrew text that contains a section, "The Book of Watchers," which describes the fall of certain angels who had become enamored with women. This interest accords with a curious passage in Genesis (6:1–4) that speaks of the sons of God who found the daughters of men to be fair, and who took them as wives. The biblical passage then goes on to mention the Nephilim, apparently giants from an earlier time. These fallen angels, however, are not the ones that are taken up by Christian theologians and seen as those who rebelled directly and purely against God. These fallen angels from Enoch and Genesis are surrogates for Adam and Eve. These angels are not tempted by their very identity, as are Adam and Eve on my interpretation, but rather are tempted by fleshly desire. They suffer concupiscence of the flesh, whether or not they are fleshly themselves.

There is in fact no absolutely explicit testimony in the Bible and Apocrypha of the fall of the devil and his cohort. The following biblical passages are often cited as indirect testimony for the fall, and taken collectively may provide sufficient foundation.

Directed against Babylon and its king, Isaiah exclaims (14:12–15):

> [12] How you are fallen from heaven,
>   O Day Star, son of Dawn!
> How you are cut down to the ground,
>   You who laid the nations low!
> [13] You said in your heart,
>   [14] "I will ascend to heaven;
> above the stars of God
>   I will make myself like the Most High."
> [15] But you are brought down to Sheol,
>   To the depths of the Pit. (Isa 14)

The Day Star, often identified with Venus, is in this tradition seen as Lucifer, the son of Dawn. I am unfamiliar with any further connection between the concupiscent angels mentioned above and the goddess of love and beauty, Venus.

While teaching on the Mount of Olives, Jesus describes the final judgment by the Son of Man.

> [41] Then he will say to those at his left hand, "Depart from me, you cursed, into the eternal fire prepared for the devil and his angels." (Matt 25)

The newly appointed seventy disciples found that even the demons were subject to the name of the Son of Man. Having been informed of this power, Jesus responded.

> [18] I saw Satan fall like lightning from heaven. [19] Behold, I have given you authority to tread upon serpents and scorpions, and over all the power of the enemy, and nothing shall hurt you. (Luke 10)

The apostle Paul exhorted the Corinthians to drive out of the church the immoral people within their membership. Paul claims that God will judge the outsiders, but that we followers of Christ will judge those within. Do not take one another to public court, but rather take care of disputes within the church.

> [2] Do you not know that the saints will judge the world? And if the world is to be judged by you, are you incompetent to try trivial cases? [3] Do you not know that we are to judge angels? How much more, matters pertaining to this life! (1 Cor 6)

In the Second Letter of Peter, the author writes about God's ability to judge correctly, and to reward the righteous and to punish the wicked.

> [4] For if God did not spare the angels when they sinned, but cast them into hell and committed them to pits of nether gloom to be kept until the judgment . . . [9] then the Lord knows how to rescue the godly from trial, and to keep the unrighteous under punishment until the day of judgment. (2 Pet 2)

A similar sentiment is expressed in the Letter of Jude.

> [6] And the angels that did not keep their own position but left their proper dwelling have been kept by him in eternal chains in the nether gloom until the judgment of the great day. (Jude 1)

Finally, there are several passages from the book of Revelation that can be interpreted as testimony for the fall of angels. In chapter 12, the great dragon of heaven is identified as the devil and as Satan. He is further identified as that "ancient serpent," presumably the one at the beginning of Genesis, chapter 3.

> [3] And another portent appeared in heaven; behold, a great red dragon, with seven heads and ten horns, and seven diadems upon his heads. [4] His tail swept down a third of the stars of heaven, and cast them to the death . . .

> ⁹ And the great dragon was thrown down, that ancient serpent, who is called the Devil and Satan, the deceiver of the whole world—he was thrown down to earth, and his angels were thrown down with him. (Rev 12)

In chapter 20, the author reveals a final conflict with "that ancient serpent, who is the Devil and Satan." After having been bound for one thousand years in the bottomless pit, he will be freed to wage war against the camp of saints. But he and his army will be consumed by heavenly fire.

> ¹⁰ And the devil who had deceived them was thrown into the lake of fire and sulphur where the beast and the false prophet were, and they will be tormented day and night for ever and ever. (Rev 20)

Surely the most elaborate and well-known account of the fallen angels occurs at the beginning of Milton's *Paradise Lost*. That account hints at the reason for any consideration here of this fall, specifically the pride that might be associated with the free choice to turn away from God. The matters of cause and effect and the freedom of choice, Kierkegaard's *possibility*, will be considered later, but here let us summarize briefly the accounts and rationales given by Augustine, Anselm, and Aquinas. In anticipation, however, I note that the task here is to give an account for disobedience, to provide a narrative and a rationale for turning away from God and from the good.

Augustine writes frequently and at length about the fall of the angels, and he elaborates on the similarities between that fall and the fall of mankind. In this respect, I have followed his connection by combining the two falls into one, the one that initiates time. Among the many sources for Augustine's thought on the matter, *The Literal Meaning of Genesis*, *On the Free Choice of the Will*, and *The City of God* are especially informative. Augustine is chiefly concerned with establishing the absolute culpability of the fallen angels, or at least of the devil (Lucifer or Satan). In order to do so, Augustine must give an account of the devil's decision to disobey that relies on no exterior causes whatsoever. This sentiment that motivated Augustine is the same sentiment that has led me to my interpretation of the fall of mankind, and accordingly to be obliged to take up the matter of the fallen angels in the first place.

Among the various accounts of why the devil so chose to disobey God—indeed if we can even ask the question "Why?" in this respect—one finds that the Christian writers remain unified in attributing the action solely to the will of the devil. Piety apparently demands that in no way must evil in God's creation be traceable back to the creator himself.[15] (Hegel was not pious.) In his treatment, Peter King introduces an apparently critical distinction between cause and reason in the sense that to provide a reason for an action differs from identifying the cause for the action. I shall return to this important matter below when I discuss freedom of choice and foreknowledge. But at this stage in the argument, one can readily foresee the difficulties that must attend the difference between cause and reason or rationale. How are we to evaluate the workings of what is generally referred to as the will?

For Augustine, pride is the reason for the fall of the devil because pride is the basis for all sin. He quotes the book of Sirach on the matter (10:13), "The beginning of all sin is pride."[16] This angelic sin is connected to the first human sin. In the form of the serpent, the devil told the woman that she would be like God. "When would the woman have believed this assertion, telling them they had been held back by God from something good and beneficial, if there had not already been in her mind that love of her own independent authority and a certain proud over-confidence in herself, of which she had to be convicted and then humbled by that very temptation."[17] What does it mean to be like God, and is it desirable?

Augustine goes to some length to explain that this desire to be like God, this sin of pride, is not indirectly caused by God himself who had created the devil and subsequently Adam and Eve. The devil was not created evil, although he never stood in truth nor lived a blessed life. "But the very moment he was made, he turned away from the light of truth."[18] Thus of his own accord, the devil refused the blessed life of the good angels, a life that entails knowledge that they will not sin in the future. In this regard, the faithful angels inhabit a state of timeless-ness.

With his interlocutor Evodius, Augustine emphasizes that God created both the devil and man to be good.

> Evodius: In addition, I proposed and you granted that everything good is from God; human beings can also be understood to be from God on this score. For a human being *qua* human being is something good, since he can live rightly when he wills to.

---

15. Especially helpful in navigating these accounts is the discussion of the matter provided by Peter King, "Angelic Sin."

16. Augustine, *Literal Meaning of Genesis* XI.15.19.

17. Augustine, *Literal Meaning of Genesis* XI.30.39.

18. Augustine, *Literal Meaning of Genesis* XI.23.30; see also *On the Free Choice* I.2.4.

> Augustine: Obviously, if these things are so, the question you raised has been solved. If a person is something good and could act rightly only because he willed to, then he ought to have free will (*libera voluntas*), without which he could not act rightly. We should not believe that, because a person also sins through it, God gave it to him for this purpose. The fact that a person cannot live rightly without it is therefore a sufficient reason why it should have been given to him. Free will can also be understood to be given for this reason.[19]

Augustine here provides a response to those who question why man was given freedom in the first place if he was subsequently to misuse this power. According to Augustine, without freedom man would be unable to live rightly (*ut recte vivertur*). He may be able to live entirely in accord with creation and to do so naturally, but not *rightly*, as a stone naturally but not rightly falls toward the center of the earth. Nonetheless, the individual's right action, although commanded by eternal law, is in no way personally meritorious, for if it were, the person would have a basis for pride.

The will, angelic or human, is an intermediate good that may choose to adhere to the common and unchangeable good. "But the will sins when it is turned away from the unchangeable and common good, towards its private good, or towards something external, or towards something lower."[20] Augustine acknowledges to Evodius that he cannot answer the question, Where does the first sin come from? This is so, according to Augustine, because it does not come from anywhere. "If this movement, namely turning the will away from the Lord God, is undoubtedly a sin, then surely can we not say that God is the author of sin? Therefore, this movement will not be from God. Then where does it come from? If I were to reply to your question that I do not know, perhaps you will then be the sadder, but I will at least have replied truthfully. What is nothing cannot be known."[21] This much of the argument accords well with Augustine's understanding of God as not only the source of all being but, in a way, all being himself. If, then, some substance could be identified as the cause of the devil's sin, this substance in turn would have its being from God. The soul, then, turns from God absolutely spontaneously, and the search for the cause of a free act is a wild goose chase. Finding a cause for this

---

19. Augustine, *On the Free Choice* II.1.2–3.
20. Augustine, *On the Free Choice* II.19.53.
21. Augustine, *On the Free Choice* II.19.54.

disobedience would in fact exculpate the offender by rendering the sin an effect.

With this much of the argument in place, Augustine must account for the timing of the devil's first sin, since the devil must enjoy no time living the blessed life on the one hand, but on the other hand the sinful nature of pride in the devil must not be attributed to God. Augustine quotes the Gospel of John regarding the origin of sin. The devil "was a murderer from the beginning" (8:44). Augustine elaborates by claiming that the devil fell from the beginning, i.e., the devil enjoyed no time living in the bliss associated with the holy angels. First he did not stand in the truth, and then from the time that man could be murdered, the devil became a murderer.[22]

Augustine also cites the First Letter of John regarding the *beginning* of sin. "As for what John says about the devil, The devil sins from the beginning 1 John 3:8, they who suppose it is meant hereby that the devil was made with a sinful nature, misunderstand it; for if sin be natural, it is not sin at all. . . . And from this passage, The devil sins from the beginning, it is not to be supposed that he sinned from the beginning of his created existence, but from the beginning of his sin, when by his pride he had once commenced to sin."[23] Thus Augustine has multiple interpretations of the meaning of "beginning," and these are crucial to my argument regarding free choice and the origin of sin. It is crucial for Augustine's understanding, however, that the devil not partake at all of the blessedness of the holy angels, a blessedness that includes absolute assurance of total fidelity to God.

> From all this, it will readily occur to any one that the blessedness which an intelligent being desires as its legitimate object results from a combination of these two things, namely, that it uninterruptedly enjoy the unchangeable good, which is God; and that it be delivered from all dubiety, and know certainly that it shall eternally abide in the same enjoyment. That it is so with the angels of light we piously believe; but that the fallen angels, who by their own default lost that light, did not enjoy this blessedness even before they sinned, reason bids us conclude.[24]

---

22. Augustine, *Literal Meaning of Genesis* XI.16.21.
23. Augustine, *City of God* XI.15.
24. Augustine, *City of God* XI.13.

Thus even the faithful angels experience time, although perhaps not as a suffering, since they are assured of their faithfulness. This assurance entails a context, a Kierkegaardian possibility. This possibility must consist of the following: the angel now knows that at some moment, not now, the angel will be faithful to God as he now is. This angel then must somehow experience time without suffering it. This is a kind of time that has been cleansed of sinfulness, a kind of time unknown to us human beings, a time in which there is no doubt concerning right action.

Anselm devotes an entire treatise to the fall of the devil, which was considered in some detail above in the section on perseverance (chapter 5). I add here the following observations. Anselm determines two goods and two evils: justice and injustice, and advantage and disadvantage.[25] Accordingly God created two wills, one for happiness (advantage) and one for rectitude (justice).[26] The devil, therefore, exercised only the will for happiness, and did so incorrectly. But there was no cause for the devil's failure to will justice. "He abandoned justice *because* he willed what he ought not to will, and he abandoned it *by* willing what he ought not to will. . . . No cause preceded this will, except that he was able to will . . . there was no other cause by which his will was in any way incited or attracted. Instead, his will was its own efficient cause, if I may put the matter that way, and its own effect."[27] Thus, although Anselm adds to Augustine's interpretation of the devil's fall by distinguishing between two wills, he agrees entirely with Augustine that there was no cause for the devil's fall. Spontaneous action *is* uncaused action. Specifically, God did not indirectly cause the devil to fall by creating him with a particular nature or disposition. This interpretation accords with Augustine's thinking that God is being. To seek a cause, even to appeal to the notion of cause betrays a misunderstanding of freedom.

Aquinas concurs with the accounts given by Augustine and Anselm, and elaborates on certain matters. Following Augustine's argument that pride is the origin of all sin, Aquinas claims that the first sin of the fallen angels can be none other than pride.

> Yet, as a consequence, it was possible for envy also to be in them, since for the appetite to tend to the desire of something involves on its part resistance to anything contrary. Now the envious man

---

25. Anselm, *On the Fall*, ch. 12.
26. Anselm, *On the Fall*, ch. 14.
27. Anselm, *On the Fall*, 211.

> repines over the good possessed by another, inasmuch as he deems his neighbor's good to be a hindrance to his own. But another's good could not be deemed a hindrance to the good coveted by the wicked angel, except inasmuch as he coveted a singular excellence, which would cease to be singular because of the excellence of some other. So, after the sin of pride, there followed the evil of envy in the sinning angel, whereby he grieved over man's good, and also over the Divine excellence, according as against the devil's will God makes use of man for the Divine glory.[28]

This is how Aquinas accounts for the tradition that ascribes envy to the devil because of the creation of mankind. Out of pride, the devil seeks to exult himself above his creator, to exult himself above all. Accordingly, the existence of any other good can lead to the conclusion that the highest good may not be all good. The devil is not responsible for the creation of Adam and Eve, and consequently his basic pride leads him to envy their natural goodness.

Aquinas also elaborates on the notion that the devil's choice to sin was uncaused. He notes that mortal sin occurs in two ways in the act of free will. The first way comes about because of ignorance or error, and because of the passions or habit. Aquinas gives as an example the adulterer.

> In this way there can be no sin in the angel; because there are no passions in the angels to fetter reason or intellect . . .; nor, again, could any habit inclining to sin precede their first sin. In another way sin comes of free-will by choosing something good in itself, but not according to proper measure or rule; so that the defect which induces sin is only on the part of the choice which is not properly regulated, but not on the part of the thing chosen; as if one were to pray, without heeding the order established by the Church. Such a sin does not presuppose ignorance, but merely absence of consideration of the things which ought to be considered. In this way the angel sinned, by seeking his own good, from his own free-will, insubordinately to the rule of the Divine will.[29]

Unlike the apostle Paul, the devil, therefore, made his choice unimpeded by passion or ignorance or habit. For the devil, there were no extenuating circumstances, no fleshly concupiscence. In this sense, Aquinas has presented the case for why I have considered the fallen angels in the first place. For from the position of Aquinas, and of Anselm and Augustine

---

28. Aquinas, *Summa theologica* I, Q.63, A.2.
29. Aquinas, *Summa theologica* I, Q.63, A.1.

THE FALL (THE CHOICE OR THE EVENT)   163

too, there is no precedent for the angels' fall. There is nothing external that could be considered in the form of temptation. The angels are without passion, without concupiscence of the flesh. They move themselves by willing.

Aquinas makes a very fine distinction regarding "when" this first sin occurred. In fact, the devil was truly wicked by his own choice, but such action was not an inordinate act of the will. In short, the devil was not created with an evil will, logically bound to sin, and thus in a way he did not sin in the first instance of his creation. Here, Aquinas is trying to distinguish between logical priority—the devil's created constitution, which is good—and temporal order. The argument that the devil sinned in the first instant would hold only for movements of the will that are measured by time.

> For [the argument] holds good only in such movements as are measured by time, and take place successively; thus, if local movement follows a change, then the change and the local movement cannot be terminated in the same instant. But if the changes are instantaneous, then all at once and in the same instant there can be a term to the first and the second change; thus in the same instant in which the moon is lit up by the sun, the atmosphere is lit up by the moon. Now, it is manifest that creation is instantaneous; so also is the movement of free-will in the angels; for, as has been already stated, they have no occasion for comparison or discursive reasoning [I:58:3]. Consequently, there is nothing to hinder the term of creation and of free-will from existing in the same instant. The free choice of the angels depends logically and necessarily on God's creation but not temporally.
>
> We must therefore reply that, on the contrary, it was impossible for the angel to sin in the first instant by an inordinate act of free-will. For although a thing can begin to act in the first instant [*in primo instanti*] of its existence, nevertheless, that operation which begins with the existence comes of the agent from which it drew its nature; just as upward movement in fire comes of its productive cause. Therefore, if there be anything which derives its nature from a defective cause, which can be the cause of a defective action, it can in the first instant of its existence have a defective operation; just as the leg, which is defective from birth, through a defect in the principle of generation, begins at once to limp. But the agent which brought the angels into existence, namely, God, cannot be the cause of sin.

> Consequently it cannot be said that the devil was wicked in the first instant of his creation.[30]

My interpretation of the passage is that Aquinas is eliminating the temporal backdrop from the devil's disobedience.

With regard to the passage of time, Aquinas concludes that there was no passage of time from the creation of the devil to his choice to rebel against God.

> There is a twofold opinion on this point. But the more probable one, which is also more in harmony with the teachings of the Saints, is that the devil sinned at once after the first instant of his creation. This must be maintained if it be held that he elicited an act of free-will in the first instant of his creation, and that he was created in grace; as we have said [I:62:3]. For since the angels attain beatitude by one meritorious act, as was said above [I:62:5], if the devil, created in grace, merited in the first instant, he would at once have received beatitude after that first instant, if he had not placed an impediment by sinning.[31]

The verb that is translated here as "to exist" and its substantial form as "existence" is *esse*. In translating these passages into English, one is forced to choose between *to be* and *to exist*, between *being* and *existence*.

What might seem to be a scholastic and metaphysical subtlety, i.e., whether or not the angels that fell enjoyed a moment of heavenly blessedness after creation but before their sinful choice, turns out to be significant regarding the association of time with original sin.[32] These are matters that will be pursued further in the section on freedom and foreknowledge. At this point, however, I can summarize one concern that runs from Augustine to Aquinas.

The good angels and the fallen angels are created with identical, good natures. If the good angels experienced any passage of time after creation in uncertainty that they would remain faithful to God, then their existence could not be considered truly blessed, at least not until

---

30. Aquinas, *Summa theologica* I, Q.63, A.5.
31. Aquinas, *Summa theologica* I, Q.63, A.6.
32. Much has been written, no doubt piously motivated, in an attempt to separate God's good creation from the creature's choice to sin, whether the creature be angel or man. Taylor O'Neill puts it thus: "The goal is to distance God from the fact of sin, to explain how it could be that man can sin without God's being able to be taken to task for not giving the grace whereby man will not sin," *Grace, Predestination*, 304. The writers, especially Aquinas, seek to distinguish between divine permission and cause. O'Neill, *Grace, Predestination*, 304–8. For example, see Aquinas, *Summa theologica* I, Q.19, A.9.

they made their choice. Only subsequently would they have the knowledge that they had chosen once for all the good. But the good angels are truly blessed, and therefore they must have experienced no period of uncertainty regarding their steadfastness. This blessedness, however, as portrayed by these theologians is a temporal state, or so it seems to be. Specifically, the faithful angels enjoy an ongoing blessed state, assured of their faithfulness.[33] These angels, as so characterized, are certain in the face of uncertainty, resolute in the context of possibility.

When the theologians take up the same concerns with respect to the bad angels, the succession must be the same, but on the side of evil. In other words, the choice of the bad angels must have been made in identical fashion to the choice of the good angels. Specifically, no time intervened. This much of the argument regarding the bad angels conforms exactly with our treatment of the fall of mankind in the following sense. Were the devil to spend merely a moment in a state of ignorance regarding his future choice, then he would have been subject to time. He would have suffered time, and accordingly there would have been extenuating circumstances attending his choice.

---

33. Can there be a-temporal assurance?

7

Time as Sin

IN THIS CHAPTER I take up the centerpiece of my inquiry, the assertion that time is sin. It is my intent to give an account of this assertion, to explain its origins, and to argue for its credibility. The task before me is daunting and will require that I write about some of our most fundamental and innermost cognitions and perceptions, although I do so in the light of Christian revelation. (The task might be characterized generally as phenomenological, although one wonders if there is any room for sin in phenomenology.) Cognition and perception refer to all aspects of human awareness including sensations, even those stimuli that we are not explicitly aware of, for example the biochemical processes of digestion. If I am able to identify the source of our sinfulness, and if I can show this source to be also that from which time, or what we usually call time, unfolds, then I shall have established the origin of sin, and in particular the origin of sin as time. I intend to show that there is one time, but that it is most commonly understood from two seemingly separate perspectives. I intend to show that the one time *is* our sin, that it originates with our sin, and most fundamentally that time is indistinguishable from sin.

Terms like "cognition," "perception," and "stimulus" may seem to promise an investigation characteristic of either epistemology or neuroscience. Both branches of study may have something to contribute to this study, but it will come as no surprise to the reader that this inquiry is neither strictly epistemological nor "scientific" in the sense of giving accounts of electrical-biochemical processes. The subject of sin may not exclude contributions from these and other branches of learning, but sin always and everywhere is concerned with praise and blame, and this concern is not touched essentially in any way by these other contributions. To this extent, these remarks accord with those of Augustine, above, regarding the location of sin in the soul and not in the senses. In a narrow sense, philosophy too has nothing to say about sin, Kierkegaard's discussion of Socratic sin notwithstanding.[1] These remarks, however, depend upon the individual human being's ability to cognize its individuality, and in that regard these other ways of knowing and learning—philosophical, psychological—may be related to accounts of how we know what we know. This also is where phenomenology with its concern of consciousness may come in.

This endeavor will not, however, succeed in originating an adequate description of the reconciliation of our sinful condition. Some writers, such as Karl Barth, would say that the entire project is misguided at best and perhaps heretical and blasphemous in its attempt to argue synthetically in the first place. Specifically, it may be considered by some impious to attempt to give this account of time as sin because in so doing one may entertain the thought that an adequate accounting would suffice, if not for a remedy at least for a state of satisfaction on the part of the human being. One might settle for a seemingly suitable explanation. It is what it is.

I harbor no such delusions. The synthesis here in no way attains to the summit, the fix, the Son of God become man. Even if my argument is deductively sound, this does not entail that knowledge is power. *Understanding* sin as I shall explain it will not enable one to rectify the situation. We can't forgive ourselves. At the end of the day, one must jump to the other side and continue on analytically, downward, from salvation to sin. One must acknowledge that a full understanding of original sin ultimately requires knowledge of its expiation and of the thoroughgoing transformation of the salvation of Jesus Christ. But the only theological treatment of the matter is synthetic, from the ground up. Theology, as vain as it may be, attempts to give an account of the creator and his creation. Theology is excusable among us because it is exclusively a human activity, a cross between anthropology and theater. We want to know. Piety accounts for nothing.

---

1. Kierkegaard, *Sickness unto Death*, 87–96.

Some portions or aspects of the argument set forth here are similar to that given by Plotinus in "On the Three Primary Hypostases" and in other places, where he discusses the descent of the soul from the intellect, and the intellect from the One.[2] This similarity is most distinct where the discussion concerns the apperceiving soul, the I who says "I."

Above, in chapters 2 and 3, we encountered descriptions of time and of sin. The task here is to show how the two descriptions entail and in fact presuppose one another.

We saw that most commonly if imprecisely time may be considered as one of the ways events are related to one another, or perhaps more precisely, time is what makes events events. These events, when external, reveal an inherently spatial conception of time. One appearance is coordinated with another appearance. We human beings establish the coordination. The appearances are thought of as being in the same place or in different places. And they are thought of as being at the same time or at different times. This is the coordination of which we are capable because we know the meaning of simultaneous, although we may be hard pressed to explain what we know without presupposing simultaneity to begin with. Even when internal, in which case of course they are immaterial, the events are coordinated by us, and in our imagination usually given a spatial representation. (The neuro-scientist might object here to the designation of inner events as immaterial. I do not deny in any way the possibility of biochemical changes that may accompany successive thoughts, feelings, or generally perceptions, nor am I opposed in some instances to the management of these thoughts and feelings by means of material interference: drugs. But these material changes, by being material, are not the subject of our concern about immaterial events.) We think of ourselves in the past and in the present, then and now. We connect the two times with our individuality and we *imagine* them connected by a line.

To the extent that change is concomitant with our temporal designations, we must posit the permanent, the Kantian substrate, to account for the difference between here and there, now and then, this and that. These two "locations" for temporal cognizance, outer and inner, may correspond to Eva Brann's first two classifications of time, what she calls succession time and the counting soul. The first of these two, which Brann associates with motion, I have labeled the alien, but the second may just

---

2. See especially Plotinus, *Enneads* III.7.11, V.1.1, and V.3.13.

as well be seen as an alien to the extent that we suffer it, even as mere souls who count. And this activity, counting, is one that Plotinus, a representative of Brann's third category, relates back to the descent from the One. The being who counts, counts by one's as well as counting by One, i.e., on account of the One, enabled by the One.

The third kind of time identified by Brann is the grounded time, although this turns out to be, for my consideration, merely an aspect of the two fundamental temporal appearances, succession time and phase time. That time be grounded in the soul will be seen ultimately to be just another way of acknowledging the connection of time to sin. Time, even when viewed as an alien, is *our* alien, and thereby it is in a sense our responsibility. In this limited way, I follow Heidegger's thinking about *Dasein*.

Finally there is the stretching of the mind, Brann's fourth category. This corresponds to Augustine's treatment of time as a distension of the mind. Here is where we encounter phase time, which has been described in somewhat Kantian terms as the source of all inner organization. It is Augustine's three presents: past, present, and future. Experience, which is phenomenally indisputable, presupposes the permanent as well as cause and effect. Even if the last three categories all contribute to phase time, they share with the first category the same name, time, and for good reason. All these conceptions are ours. Kant, no doubt, would object to my description of succession time as being ours because in so doing I seem to give credence to the notion of time as subsistent and independent of things. (One wonders if Kant ever had to wait anxiously for something.) One of the principal corollaries of original sin, however, is that we suffer it at our own hands. We are responsible for the outer as outer, and for the other as other. We are the enemy.

It will be best to limit further discussion of the matter to the two large categories determined in chapter 2, succession time and phase time. Both times are our time, and as we shall see, it is for this very reason that time in general can be considered as sin, and in particular as original sin. This amounts to an enunciation of the proposition of my entire inquiry.

Sin has been described as an event not merely to indicate that it consists of an act freely committed by a being who is rational, faithful, hopeful, and loving. There would be no sin without faith. In a way, Kierkegaard recognizes this when he claims that faith is the opposite of sin.[3] In addition to this connection, we must emphasize the deep temporal

---

3. Kierkegaard, *Sickness unto Death*, 82.

nature of all sin, and it is the task of this entire chapter to justify this association. A more precise statement is sins are events, and an individual sin is an event. The general concept or notion of sin and its accompanying sinfulness are not events. Sin, per se, is a qualification for sinfulness, the negative quality that results, not temporally, in sinful events.

Sin is a relational disorder brought about, at least according to Augustine and Aquinas, by violating eternal law, the law that directs all that is. If not entirely rational, then at least eternal law is in accord with reason. The importance of connecting sin to reason is to provide a basis for culpability and blame. The sinner must acknowledge cause and effect, he being the cause and the effect being disorder. If the individual is truly ignorant of the governance of eternal law, then it would seem to be inconceivable to attach blame to a violation of this law, even if the violation brought with it some kind of punishment or misfortune. For who would *blame* whom? Thus some level of responsibility is presupposed for all considerations of sin. Without fail, we find it comical that Xerxes flogged the sea that destroyed his bridges.

What has been described as willful disorder has many other worthy descriptions: missing the mark, lawlessness, estrangement, imbalance, going astray. Sin is a predator that has leaped into the world. All of these may require accompanying notions of occurrence, responsibility, freedom, and punishment. But does sin also convey the notion of a condition, specifically that of fallen-ness, and can this condition be willed or chosen? After all, if sinfulness is something suffered by mankind, a passion, then it might seem to be the result of divine malice, an unmerited burden of life. A considerable amount of contemporary religious preaching emphasizes the existence of evil in the world as if evil were substantial, perhaps the accomplished work of the devil. Such accounts and questions attempt to take the sinfulness out of sin, to reduce sin to the realm of failure, mistake, and misfortune, and to render the alleged sinner a victim, prey to the evil lurking at the door. Other accounts render sin as a subject for psychology and anthropology. These are the accounts given by those engaged in self-help, by those for whom mankind is in a way all powerful, so much so that we can fix our own problems by renaming them. These are the accounts that in some way would reject one or more of the three axioms with which we began, that acknowledge the creator, the individual who says "I," and the evidence of suffering. These accounts describe a human being who is on his way somewhere and who may justly take pride if not in his arrival at least in his journey.

Having reviewed briefly earlier comments about time and sin, I shall begin to make explicit the link between the two. The reader should keep in mind, however, that on the face of things the task at hand is inherently contradictory and accordingly impossible. For if time is order, i.e., inner organization, and if sin is disorder, i.e., willful violation of eternal law, then time and sin would be linked only in opposition. And even if I am successful in forging the connection between time and sin, the matter of rectification would still lie before us. Strictly speaking, salvation lies beyond us. In the wake of inherently contradictory lives, how can one hope for justification and a reestablishment of balance? How can one hope for forgiveness? "For in this hope we were saved. Now hope that is seen is not hope. For who hopes for what he sees?" (Rom 8:24). To see is to understand. Therefore, one does not hope for what is understood.

Here is the course of the rest of this chapter. Evidence for time as sin is found in desire and waiting. Desire depends on an urge that betrays imbalance, which further depends upon change. Change then entails the permanent as well as the other. All this evidence requires a soul, one who has enough *one* in itself in order to say "I." But this "I" is disruptive, necessarily distinguishing between itself and other, and thereby entertaining both possibility and obligation. This is the very "I" which in its being *commits* the problem of self-reference. This is the "I" that erects an encircling fence and then proclaims to stand both inside and outside the enclosure. The name for this condition is time, or sin, and it is a condition of suffering for which there is no rational reconciliation.

In a worldly way, one does not hope for the impossible or unforeseeable. For example, one does not say meaningfully: "I hope to win the lottery last week." Generally, one hopes for what might be, and not for that which definitely is not. One hopes to win lotteries that have yet to be decided. One may wish that one had better luck in the past, specifically by having won the lottery. (Such a wish may exemplify Augustine's distended mind that has taken up the present-past.) But this is not how the word "hope" is usually employed. Here, however, we must vary from convention in saying that one can *only* hope for salvation, the ultimate reconciliation and justification. This is so not because salvation is in the future. It certainly is not. One *only* hopes for salvation because it is impossible.

A. EVIDENCE: DESIRE AND WAITING

Desire and waiting provide the keys to understanding time as sin.[4] Desire and waiting, however, are not two distinct elements of the sinful condition, but rather two aspects or two views of the same thing. One might say that desire is equivalent to waiting but in a noisy sense. Another rendition might be that waiting is the soul of desire. Desire is waiting with the distraction of particulars. These distractions might be fleshly, concupiscence of the flesh, such as physical pleasure and relief from physical pain. They also may be intellectual, emotional, psychological, and even spiritual. Along with Paul and Augustine, one may have concupiscence of the spirit, against the flesh and inclining toward wisdom.

Desire certainly is an indispensable part of what we know as life, and it is hard to disagree with Hobbes when he claims that the end of desire means the end of life, death. But these observations, although general and seemingly widely applicable, are superficial at best. There is also a great deal of commentary, especially in Greek antiquity, on the subject of ἔρος. As vital as desire may seem to be, it merely points to an underlying condition, the state of the desirous being. Anselm might argue that desire is a sign of the lack of original justice, an imbalance. And this condition needs deeper analysis.

Desire, of course, also entails satisfaction, or at least the hope for satisfaction (εὐκολία—contentedness, or perhaps even εὐδαιμονία—blessedness). It would seem that desire has no meaning devoid of satisfaction. Nevertheless, we can engage in some play, a thought experiment, by separating desire from satisfaction and considering it alone. I propose to do exactly that, and to postpone any consideration of satisfaction until the very end of this study. There it will be necessary to take up the notion of non-temporal satisfaction, and to determine whether or not it is meaningful, specifically whether or not one can be satisfied without desire. (Can one know the answer as answer without knowing the question?) Terms such as "blessedness" and to a lesser extent "contentedness" have sufficiently broad connotation to hold at bay the notion of desire, at least temporarily.

Above we saw a treatment of desire as concupiscence, such treatment being a Christian theological interpretation of this urge. In highly truncated form, the Letter of James summarizes the relationships. "Each

---

4. Aquinas even has the saints in heaven waiting for and desirous of return of their earthly bodies. *Summa theologica* I-II, Q.4, A.5–6.

person is tempted when he is lured and enticed by his own desire. Then desire when it has conceived gives birth to sin; and sin when it is full-grown brings forth death" (Jas 1:14–15). The Vulgate has *concupiscentia* for desire here, and it is this notion that we have traced from Paul's letters (Greek ἐπιθυμία) through Augustine to Luther and Calvin. All the authors considered above, including Anselm with his emendation and addition of original justice, consider concupiscence broadly to be a part of human nature. Fleshly concupiscence, according to Augustine, is the remnant or scar of original sin. It is a tendency toward sin that is natural to mankind. This tendency is correlated with the Hebrew *yetzer hara*, an evil purpose or inclination among men. It resides continually in the heart of man, from his youth (Gen 6:5, 8:21).

Augustine distinguishes between fleshly concupiscence and concupiscence of the spirit, the latter, according to him, not necessarily being a vestige of original sin. As simple and perhaps trivial examples of this kind of desire, I have suggested some unsolved conjectures of number theory. The Reformers, however, reject this distinction, and rather point to all desire as indicative of man's sinfulness. And in this regard, I follow Luther and Calvin, considering here all kinds of want: concupiscence, lust, covetousness, passion, estrangement. These are names for the surface of desire.

Luther points to an important aspect of desire in considering the entire kingdom of sin, for he connects concupiscence with wrath, pride, and impatience. The latter is directly our concern here, because by our sense of impatience we acknowledge our inherent disorder and imbalance. By waiting, strictly, purely, and solely waiting, we confront our fundamental misalignment. We anticipate the future in ignorance. We look forward, see nothing, and persist in looking.

Estragon	So long as one knows.
Vladimir	One can bide one's time.
Estragon	One knows what to expect.
Vladimir	No further need to worry.
Estragon	Simply wait.
Vladimir	We're used to it.[5]

---

5. Beckett, *Waiting for Godot*, 26.

This is a principal subject of the Temporal Garden, where our condition was heightened by the central command: Forbidden!

Pozzo	Wait. (*Ponders.*) Well now isn't that . . . (*He raises his head.*) Help me!
Estragon	Wait!
Vladimir	Wait!
Pozzo	Wait![6]

Thus waiting is the sure sign of our fallen state, of our original sin, for in waiting we receive our clearest indication that time is the enemy. In arriving at this conclusion it has been necessary to interpret the story of Adam and Eve, first by distorting the story in the Temporal Garden. In the Temporal Garden there is no beguiling serpent. There is little or no concern for material sustenance: the garden is full of trees with fruit that is good to eat. In this garden, Adam and Eve are condemned to wait, and in particular, to wait for themselves. In a way, it may have been incorrect to claim that the condition of sin is waiting in ignorance. In a way, the condition of sin is waiting in full knowledge, knowledge of oneself, and waiting nonetheless, waiting for nothing. One applies the screws to oneself. (Estragon: So long as one knows. Vladimir: One can bide one's time.)

The Temporal Garden, of course, is a distortion of the story of Adam and Eve. It is not the story of *original* sin, but merely the story of sin, the story of events. In this regard, the Bible has a literary quality to it. The Bible consists of the words of men that both reveal and conceal the word of God. The sinful condition is presupposed in the Temporal Garden. By means of this fanciful distortion we have in effect excluded the Temporal Garden from our consideration. For now we have arrived at the critical aspect of the story. We have arrived at what Karl Barth describes as "the truth concerning us as it is known to God and told to us."[7] The sexuality present in the garden story, the serpent and the nakedness, provides a penumbra to the central message or meaning, but an ambiance that is undoubtedly one of desire and imbalance. In that respect, the sexuality is pertinent to the origin of sin, but only in that respect, only as nisus.

Although desire and waiting are the superficial indications of time as sin, and although imbalance is a general description of the fallen condition—Anselm's loss of original justice—change may be a better or

---

6. Beckett, *Waiting for Godot*, 27.
7. Barth, *Church Dogmatics*, 4/1:510.

more fundamental term to analyze the state of man. Change points to Kierkegaard's *possibility*, Kant's *ought*, and eventually to Christianity's *unrighteousness*, *ungodliness*. Change points to other, which in turn presupposes permanence. The imbalance of the sinful condition, the violation of eternal law, presupposes change, and of course freedom. But here, let us concentrate solely on the change implied by correction, and even more narrowly on permanence.

Does the permanent, conversely, presuppose change? Can there be meaning to the Kantian substrate in the absence of change and possibility? Must we always and everywhere not only begin in the middle of things but also end up, along with *Dasein*, in the middle of things? I concur with Kant's analysis here. Experience is indisputable. We find ourselves in the middle of things. Although the permanent, when characterized as such, implies change—we experience only in a sea of change—experience entails appearances, which in turn necessitate a substrate, substance itself, something objective, that which is experienced.[8] We encounter the permanent in the context of change, but this encounter is acknowledgment of the temporal nature of experience. Our encounters are events. All knowledge may begin with experience and thereby presuppose time and change. But knowledge does not originate with experience. Quite the opposite is true. Experience originates from the permanent. In short, things come first. In the Heraclitan expression "Everything is in flux," the word "Everything" has no denotation. It does have, however, connotation, meaning that is derived from that which is. To call this "unchanging," or "permanent," or even "being" is to run the risk of confusing the issue, a confusion that some writers—Husserl's "continuance" and Ricoeur's "permanence of time"—are willing to accept.

It is important to keep in mind that the "things" referred to here are be-ings. The mind easily confuses or limits things to material objects. Substances must have matter, or at least locations in a force field. But the things that come first have a much broader designation, one that includes act, especially non-temporal action. (These observations about permanence of "things" can be extended to justice, the good, and satisfaction.)

One might object that in the case of eternal action, described above in chapter 2, we presuppose change in order for the action to be. Just as "permanent" initially brings with it a connotation of change, so does "act" or "action." Thus one might conclude that in this case, outside the realm

---

8. Kant, *Critique of Pure Reason* B224–25 ("Principle of the Permanence of Substance").

of experience, we have vacillation between the permanent and change. But even here, where we are considering necessary relations, the things that are related must ultimately be presupposed. Here I am trying to distinguish between our experience and the things that we experience, to put it loosely. I am pointing to Kant's *noumenon*, the thing in itself, *the* object. And I am pointing to Kant's substrate. One might do well to rely on technical terms that display their Greek and Latin origins in ostentatious fashion, rather than to use words such as "permanent." For then we think of maintaining through, *per*. The substrate, not as that which maintains but simply that which is, does not presuppose change.

B. ONE: SOUL (I) AND DISRUPTION

Thus the permanent, the thing, the soul *is*. It is crucial that we do not call it the immortal soul. The immortal soul is surrounded by death. It continuously interacts with death and is defined by death. It spends all its time not dying. Immortality entails time, and although the soul will turn out to be the origin of time, it is not purely in itself in time. It is incorrect also to say that the soul exists. Rather, it *is*. Of course the soul participates in time and, in an entirely negative way, originates time. But the soul itself is not time and strictly speaking is fundamentally independent of time. As we shall see, however, the soul conditions itself in time. Clearly this is the unredeemed soul, the fallen soul.

And this is where we come in, since we are souls. All men are created equal. This is the second axiom from the introductory chapter. The human being, by possessing a soul, meaningfully, but confusedly, says "I." The *saying* of "I" is not strictly a verbal deed or expression. The saying is both active and passive. The saying is a thing. The saying of "I" is an act performed by the soul, but the act is also correctly seen as mere acknowledgment. It is recognition. The soul finds itself, but only in a way. It finds itself encumbered, and from this encumbrance it deduces its being. It discovers the noumenal as noumenal. In doing so, the soul also confuses the noumenal with the phenomenal.

It is not quite correct to say that the human being possesses a soul in the same way that the human being possesses a head, a heart, two eyes, and so forth. A soul is not a possession of the human being, but rather it is a qualification of a human being. This is not to say that it is a quality of the human being, but that it qualifies a being as human. The soul makes the man. The soul acts.

Analytically one might say that a human being is a rational animal that has a soul. But this analysis undervalues the activity entailed by a soul. (Its original act is the saying of "I.") There is not a human being without a soul, by which I mean, there is not some thing or creature or body which if it had a soul would then be this particular human being. This particular human being is a human being first and foremost because of its soul. The soul is that which not only makes a being human, but also makes *this* being human. There may be other necessary "parts" that go into making this particular human being what it is, a human being, but it is the soul that indispensably makes the being human, and really makes the being in any sense.

This soul, this "I" by saying "I" will initiate the entire process of distinction, the establishment of other. This "act" can be seen as the individual's response to the prohibition in the Garden of Eden.[9] There we saw that the kernel of the prohibition has nothing to do with fruit that is desirable to look at and good for food, nothing to do with a subtle serpent providing information that is easily misconstrued. The heart of the prohibition, rather than concerning any of these goods and advice, is the prohibition itself: *Don't!* This command did not fall on deaf ears. It was fully understood because Adam and Eve were capable of understanding it.

In anticipation of the forthcoming account of the self-affirming "I," let us note similarities between this argument and that given by Plotinus in his explanation for why the Intellect is not the One, or is no longer the one. (Time intrudes everywhere.) "Beginning as one it did not stay as it began, but, without noticing it, became many, as if heavy [with drunken sleep], and unrolled itself because it wanted to possess everything [πάντα ἔχειν θέλων]—how much better it would have been for it not to want this, for it became the second!"[10] This poor choice, according to Plotinus, can be characterized as audacious (τόλμα—audacity, courage), the act of an overly bold self-will.[11] If I succeed in presenting my argument, then we

---

9. Commenting on Plotinus, *Enneads* V.i.1, Halfwassen writes: "Since Soul loses the entirety of Being, with which it was originally identical, on account of its individuation, Plotinus understands the act of individuation, just like Plato, as a *fall* of Soul." *Plotinus*, 93. See also Plato, *Phaedrus* 248C.

10. Plotinus, *Enneads* III.8.8.

11. Plotinus, *Enneads* V.1.1. As Halfwassen asserts, "Time is generated by means of the self-unfolding of the Soul. However, the Soul comes to itself by making its respective individuality opposed to the undivided entirety of Being valid by means of an act of

shall be able to retain, if we like, an expression such as "poor choice," while at the same time eliminating commentary along the lines of how things might have been better. The argument of Plotinus also appears in Augustine's treatment of the fall of the devil.[12]

Souls, at least the souls of human beings, say "I." This non-temporal act demarcates all being and uniquely distinguishes the self, all ambient clatter and degeneration notwithstanding. The self-referential statement of "I" disrupts all being, dividing it into two. (Plotinus would characterize this act as the separation of the Intellect from the One.) This act also opens the being who says "I" to change. In particular, the I, by its divisive statement, admits a "this" and a "that." It establishes for itself a distinction, wrought by means of identity. In one regard, then, the act seems to have a creative quality to it, at least to the extent that it brings the recognition of things into being. This apparent quality, which properly is reserved totally and exclusively for the divine, may betray the creator's fingerprints, evidence of the creature having been made in the image of the creator. Unlike the biblical creator and creation, however, the *I* has no foresight when it performs its original action. The act is strictly phenomenal and therefore completely devoid of good intentions. Strictly speaking, the apperceiving *I* is both observational and contradictory because the *I* "sees" what cannot be seen. The action seems in an entirely worldly and temporal way to be creative. (Hegel would recast many of these assertions into the progression of consciousness along a "logical" series according to a necessary development.)

In its observation, however, the apperceiving *I* encounters the confusion of all systematic self-references, the confusion of antinomies and paradoxes. This is the confusion of the Liar Paradox ("This statement is false."), and it is the incompleteness of representational systems that are the subject of Gödel's famous proofs. In both cases, the system (for us the "I") is represented within the system. The strictly noumenal is rendered phenomenal, and it is done so by the noumenal itself. The confusion here is one of mistaking understanding for comprehension. The noumenal is understood as phenomenal. This occurs in a superficial way every time one person identifies another person as such, as well as himself. But here the identifier and the "object" identified are the same; they are confused.

---

primal spontaneity and issuing in this way from the whole." *Plotinus*, 93.

12. Augustine, *On the Free Choice* III.25.76.

The apperceiving *I* "thinks" that it has comprehensively referred to itself when in fact it has merely discovered that the *I* is.

The saying of "I" nevertheless is an original distinction, the origin of distinction. Saying "I" is an exercise of the capacity to distinguish. It is the statement that never could be made by the *all*. But the saying of "I" is not strictly uncaused. This statement, this *word* of saying, is a capacity that we discover by means of its very exercise. It is the capacity that unites Kierkegaard's *possibility*, Kant's *ought*, and Augustine's and Calvin's *perseverance*. It is the capacity by which we come to know that things might be otherwise. It is the capacity by which we encounter our own spontaneity, or at least what seems to us to be spontaneity, what feels like freedom. It is the capacity by which we recognize what is commonly referred to as consciousness and even eventually conscience. In a limited sense, it is the capacity by which we follow the command of the Delphic oracle.[13]

For these reasons, Augustine attempts to distinguish between the origin of sin and the origin of the sinner. Augustine's comment concerns the devil, who, according to the Letter of John, "sins from the beginning" (1 John 3:8). Sin is not natural, although it is spontaneous. (To some extent, freedom and nature are contradictory notions.) From this passage about the devil, "it is not to be supposed that he sinned from the beginning of his created existence, but from the beginning of his sin, when by his pride he had once commenced to sin."[14] Augustine is eager to acquit the creator from any responsibility for the devil's poor choice while at the same time maintaining the argument that all creation is good in itself. As we saw above, the sequence of the devil's creation and his disobedience is logical but not temporal. The sequence is devoid of context or location.

Even if God is not the origin of sin per se, one might wonder why God permits sin in all its negativity to be, to persist, to be in time and to be time. Paul Tillich provides the following apology.

> If one is asked how a loving and almighty God can permit evil, one cannot answer in the terms of the question as it was asked. One must first insist on an answer to the question How could he permit

---

13. "For intimate self-consciousness [συναίσθησις] is a consciousness of something which is many: even the name bears witness to this." Plotinus, *Enneads* V.3.13. Halfwassen comments, "Time is this form of Being of the self-differentiating soul and its life determined through the differentiation. Soul separates itself from the entirety of Being in order to possess itself. Self-possession, however, is only possible by means of self-consciousness (*synaisthêsis*), that is, by the means through which an entirety is present to itself and to which it knows and possesses itself." *Plotinus*, 94.

14. Augustine, *City of God* XI.15.

> sin?—a question which is answered the moment it is asked. Not permitting sin would mean not permitting freedom; this would deny the very nature of man, his finite freedom. Only after this answer can one describe evil as the structure of self-destruction which is implicit in the nature of universal estrangement.[15]

Following this line of thought, the finite freedom that may be associated with the origin of sin should actually be considered a gift, one by which the recipient, man, is enabled to choose rightly, to obey. (One might also consider as a gift having been given a loaded gun for self-protection.)

In considering descriptions and consequences of the disruptive act, the saying of "I," we have run ahead of ourselves. If this were the end of it, the *word* complete, the mere and unanalyzed saying of "I," we may never arrive at sin. But in fact this singular distinction is the origin of all morality, and therefore the origin of merit and blame. It is the origin of sin. At this point, at least, I am not trying to give an account of God's goodness.

We bring about "this" and "that," but "this" and "that" are not merely "this" and "that." They are all-ways "this" in relation to "that" and "that" in relation to "this." Here there is no appeal to a Kantian substrate, to the primacy of justice or goodness. The saying of "I" is disruptive, and with this disruption enters the possibility, or to give a name to the possibility, the possibility of "other." The capacity to make distinctions brings with it infinite richness, perhaps including the opportunity to align our will with eternal law, but the price of distinction is possibility, and the price of possibility is the possibility of sin. Adam and Eve understood the most important aspect of the command "Don't!" which is the possibility of "Do!"

"Other" in itself may seem to be analytically neutral, neither good nor bad, and not necessarily the near occasion of sin. It turns out, however, that "other" as possibility brings with it the very condition of imbalance that will serve as foundation for sin. In our original myth, the LORD God presents this distinction to Adam and Eve. He does so by singling out from all the trees in the garden one, the tree of the knowledge of good and evil. The name of the tree is intriguing, perhaps even delightful. But the name is merely decorative, for in the story God has already brought to the consciousness of Adam and Eve *the* distinction: "this" tree, not "that" tree. This kind of distinction is hinted at by Aquinas when he attributes envy as well as pride to the wicked angel. "But another's good could not be deemed a hindrance to the good coveted by the wicked angel, except inasmuch as

---

15. Tillich, *Systematic Theology*, 2:61.

he coveted a singular excellence, which would cease to be singular because of the excellence of some other. So, after the sin of pride, there followed the evil of envy in the sinning angel."[16] The simple distinction of "this" and "that," the disruptive "I" is seed sufficient to sprout comparisons.

After stripping away all ornamentation, we encounter in Adam and Eve the unencumbered will. "Eat fruit from those trees, but don't eat fruit from this tree! That is all you need to know." And what do Adam and Eve know, what do our first parents now understand? They understand distinction pure and simple. Adam and Eve each are an "I," and this fundamental self-awareness, this original self-awareness is depicted in our story as the command *to obey*. Of course a commandment, *the* commandment, is meaningless without the possibility of disobedience. And this much they completely understand.

Adam and Eve and each one of us are responsible for our encounter with this possibility, for we are the ones who bring the possibility into being; it is what we do. A prohibition such as "Don't eat!" has in it, by a quirk of English, the verb *to do*. Accordingly, our saying of "I," our completed *word*, is an act. We do it. We say "I." This fundamental distinction, the disruption of all that is by means of a single division, is committed by us.

Perhaps it is not quite correct to claim that God issues the command. More in keeping with this account, we must say that Adam and Eve hear or receive a command. Are they delusional? Who issued the command? This important detail must be left for the end of this study, for the argument that creation itself issues the command, and it does so simply by being God's creation. The disruptive *I* has heard the command. The phenomenon is undeniable, and as I complete this chapter it will become clear that the consequences are equally undeniable. This much can be accounted for. An account of the command itself however requires revelation.

In summary, the argument thus far consists of the following. From the general and superficial state of desire, manifested most acutely in us by waiting, we encounter change, or at least we come to understand change. Change, in turn, is meaningful only on the condition of permanent. The permanent is the soul, the "I." (I shall address presently the notion of the *empty I*). This is the "I" that confusedly says "I" and thereby presents to itself distinction. The other comes on the scene, and with it comes possibility. Now we must show that *time* is the correct word or notion to describe this sinful condition.

---

16. Aquinas, *Summa theologica* I, Q.63, A.2.

C. TIME

> Is there sin without time?
> Is there eternal sin?
> What do the fallen angels suffer?

Being able to answer the first of these questions might enable us to answer the other two, but it shall be easier to address the third one first. The fallen angels, of course, are not our concern at all. It was necessary, however, to consider some of the commentary about the fall of the devil because this story has been conflated, not confused, with the fall of mankind. The conflation is necessary in order to consider time as sin.

Do the fallen angels eternally recommit their sin? Do they repeatedly commit their sin? Kierkegaard writes about "the continuance of sin." "Every state of sin is a new sin."[17] But Kierkegaard is writing about human sinners. It is incorrect to say that the fallen angels committed their sin once and for all, but it may be correct to claim that they commit it once and for all. We might say that they persevere in their rebellion. They rebel once and for all. Their sin is phrased this way in order to remove the element of time. The commentary of Augustine, Anselm, and others points to the eternality of the devil's sin, but does so in a temporal way. We are left to think about and to try to imagine a being in time that spends absolutely no time in a blessed state, even though the being was created good. From here it might seem reasonable to ask if the devil perseveres in his sin, and if we are to think of him temporally, then we must concur. The devil condemns himself to perseverance. But the commission of the sin must not be *an* event. It must not have a place and most especially not have a time. There is no context for the commission of sin by the fallen angels, Milton's fantastic portrayal notwithstanding. In a sense, however, it is correct to say that the devil perseveres in his sin because his sin is the essence of temporality: waiting.

There is an aspect to the theologians' treatment of the fallen angels, however, that is both perverse and helpful. What does their condition say about the fallen angels? How odd! They insist on waiting. They choose to wait. What are they afraid of such that they choose to wait rather than to go on, to arrive, to finish, to be joyous and satisfied? Augustine, Aquinas, and others describe their choice as willful inversion of the less good for the greater good, inverting the goodness that each and every creature of

---

17. Kierkegaard, *Sickness unto Death*, 105.

God has in its very being for the source of all being, God himself. It is as if the fallen angels reject the living water (ὕδωρ ζῶν) offered by Jesus to the Samaritan woman at the well if favor of waiting to drink the water after which they will thirst again (John 4:7–15). They choose thirst.

What will the angels lose, or think they will lose if they give in and selflessly say "I" and wait no longer? They have identified the "I" with the waiting, and on the face of it this is not an absurd identification. But they concretize the waiting; they fulfill it, and in so doing they make the temporal eternal. In so doing, they persevere as no others. They do so not in some glorious, salvific way in which the fullness of time has been transformed into the beatific vision. Rather than this, they make the opposite transformation, Augustine's willful inversion. All becomes temporal and it remains temporal in all ways. All passes, always. The fullness of time for the fallen angels consists of all waiting, i.e., it consists of nothing. In the battle between permanence and change, change wins. It is as if they took all eternal action described above in chapter 2 and turned it on its head. Necessary consequence is made contingent. The world of evil is truly chaotic. One thing happens, and then another thing. This is the world of facts.

In at least one miserable respect, we are like the fallen angels in that we continually succumb to time. In a way, time becomes a predator, like the sin that lurks at Cain's door. Not only is Kant correct in asserting time to be our inner intuition, but so is Heidegger in maintaining that *Dasein* is temporal. To some degree we live our lives in the world of Hobbes, Kant, and Heidegger, and in that regard, we live the lives of the fallen angels. We are. We experience. We wait. In a sense we abhor the present, preferring to review the past and to anticipate the future. Perhaps that is what we are, *and no more*. We live in a world full of waiters. We fall in love with time and we desire it, but our desire is insatiable and necessarily so, since what we desire, or seem to, is to desire more desire. Anticipation is our end, and thus are we condemned.

We can characterize our sinful condition in three ways. First there are the sins of the rational being. Kant would point to consistency or more properly inconsistency, violation of the law of non-contradiction. This is good as far as it goes, and if reason were the final judge that many people would like it to be, or so they say, we could stop with this single characterization of sin. The categorical imperative would provide the entire moral framework for our being, and the victory over sin would be grounded in reason. But, second, there are also the sins of the empirical being, the sins that always are buried in extenuating circumstances. Time is the fundamental and all-encompassing extenuating circumstance. Can the human being, the being of reason, faith, hope, and charity, produce enough din of extenuating circumstances to drown out the signal of *ought*? Can the human being render himself entirely empirical, entirely circumstantial, thereby annihilating the *ought* and its force? No, of course not. Even Heidegger acknowledges the reifying (*Verdinglichung*) that continually reasserts itself in our lives.[18] Even Lucretius appeals to reason. In fact, we have souls. Even if somehow we managed to live a life of perfect evasion, finding a context for all our actions, even then we would be buffeted by time. Indeed, our victory over the sins of obligation would be bought at the cost of never-ending and all pervasive suffering. And third, there are the sins of the apperceiving being, the apperceiver, i.e., the one who says "I" but necessarily in the disruptive, selfish way that ensures sinfulness.

Thus the never-ending battle between the sins of reason and the sins of circumstance plays out in our lives, but these sins are both subsumed, originally, by the sin of apperception. This is the sin of saying "I" exclusively, the sin that recognizes "this" and "that," and thereby the element of change. This assertion is even more fundamental than the theologians' account of inverted goods. One might here finish the account by claiming that it is change that is the culprit, the origin of sin, and thereby that which underlies time.

"Change," however, is finally not the correct name for this third, original, and culminating sin. The apperceiver distinguishes between "I" and "not I" in an organized way. I think that Kant would like to label this distinction as time, and to some extent I am in accord with him. But calling the awareness of the distinction, the awareness of "I" time is not the whole story of time. The "not I" is the alien, and it is the alien or other that has its origin in the apperceiver while "at the same time" being other, alien. One might see here a kind of reverse Hegelian dialectic, one where the third item after thesis and antithesis is sin. Thesis and antithesis do not produce dialectically something, a something. They produce nothing, a nothing. Rather than the Hegelian *kenosis* of spirit in the world, we would have an extraction, the sucking out of all good: spiritless-ness. This is the victory of sin, the primary evidence of which is death. Under such an account, then, Jesus Christ undoes the dialectical movement. He

---

18. Heidegger, *Being and Time* H437.

reverses it. I reserve further elaboration about this aspect of the story of sin for later in this inquiry, for the end.

Time begins with the free choice of Adam and Eve to disobey God's single command. With this choice they transform their inner organization, that by which they are able to be and to be aware that they are, into an alien. Adam and Eve make time double, and accordingly they suffer. Eve "takes of the fruit and eats." She wills the act. Eve is Eve, and she knows it. She chooses Eve, and in so doing she mistakes the source of her identity. She falls from her source of being.

The language used here is entirely too sequential, and perhaps it should not even be consequential. The choice of the selfish "I," the proud choice expressed as disobedience of God's single prohibition, undoubtedly initiates a sequence of events. It ushers in all time and all sin, such as envy as Aquinas noted. But it is incorrect to see the establishment of all inner organization and thought, phase time in its temporal manifestation, as the cause of the alien, succession time which is to be suffered. The apperceiving "I," by being just that and by doing just that, apperceiving, originates both inner organization and outer assault. The apperceiving "I" has characterized inner organization as outer assault. The serpent is merely an image of the alien that Eve has generated. The serpent's name is Eve. The serpent is a partial and deformed image of time. But the serpent is equally within. The serpent is ours.

Thus begins the experience of alienation, for Adam and Eve and each one of us, alienation from one another, alienation from ourselves, and alienation from God. Thus begins time, and with this beginning comes disintegration.[19] If there is any meaning to the term *nonbeing*, then it is here, for it is in the apperceiving act that the sinner encounters nonbeing. Other. Nothing.

I have acknowledged above the dark character of my account of sin. One could—and I presume many would—dispense with this account by accepting it in its near entirety. One might acknowledge my story of disruption with a slightly weary smile. One might even humor me by accepting my designation of our temporal state—time as it is and time as we understand it to be—without going so far as to use expressions like "deformation of human nature" or "sin." Apparently for some people, it is okay that things happen to us. Suffering is the way things are. How poor

---

19. "For time is by its nature the cause rather of decay, since it is the number of change, and change removes what is." Aristotle, *Physics* iv.12.221b.

an opinion of the creator and his creation! The best he could do was to produce a timorous species that knows how to lie.

D. SUFFERING

We know that Augustine suffered time. "Time is not inert. It does not roll on through our senses without affecting us. Its passing has remarkable effects on the mind."[20] Of course, Augustine viewed time as part of God's creation, but he also saw the predatory nature of time that we find in sin lurking at Cain's door (Gen 4:7). In a series of remarks concerning Ps 4, Augustine writes, "I had not desire for earthly goods to be multiplied, nor to devour time and to be devoured by it."[21] Augustine desired to know what time is. He wondered at it and about it. But he also feared time, as one should, because time is both our source of control and a condition beyond our control. It is our contradiction. In *Waiting for Godot*, Vladimir and Estragon converse with Pozzo, then Lucky and Pozzo exit.

> Vladimir   That passed the time.
> Estragon   It would have passed in any case.
> Vladimir   Yes, but not so rapidly.[22]

This is hell, not eternal damnation but temporal damnation. Hell lasts forever, and therefore it is hardly temporary, despite being temporal. Hell is the permanence of original sin, an odd claim, since in a way hell is also and absolutely nothing. Hell is always here and always now, but it also is nowhere and at no time. Hell is here and now for one who wants to be anywhere but here at any time but now. Hell is the insatiable desire for *then not now*. That precisely is the problem with hell, and all the hellish episodes of our lives. In these episodes, we experience nonbeing. We undergo nothingness, the absence of all meaning and of all love. In these episodes, our desire reaches perfection. We want, and we do so absolutely. We attain the full dissatisfaction of absolute lacking, for we lack all that is. Empty. And we know we lack because we are waiting for the void to be filled. The absolute terror of these episodes consists in the knowledge that

---

20. Augustine, *Confessions* IV.viii.13.
21. Augustine, *Confessions* IX.iv.11.
22. Beckett, *Waiting for Godot*, 32.

what we await is totally and only more waiting. We exchange nothing for nothing, continually. We get nothing in return.

How dispiriting! Perhaps we could retrieve final cause. Perhaps we could obtain an end, something for which we can recharacterize waiting as perseverance. Perseverance presupposes not only time but also an end, if not to time, at least to waiting in a limited or circumscribed sense. In many instances, the limit to perseverance, the temporal aspect of the goal, is specified. Engage in a sporting contest for one hour, at the end of which the team with the higher score shall be declared the winner. Even in defeat, there is release and relief after sixty minutes of engagement. The waiting stops.

With regard to sin, we have seen that Augustine takes a score-keeping approach, in which the game lasts for a lifetime. There is a statute of limitations. Therefore, perseverance may relieve to some extent the hellishness of endless-ness, the lack of any goal. But perseverance in no way obviates the temporality of sin. Indeed, the opposite is true. Perseverance confronts sin or failure directly in its temporal nature. Perseverance amplifies sin as did the law for Paul. The person who perseveres acknowledges time to be sin, at least succession time. With considerations such as these, one can understand Calvin's assertion that death was a gift of the creator to fallen man, an end to his suffering. Even in sinfulness, man is finite. One can understand Augustine's desire to rest in the Lord (*requiescat in te*), in the Sabbath of eternal life (*sabbato vitae aeternae requiescamus in te*), in repose outside of time (*quietem ex tempore*).[23]

According to Aquinas, the only way fallen man, who, as we have seen, is the originator of time as sin, can resist the alien is by means of grace. He is able to withstand each temptation, each near occasion of sin, but he is unable to withstand them all. On the assumption that the individual is able to sin, to choose to invert the order of goodness by placing the lower above the higher, then his inability to remain sinless is owing to the magnitude of life and the infinite subdivision of time. All time is sin, in that every instant of time is a suffering, a consequence of original sin, and a sign of man's fallen state. Sins, however, are events, and apparently according to Aquinas, countable. In terms that are decidedly not those of Aquinas, the cardinality of the temporal moments of a human life is that of the continuum (at least). Specifically, its cardinality is greater than that of the natural numbers. The individual, therefore, is certain to sin since

---

23. Augustine, *Confessions* I.i.1, XIII.xxxvi.51–xxxvii.52.

he can resist each temporal moment of sin but not all such moments. The continuum devours the infinitely many instances.

Aquinas does not despair under this realization but rather relies on his faith in God, a loving, merciful, and purposive creator, who can and will provide the grace to resist sin. This is the faith and hope of the believer. In the face not of overwhelming odds but rather of certain failure, the faithful person places his hope for perseverance in a gift. This is the kind of hope that is described above, a virtue by which one hopes only for the impossible. This is the kind of hope harbored by a fool for Christ. "For in this hope we were saved. Now hope that is seen is not hope. For who hopes for what he sees?" (Rom 8:24).

Some recourse, perhaps to grace, would seem to be necessary once we realize that we are the source of our parlous state. Augustine writes, "I know myself to be conditioned by time,"[24] but for Augustine time is a distension of his own mind. Accordingly, sin is not only in the world, out there someplace. Sin is also inside, in here with me. The time that we suffer, explicitly, is succession time, the time in which we wait, during which we attempt to persevere, the time that happens to us. But this time is simply the other face of phase time, that by which I am able to think, to feel, and to say "I." I, by being who I am, am the source of my suffering. I am the alien to myself. Augustine, I believe, would agree with nearly all of my comments here, although for him time is a creation of God, a thing, substantial, and therefore inherently good.[25]

Perhaps our fallen state is peculiar to our humanity. I engage in the following thought experiments, not, as I have mentioned before, to work out matters for angels and for dogs, but to try to give an account of our human condition.

Could there be a being with only succession time or only phase time? The succession-time being would exist without being able to say "I," a true sufferer and only a sufferer. Perhaps not even an animal or a plant qualifies in this regard. Time for this thing would be exclusively external, Kant's subsistent time. Necessarily, of course, this thing would not be a sinner. It could take no position before God.

A phase-time–only being thinks, but with nothing to think. Is this Aristotle's *nous* thinking itself? Is this the mind of God? Kant would definitely deny the latter possibility, because for him the divine intellect

---

24. Augustine, *Confessions* XI.xxv.32.

25. See above, ch. 3, n. 41, where Pelikan claims that Augustine comes close to equating time with evil.

knows things directly, without thinking. One might suggest that we let the rational being with only phase time vacillate between thoughts of freedom and God, or for variety, freedom, God, and the soul. These thoughts or notions may truly be beyond or outside of outer intuition and experience. I do not know, however, how a rational being would come up with these notions on its own. What meaning, what connotation could they have for such a being? And revelation is out of the question in this consideration since revelation by its very nature comes from without. Our imagined being has no sensation whatsoever: no sense.

Could the phase-time–only being vacillate between the pure, unattended "I" and "not I"? This might at first seem to be a good test case since it appears to rely solely on apperception. But here, the Humean argument may have some credibility, and it is here that Hume's argument is acknowledged by Kant. My earlier remarks about apperception were naïve. For this "I" under present consideration would be completely devoid of character. It would be the pure "I" upon which no one can gaze. This is the "I" that cannot even say "I," the unconscious consciousness, although this I most truly *is*. But *is* this "I" if it is entirely empty? What is an empty soul? It is not an individual because it is utterly undistinguished. Distinction, however, is what got the soul into trouble in the first place. I shall say more about the "empty I" presently.

At this point, however, it is sufficient to acknowledge that the origin of sin rests in the juxtaposition of time with time, the confrontation of the organizing principle of all our cognition, our very *I*, with all that seems to happen to us, with all *other* that always and everywhere attends the *I*. This juxtaposition is the mirror of our problem with self-reference. The *other* is the *I* that is referred to by the apperceiving *I*. It is with or against succession time that we seek to endure and to persevere because the latter attacks us. We seek to maintain the *I* in the face of *not I*. And all this is entirely our doing. We are, therefore, entirely responsible for the state of things, not only for our own inconstancy, infidelity, hypocrisy, idolatry, and cruelty, as well as for the sins of others, but also for all those so-called natural disasters and extenuating circumstances that we like to dismiss as simply happening. The hurricane, the earthquake, the volcanic eruption, each is our fault. Like Markel, the brother of Zosima in the *Brothers Karamazov*, "each of us is guilty in everything before everyone, and I most of all."[26]

---

26. See above, ch. 3 and n. 37.

We arrive here at the origin of sin, ur-sin, wherein sin becomes possible. But can the mere saying of "I" constitute sinful action? I have argued above that salvation, *the* redemption consists of the final integration of the individual, an integration in which the individual says "I" without sinning. This is the transformation of all being accomplished by God's love for us, and carried out by the seemingly contradictory Jesus Christ. He only *seems* to be a contradiction because he is the Truth, but he necessarily is contradiction in his divine and human natures. (When Aquinas writes about errors of reason, I presume that he has in mind the assault on reason carried out by Jesus Christ, an assault that is emphatically promoted by Luther and enticingly named as "paradox" by Kierkegaard.) This is the reconciliation of the distinction of the individual with the attending possibility in that the possibility is transformed into actuality, into act, but not act as other. There is a difference, however, between the mere saying of "I" and each and every such statement, each and every "act" of apperception. The apperception referred to here is that of the human being. Angels and dogs will need to get their treatments of these matters from elsewhere.

E. NO RECONCILIATION

The argument, at least from a rational and deductive perspective, is complete. There is no reconciliation for the apperceiver and the world. There is no reason for the person who says "I" and thereby disrupts all being to expect relief. In no way can we achieve a reintegration of ourselves while retaining our individuality. Perhaps we can become one with everything. For the Epicurean, that is what happens after death. But the Epicurean is a slave to time, and like all slaves, he loses himself. In the end, there is still time, but the Epicurean is not. The noumenal has been completely absorbed into the phenomenal. Thus we live unreconciled, and only in death do we become reconciled with nothingness as nothing. Even with death, however, the Epicurean remains a slave to time for having lived at all. He has a history, an external time stamp on his life. Becoming one with everything does not transform time, it forgets time. Becoming one with everything is equivalent to becoming a succession-time–only being.

There is memory, even world memory. The individual may pass away, but others, perhaps offspring, may remember him for a while. The others, too, will pass away, but there will be yet more others. This is the way that the sinner, without acknowledging his sin, attempts to achieve immortality. We keep family photo albums. And if by immortality is meant something so feeble as a little more time, then in some very general and supremely impersonal way, the individual receives an extension beyond his allotted time. But an extension of what? More time. Those who seek to live forever in memory truly deny their sinfulness when in fact they are embracing it.

Perhaps we should circle back, one more time, to the very expression "I." What is necessary to say "I" in the first place? Perhaps we could sever time from the notion of sin if we attempt to approach the soul per se. We have seen that each and every apperception—which in Humean nomenclature is not in any way a perception—is indeed sinful. These apperceptions are the origin of sin; they comprise original sin. But can we consider a blessed state, not one transformed by Jesus Christ in the fullness of time, but a proto-apperception of sorts? Are we searching for prelapsarian man? Perhaps we are inquiring about Adam and Eve before their decision to disobey. Could they have been logicians that praise God? Dealing with this question must await the final chapter.

The theologians have much to say about the nature of man before his act of disobedience, but this being is far from the one described here, and it is one that is usually manifestly contradictory and nonsensical. Milton's Adam and Eve before the fall are exemplary in this regard since they suffer all the pains of original sin before they disobey. This, of course, is not surprising since all these other accounts subject prelapsarian man to time, i.e., they make him a sinner from the beginning, just like Augustine's devil.

I do not know what to say about what I am seeking, this primitive, pure apperception in terms of its being, other than to give it a name, the *empty I*. One can say for certain that it does not occur, for in occurring it would be subject to time. It would already be sinful, like Milton's Eve tormented by dreams. We might construct syntactically and grammatically correct statements about this proto-apperception, the apperception that allegedly knows the "I" absolutely independent of any stimulation, i.e., independent of the other. This "I," however, is deduced or discovered only by first considering the perceiving "I." "There can be no doubt that all our cognition begins with experience."[27] Then, from this self that sees itself as this or that, by analysis or deduction or inference we might arrive

---

27. Kant, *Critique of Pure Reason* B1.

at the permanent self, the indivisible and immortal soul, the *noumenon*. In fact, this is exactly how knowledge of the self is achieved. This *is* apperception. All cognition may begin with experience but it does not originate with experience. Cognition originates with the one who can think, the one who apperceives, the created soul, *noumenal* in its objectivity. At this point, however, we are left with the apperception of a soul without a world. In other words, it is apperception that is absolutely empty in every respect. It is the utterly meaningless "I," so terribly isolated as not even to have a creator. This soul is a cipher, unworthy to be a subject. It may not be a sinner, but it is hardly correct to call it sinless. Sin demands possibility, and the completely isolated and abandoned soul has none. It is alone. It is no more than Lucretius after he has died and disintegrated. In fact, it is less since it has no famous book to its name, no history. This soul is not even forgotten. It is, truly, in name only, as it is testimony to the opposite of the famous Hegelian claim about language: that we often speak the truth in language although we do not say what we mean. In the case of the "empty I" we say exactly what we mean, and we do so with syntactic correctness. But we do not mean anything.

Creation is good, and therefore we are dealing with the apperceiver who in fact has something to perceive, and consequently is led to apperception. Experience is a fact. In other words, there is a world, and it is in this world that the apperceiver perceives, and in so doing he connects these perceptions and cognitions with himself. They are his, and he possesses them. The apperceiver does not perceive himself as one of his perceptions. To do so would be to perceive the soul directly, thereby limiting the soul to the conditions of perception. About this, Kant and Hume were in agreement. Hume, however, remained skeptical about the self (soul) for the very reason that it did not present itself as a perception. He established at the beginning of his inquiry a principle that effectively blocked this acknowledgment of the self (soul).[28] It is precisely in recognizing that these perceptions and cognitions are *my* perceptions and cognitions that I become aware of myself, and ultimately and rationally infer or deduce that there is the self, my soul, which I cognize directly but never solely and always confusedly. Should not I be grateful that I am not so terribly alone as to have no cognitions to call my own?

It is in cognizing my soul that I make the critical division between mine and not mine, between "I" and "not I," between the comprehensive

---

28. Hume, *Treatise of Human Nature* I.I.i.1.

"I" and the specified "I." This critical division generates or more properly discloses the dual manifestation of time, i.e., time as inner organization or phase time on one hand, and succession time on the other hand. Both manifestations have a single origin, and the origin is both divisive and entirely mine. In realizing the dual manifestation I become aware, rarely in exactly these terms, that I have sinned. I have originated sin. I have separated myself from God, my creator, and the separation is truly and strictly my fault because only I can claim both manifestations of time to be both one and mine. It is as if *my* inner organization and capacity to think at all is identical in being with the alien under which I labor and suffer. I produce my adversary, I do so necessarily as soon as I say "I," and accordingly I am culpable for my action. I am my own worst enemy.

It may seem to be patently unjust that there be a world created by the creator in which the individual, solely by recognizing his or her individuality, becomes blameworthy, becomes a sinner, and then accordingly is punished by the consequence of having said "I," the consequence that is succession time, which of course is also the phase time of myself but seen from a different perspective. Perhaps uniquely in this case, defense is an admission of guilt. The individual simply and strictly *cannot* defend himself. This is so because the defense has no footing that is not simply contradictory. As soon as the individual begins his defense, by saying "I," he is convicted.

Creation is good. Proof that creation is good comes ultimately and perhaps even solely through Jesus Christ, because only by the Son of God becoming man can the distinguishing soul that says "I" be reconciled with the time, i.e., the possibility that the act of distinction ushers in. The *other* that comes with the distinguishing "I" must be remade, reborn so to speak, in a way that harmonizes with the apperceiver. All time must be reconciled, and thus Jesus Christ comes, so to speak, only in the fullness of time.

Vladimir, having fallen	Well I suppose in the end I'll get up by myself. (*He tries, fails.*) In the fullness of time.[29]

Vladimir will rise again, of his own accord, but only to fall again. Time itself must be superseded, even vanquished as we know it, in order for each of us to rise finally.

---

29. Beckett, *Waiting for Godot*, 53.

I comment here on the solution, the salvation, to repeat some of the concerns that were expressed above. I speak against those who would accept the world as it is, and themselves as they are. I speak against those who are so learned and experienced that they acknowledge the ways of man to include pride, envy, avarice, and cruelty. We must admit that this is the way human beings are, they say, and we must learn to live with this state of affairs and to mitigate to some extent the undesirable effects of our condition. We initiate the process of mitigation by talking to one another and to ourselves about our condition. We *explain* things to ourselves. The same also goes, they—the explainers—say, for natural disasters. Hurricanes, tornadoes, earthquakes, and the like simply happen. We might seek ways to minimize their effects on us, and we might further seek to modify our collective behavior in an attempt to decrease the frequency of these disasters or at least their impact upon us. We do so by learning about these "disasters," and in so doing we claim to understand their being and to explain why they occur. But they are not, per se, our fault, so they say, and in so saying they do not explain why disasters occur.

Who are these people against whom I am here speaking? We are they. I am one. Each of us is an authority, an expert on self-help, at least on the subject of helping ourselves. We are "like a shrub in the desert, and shall not see any good come." We "shall dwell in the parched places of the wilderness, in an uninhabited salt land" (Jer 17:6). Even when we acknowledge our failures, our limited and often erroneous understanding, our spineless stance against the afflictions—that is how we conceive of them—of this world, even then we do so from an assumed point of advantage. We are experts on ourselves to the very end, because there is no other way of being ourselves. We shall not bring about the fullness of time, for the only time we have is the two-faced demon that allows us to be ourselves and also punishes us for being ourselves.

Is the world this ugly? Are our lives this horrible? Are we overreacting to the fundamental equation of time with sin, and to the fact that our experience is dependent, as we understand it, on our part as originator of sin? Again I point to the revealed justification of mankind. Suffering the minor inconvenience of waiting for a certain desire to be satisfied hardly seems to merit the divine sacrifice of the Son of God, incarnate, crucified, and risen from the dead. Perhaps God overdid things with our salvation. Perhaps the prohibition against Moloch enjoined on the children of Israel was a good idea right from the beginning and should be observed by the lawgiver. These too are matters to be taken up below, where I shall consider divine foreknowledge, freedom, and the final integration of salvation.

F. SUMMARY OF THE DEDUCTION

Waiting, the soul of desire, is the sure sign of our fallen state. This is the evidence, the experience, for suspecting that we have "been conceived in sin." How can this be?

The soul discovers itself, the noumenal, by correlating the phenomenal, by collecting experience and then by inferring the repository of the collection. The soul, by naming the collection "I," acts. This action, for which the soul is responsible and ultimately blameworthy, is to identify the noumenal *I* with the phenomenal *I*, the other or object of reference. The act is one of confusion. The soul commits the sin of apperception, the sin of self-reference, the sin which encompasses all sins, both those of reason and those of circumstance.

Further evidence of our fallen-ness comes from the disintegration that we encounter regarding all souls, including our own. We suffer at the hands of time, the two-faced emanation of our inner organization and our successive experiences.

The origin of sin rests in the juxtaposition of time with time, the confrontation of the organizing principle of all our cognition, our very *I*, with all that seems to happen to us, with all *other* that always and everywhere attends the *I*. This juxtaposition is the mirror of our problem with self-reference. The *other* is the phenomenal *I* that is referred to by the noumenal *I*.

Sin and time are dually manifested in one another. The noumenal *I*, the soul, correlates with the organizational principle of all cognition, phase time. The phenomenal *I*, *other*, correlates with the serendipitous occurrences of succession.

8

Foreknowledge, Predestination, and Freedom

AT NUMEROUS INSTANCES IN this study, the argument has led us to questions of divine foreknowledge, predestination, and the freedom of the individual human being. The three questions clearly are interrelated, with the latter, freedom or free will, dependent upon the first two. At each of those instances along the way I have postponed consideration of these important matters, and have done so because a proper consideration of them requires a full explication of the relationship between original sin and time. In fact, divine foreknowledge, predestination, and human freedom can truly and properly be understood only in light of the detailed equivalence between time and sin. I believe that equivalence has been established in the previous chapters, especially the last one, and now we can address the general matter of freedom. It will be advantageous, however, to reserve direct consideration of freedom until last, after foreknowledge and predestination. Although such freedom has been presupposed, in a way, by all of the arguments about sin and culpability, free will per se has not been asserted as an axiom along with the other claims regarding the eternal God, the permanent soul, and the sinful condition of mankind, i.e., the three axioms of the introductory chapter.[1] It will become clear

---

[1]. Some sort of freedom is implied if the third axiom, sinfulness, contains within it not merely punishment but also culpability.

that the assertion of freedom will be unnecessary once the other matters are considered from the sinful nature of time. I shall begin, therefore, with divine foreknowledge and its related notion of predestination, and then move on to human freedom. The subject of investigation here is what might be called the common notion of predestination and not the beautiful rendition attributed to Karl Barth: predestination is the choice of Jesus Christ as savior.[2]

When we say that God knows what is going to happen tomorrow, we speak as sinners. Only beings in a condition of original sin say things like that. For this language imputes sin to God. It does so by attributing to God our understanding of foreknowledge and predestination. When we speak this way, we bind God with time. In fact, we all speak this way and do so with great frequency, but the commonality of this kind of speech is directly reflective of our sinful condition, a condition that pervades our existence if not our being. Our careless speech betrays our original sin.

When we say that God knows what is going to happen tomorrow, what we mean to say is that if we were God then we would know what is going to happen tomorrow. More precisely, we take a fact, an event, that we are certain of, both regarding its time and place. We then invent another event, one occurring at an earlier time, a time before the initial event in question. Then we make ourselves part of the second, earlier event. We attribute our present knowledge to a previous state, even though the previous state is simply imagined.

We speak of God's plan, and that is speech for us. To say that God's plan unfolds means that we live lives, there is time, we make plans, and to varying degrees we are prudent. We know what plans are, in part because of our frustrated desires and intentions, but also because of our approximate predictive ability. We know how we feel when a much-anticipated event is canceled, perhaps because of inclement weather. We may also have an understanding of plans from so-called successes: good education tends to lead to gainful and meaningful employment. But the precise

---

2. "The doctrine of election is the sum of the Gospel because of all words that can be said or heard it is the best: that God elects man; that God is for man too the One who loves in freedom. It is grounded in the knowledge of Jesus Christ because He is both the electing God and elected man in One." Barth, *Church Dogmatics*, 2/2:3. Also regarding the rejected person, "Because Jesus Christ takes his place, He takes from him the right and possibility of his own independent being and gives him His own being. With Jesus Christ the rejected can only *have been* rejected. He cannot *be* rejected any more." Barth, *Church Dogmatics*, 2/2:453. Even Judas is "elected" among the apostles. Barth, *Church Dogmatics*, 2/2:459.

nature of a plan is most evident and clearly understood in failure, which serves not only as governor on our self-satisfaction when we predict accurately, but also enhances the thrill of correct prediction by keeping chance in the forefront of our mind.

What does it mean to say that God's plans are providential? Providential for whom? What is the purpose of revelation? Revelation for whom? For us. We understand providence and desire it for ourselves. The significance of our understanding is that we know ourselves to be sinners bound by time. We know our condition to be sinful and we know it to be temporal, and as argued in the previous chapter, these two expressions—sinful and temporal—are expressions for the same thing. Sinful and temporal are the necessary consequences of the disruptive *I* who says "I" exclusively, the *I* that confuses comprehension with specification.

It is incorrect to claim that yesterday God knew what was going to happen today. God does not know anything yesterday. We should not say that God did not know anything yesterday, because God is not in the past. We are the ones with a past, or at least a present thought of the past into which we distend our minds, and we say that God was present in our past. God may fully understand cause and effect, which is to say that God knows his own power. And God may have created a world in which there are creatures who live temporal lives, who think in terms of past, present, and future. But to say anything about God in the past as if we were speaking from God's perspective is manifestly erroneous. Such speech makes God out to be a sinner. It binds the hands of God with time, a violation of the first axiom. Such speech is in a way the apex of ingratitude, attributing *our* problem to the cause of our being. We are no better than the exasperated child exclaiming to his parents that he never asked to be born. He has not a leg to stand on. The force of his argument depends entirely on his being for which he is also entirely dependent upon others, most directly if superficially, upon his parents. This is the thinking behind the claim above that the sinner's defense is an admission of guilt. He is convicted as soon as he identifies the defendant by saying "I."

This kind of argument is dangerous, and it is easily and frequently abused. It is not uncommon, upon voicing objection to some assertion, especially regarding a failure of our conduct, that the objection itself is deemed evidence of the failure as well as its blameworthiness. In this case, the matter of sin and time, we are considering the most fundamental of all aspects of our being, indeed, our very being itself. Accordingly I grant myself license in this case to make the argument regarding admission of guilt, and I do so because the argument does not stand or fall on this single admission. This entire study points to the fallen-ness of mankind.

Why do we persist in this particular manifestation of our sinful ways, this manner of speaking about a temporal God, a God that is past and present and future? Even expressions such as the scholastic *nunc stans* that Hobbes decries, the eternal or ever-present now, is little better than the God of the past and the God of the future. The ever-present now is an expression of understanding that is entirely temporal. The expression attempts to speak of God privately, a common and well-used tactic. Indeed, it seems often to be necessary to speak about God in terms of what he is not. But placing God in the eternal now is entirely contaminated by the word "now," which effectively undoes the intent of the adjective "eternal." All that is accomplished by *nunc stans* is to acknowledge the past and the future, and then to rename them as "now." Admittedly this accomplishment seems to entail only phase time while ignoring succession time. In that regard, *nunc stans* is appealing, but it appeals to the creature who lives with, who experiences both phase time and succession time, and who does so under the onus of the latter as an alien. The sinner wants to be relieved of his sins.

We persist nonetheless with these expressions. Indeed, Scripture is full of such terminology. Let us consider here just a few occurrences. The apostle Paul brings together both foreknowledge and predestination in his Letter to the Romans.

> [28] We know that in everything God works for good with those who love him, who are called according to his purpose. [29] For those whom he foreknew he also predestined to be conformed to the image of his Son, in order that he might be the first-born among many brethren. [30] And those whom he predestined he also called; and those whom he called he also justified; and those whom he justified he also glorified. (Rom 8:28–30)

In so doing, Paul is apparently arguing in behalf of God's plan, his eternal decree that in the "fullness of time" God has sent forth his Son, so that "all men be saved and come to the knowledge of the truth" (Gal 4:4 and 1 Tim 2:4). I shall deal with the "all" of "all men" in the next chapter.

In verse 29 of Romans 8, the pertinent words are separated merely by the word "and" (καὶ). "For those whom he foreknew, he also predestined" (ὅτι οὓς προέγνω, καὶ προώρισεν). The two verbs are προγινώσκω and προορίζω.

The first, προγινώσκω (aorist προέγνων), is number 4267 in Strong's biblical concordance. Its meaning, according to Liddell and Scott, is "to know, perceive, learn," *or* "understand beforehand; to foreknow; to judge beforehand; to provide."[3] Other pertinent occurrences of the word in the Bible include the following.

Having written decisively about the fulfillment of the law by Jesus Christ, Paul goes to some length to argue that the fulfillment does not constitute a rejection of the children of Israel.

> God has not rejected his people, whom he foreknew . . . (Rom 11:2)

Also in the First Letter of Peter, we read, regarding Jesus Christ:

> He was destined [προεγνωσμένου] before the foundation of the world but was made manifest at the end of the times for your sake. (1 Pet 1:20)

The Revised Standard Version has "destined" here, but for my argument, "foreknown" would be a better translation.

The second term under consideration, προορίζω, is number 4309 in Strong's biblical concordance. Its meaning, according to Liddell and Scott, is "to determine beforehand, to predetermine, pre-ordain."[4] Other pertinent occurrences of the word in the Bible include the following.

Peter and John, praying after their release from arrest, speak about the opponents of Jesus, specifically Herod and Pontius Pilate, who were:

> to do whatever thy hand and thy plan had predestined to take place. (Acts 4:28)

Also, Paul on several occasions uses the expression to refer to God's plan.

> But we impart a secret and hidden wisdom of God, which God decreed [προώρισεν] before the ages for our glorification. (1 Cor 2:7)

> He destined [προορίσας] us in love to be his sons through Jesus Christ, according to the purpose of his will. (Eph 1:5)

> In him, according to the purpose of him who accomplishes all things according to the counsel of his will, we who first hoped

---

3. Liddell and Scott, *Greek-English Lexicon*, 673.
4. Liddell and Scott, *Greek-English Lexicon*, 682.

in Christ have been predestined [προορισθέντες] and appointed to live for the praise of his glory. (Eph 1:11–12)

I have undertaken a few etymological and philological excurses in this study with the intention solely of clarifying the argument that is presented. This is also the case here. With the two words under consideration, the root words are "to know" (γιγνώσκω) and "to bound" or "to limit" (ὁρίζω). The pertinence of these terms, however, rests on the prefix, "before" (προ-). In these passages, we find the authors writing about God's plan, what might be referred to as divine providence. These instances bring into focus what it means for God to know or to bind *before*. Especially, we ask: before what? The argument of this chapter coupled with that of the previous chapter might glibly be summarized as God knows or God binds before time, i.e., before sin.

These chapters must be connected in greater detail as we proceed, but here, in the scriptural section, let us skip ahead momentarily to the subject of human freedom. The sole instance that I shall consider is the hardening of Pharaoh's heart, an occurrence that seems to limit Pharaoh's freedom, and to do so simply as part of the temporal unfolding of God's plan, his foreknowledge and predestination.

Throughout the book of Exodus, we read about the power of the God of Israel, the God who has chosen Israel as his own since the time of Abraham. This power is made manifest especially through the interactions of Moses and Aaron with the Egyptians, especially with Pharaoh. There is in fact a competition between Pharaoh's magicians and the spokesmen of Israel with respect to the performance of spectacular, even miraculous deeds. These deeds turn out to be primarily at the expense of the Egyptians, who, under the rule of Pharaoh, kept Israel in bondage, Pharaoh "who did not know Joseph" and all the good he had done (Exod 1:8). The story is well known, and we need not go through the details here. The aim is to inquire about the condition of Pharaoh's heart, his will vis à vis the children of Israel and their desire to depart from Egypt for Canaan.

On several occasions in Exodus, we read about the hardening of Pharaoh's heart, his obstinacy. In some cases, the Hebrew verb used to describe Pharaoh's disposition, in particular his heart, is *kabed* (Strong #3513). The verb means "to be heavy, weighty, burdensome, honored; to make heavy, dull, unresponsive."[5] The word is also used adjectivally. More often, however, we read that Pharaoh's heart is hardened. Here

---

5. Brown et al., *Brown-Driver-Briggs*, 457–58.

Brown-Driver-Briggs defines the word *chazaq* (Strong #2388) thus: "to be" *or* "grow firm, strong, strengthen; make rigid, hard, i.e., *perverse, obstinate*, harden (the heart of any one)."[6]

The most common rendition of this occurrence is one wherein the Lord hardens Pharaoh's heart, and it is this version that pertains most directly to our concern with human freedom.

> And the Lord said to Moses, "When you go back to Egypt, see that you do before Pharaoh all the miracles which I have put in your power; but I will harden his heart, so that he will not let the people go." (Exod 4:21)

Here Pharaoh's intransigence seems to be not his own doing but rather that of the Lord, who is using Pharaoh in order to display his own glory. "And the Egyptians shall know that I am the Lord, when I stretch forth my hand upon Egypt and bring out the people of Israel from among them" (Exod 7:5). The Lord has done so that Moses "may tell in the hearing of [his] son and of [his] son's son how I have made sport [*alal*, Strong #5953] of the Egyptians and what signs I have done among them; that you may know that I am the Lord" (Exod 10:2).

In some cases of Pharaoh's obstinacy, the text merely reveals the condition of Pharaoh's heart without attributing cause.

> But the magicians of Egypt did the same by their secret arts; so Pharaoh's heart remained hardened and he would not listen to them, as the Lord had said. (Exod 7:22)

But in one noteworthy instance, Pharaoh is the cause himself of his hardened heart.

> But when Pharaoh saw that there was a respite, he hardened his heart, and would not listen to them; as the Lord had said. (Exod 8:15)

In summary, we have here in many, but not all, instances what looks to be examples of predestination as commonly understood, at least with respect to Pharaoh's heart. The Lord determined in advance that Pharaoh would be unmoved by the many miracles performed by Moses and Aaron, at least until the Passover when the Lord's destroyer was visited upon the Egyptian households. Our common reaction and interpretation are that Pharaoh had no choice with respect to his heart, his will. Pharaoh

---

6. Brown et al., *Brown-Driver-Briggs*, 304.

was a pawn in the divine plan to liberate Israel from Egyptian bondage and to proclaim the LORD of Israel in all his glory. God used Pharaoh to proclaim his majesty even to the point of making sport[7] of the Egyptians.

It is evident that the condition of Pharaoh's heart is related to the foreknowledge attributed to God by Paul regarding his plan of salvation. It is also manifestly related to the predestination, the decree of God. The *before* of God seems to have abridged human freedom, and if such is the case, how can the individual be held responsible for acts committed without his will? This, as I have argued before and will argue below, is the wrong question. It is a question that presupposes a specific kind of answer and does so incorrectly. It is the question of the sinner who would attribute his sin to God. It is the question of a faux-naïf who has determined the injustice in advance.

To investigate this matter more closely, let us return to our discussion of cause and effect. In my treatment of Euclidean geometry, I asked if the effects of the postulates, i.e., the propositions, are foreknown in the cause. Immediately one wants to know: foreknown by whom? The effects are formally contained in the cause, but explicit knowledge of them is another matter. It is quite common in our daily lives to encounter, often with dismay, unforeseen effects of actions that we have taken. (This is the primary component of our education regarding planning for the future.) In this respect, the consideration of foreknowledge is entirely temporal. In other words, time is the context under which the question about knowledge is being asked. But equally common in our conversation we speak about what we know and what we do not know, when what we really are saying is that someone claims to know and I believe that person. There is a non-temporal quality to such assertions. *We* know that there are approximately fifty perfect numbers. We do not know if there are infinitely many perfect numbers. When I say the latter sentence, I mean exactly what I say. I am a member of the "we," although even here I am a member in ignorance. But when I speak about the fifty perfect numbers, what I am doing is reporting some assertions that I believe. *I* do know that some numbers are perfect, e.g., 6, 28, 496, 8,128, but certainly I cannot identify all fifty off the top of my head, nor can I do it using the Euclidean formula. Thus when I say that "we know," what I mean is that humankind taken collectively knows. Reason is being represented in practical, factual, historical, and empirical fashion by being the sum

---

7. *alal*—"to make a toy of, to deal wantonly, ruthlessly." Brown et al., *Brown-Driver-Briggs*, 759.

of knowledge accumulated by human beings. This knowing is not dissimilar to claims about divine foreknowledge or assertions regarding the propositions of Euclidean geometry being foreknown in the postulates. In this regard, time is not explicitly a part of the knowledge, the factual context notwithstanding.

Above, in chapter 2, I also suggested that a machine would not know all the effects of a cause like the Fifth Postulate, a cause which was demonstrated to be non-temporal. Specifically, the Pythagorean Theorem is a non-temporal effect of the cause. If we were to define machine knowledge as the capacity to derive each and every true assertion of a system, then Gödel's incompleteness theorems demonstrate that for a consistent system (no contradictions) as rich as Euclidean geometry, there is a true statement that cannot be derived. Therefore, not all of the effects can be known by the cause, not even in the artificial and non-temporal manner described here. This claim, of course, rests on the definition of knowledge in this case, i.e., deducible.

Let us apply this result to our consideration in the following way. We ask about divine foreknowledge and in particular about what relationship it holds to our being. What we really want to know is something about our temporal being. Presumably our lives are more complex than a mathematical system such as Euclidean geometry. Yet in the case of geometry there would be unknown effects. If an individual human being were to put himself in the place of the machine, in somewhat god-like fashion, the individual would not be able to know all the effects (true propositions) following upon himself as cause. In this case, however, the machine is serving as an instrument of human knowledge, in fact, a surrogate. The machine serves in the capacity of "we" above regarding perfect numbers. The programmer of the machine would know even less, at least explicitly, about the outcomes.

Accordingly, when we ask about the relationship of divine foreknowledge and our future actions, we are pretending to be God. We are putting ourselves in the position of *the* cause. But we do not know what it means to know all the effects of the cause. We are asking about a relationship that we do not understand in its infinite complexity. All we know for certain, following Gödel, is that we do not know all the effects. With divine foreknowledge, we are asking about a relationship that we cannot comprehend. It is a relationship that we understand particularly, and even repeatedly particularly. We can follow each and every output of our machine. It is a relationship that we can understand in a non-temporal sense, although our intent is certainly temporal when we ask about divine foreknowledge and our actions, our temporal will. But it is a relationship that is qualitatively beyond our understanding. We are forming a question that meets the standards of grammar and English syntax, but we do not know what we are talking about. As the Lord said to Job, "Who is this that darkens counsel by words without knowledge" (Job 38:2)?

The argument here is not that prediction and prophecy are meaningless. As mentioned above in chapter 2, we have a clear understanding of what it means to predict an outcome, and that understanding consists of saying *now* what will be *then*. We have a test that verifies results. With this understanding, the *fore-* and *pre-* of foreknowledge and predestination are explicitly temporal. This cannot be what is meant by divine foreknowledge and predestination. The kind of language used by the apostle Paul is not meaningless. Quite to the contrary, it is more meaningful than we are accustomed to think. By referring to what seems like a simple example of temporal prediction, Paul has revealed a mystery. It is correct according to the apostle to speak of a plan, divine purpose, eternal decree realized in the fullness of time to save mankind. And it is correct for Paul to speak of divine foreknowledge and predestination such that those loved by God will conform to the image of God's son (Rom 8:28–29). This conformation, however, is not a statement about human freedom and will. It is quite incorrect to associate divine foreknowledge with human freedom, the many attempts to do so notwithstanding. I shall return to these attempts presently.

Providence is often attributed to God, both in the sense of his beneficence and also in the sense of his foresight. We shall see, at the end of this chapter, that such attributions amount to sinful action on our part, but an action that on the surface seems to be made with good intention. A remarkable incidence of beneficence and foresight occurred on Mount Moriah. In gratitude and honor of the Lord's intervention, Abraham so named the mountain. "So Abraham called the name of that place The Lord will provide, as it is said to this day, 'On the mount of the Lord it shall be provided'" (Gen 22:14). The Hebrew is *raah* (Strong #7200), most commonly translated as "to see."[8] Other meanings include "to provide, to furnish." Thus the Lord's providence means that the Lord shall be known. God's foresight, his predestination is for us a kind of knowledge, and our intent in proclaiming his providence is one of gratitude and

---

8. Brown et al., *Brown-Driver-Briggs*, 906–8.

praise. Thus we shall be seen to be sinners even when acting as our best selves, although one might counter, anthropocentrically, that even as sinners our intent is to glorify God.

We have seen already treatments of divine foreknowledge and predestination, notably that of Augustine on perseverance, which constitutes the second book of his treatise *On the Predestination of the Saints*. As inventive as some of these treatments are, they nonetheless prove to be unsatisfying. Here I shall review briefly some of these arguments with the intent of showing how each one fails to account for the fundamental error described above, the error of standing in for God. More precisely, each of these apologies or accounts makes the error of having God stand in for us. Each turns God into a sinner by subjecting him to time. In an attempt to acquit God of neglecting his creation, we convict him. Time, and particularly time as sin, is central to an understanding of the issues surrounding human freedom, and it is this central principle that is lacking in most or all traditional accounts.

In the chapter on perseverance, we saw that Augustine goes to great length to counter Pelagian accounts concerning the process of salvation. The connection to our inquiry should be quite clear. The argument attributed to Pelagius, rightly or wrongly, consists of a co-operation of sorts between the saving grace of God and the meritorious effort of the individual human being. In the extreme version, the human being owes to God only his existence, and thence he works out his own salvation, perhaps not "in fear and trembling" (Phil 2:12). This effort, if it is truly meritorious in a conventional sense, must come about freely according to the will of the individual. Its merit, or blame in the other direction, rests squarely on the spontaneity of the human act, the individual's free choice. Even if conducted in "fear and trembling," the work is his, man's. God's great gift to man was freedom.

Augustine is adamant that the human being receives or does not receive the salvific grace in no way owing to such human effort. Justification comes exclusively from God. The will, if in fact it remains faithful to God, does so only because it is assisted by God's grace, and without this assistance, the individual, subject to fleshly concupiscence, is unable to persevere in fidelity. Righteousness comes from God and only from God. Augustine relies on the very passage quoted above, Paul's Letter to the Ephesians. "In him, according to the purpose of him who accomplishes all things according to the counsel of his will, we who first hoped in Christ have been predestined [προορισθέντες] and appointed to live for the praise of his glory" (1:11–12).

We saw that even Jesus seems to confuse time and eternity in his admonition to the residents of Chorazin and Bethsaida (Luke 10:13–14; Matt 11:20–22). Jesus claims that if the Tyrians and Sidonians had been witness to the miraculous signs and preaching presented to Chorazin and Bethsaida, they would have believed, which they apparently did not. Augustine's fully temporal interpretation is that death is the statute of limitations for culpability and for merit. If the Tyrians and Sidonians had seen the signs before having died, they would have believed. Therefore, according to Augustine, they were predestined not to believe. They were not among those foreknown to receive the gift of faith. In other words, Augustine, at the suggestion of Jesus, takes the events of Chorazin and Bethsaida and temporally moves them back to the time of Tyre and Sidon. He manufactures events, and then they have the expected temporal consequences. They occur *and then* the witnesses believe. Predestination is thereby given an entirely temporal backdrop against which it unfolds. This pious argument confines God, by means of the words of Jesus, in the same way that other, more apologetic arguments do.

Augustine's argument is neither persuasive nor even entirely clear for that matter, but the argument itself does not attempt to preserve individual freedom, an attempt that we shall find in latter accounts. Augustine comes closest to my interpretation of divine foreknowledge and predestination when he takes up the efficacy of preaching, in particular preaching about the very subjects of foreknowledge and predestination. What can be the rhetorical force, the moral suasion of acknowledging that only by God's grace can one persevere in faithfulness? The efforts of the individual amount to nothing because the human contribution to salvation is a finite offering to compensate for an infinite debt. The contribution is nil. One who hears such proclamations is likely to ask himself, "Why bother?"

Augustine turns the tables on this matter. He argues in favor of such preaching, but not because of its capacity to alter human behavior. Such alteration is of no salvific value. The error of Pelagius must be condemned in every instance and every form of its appearance. Rather than making a comment in favor of or against self-help, one preaches about divine foreknowledge and predestination in order to glorify God. It is the right thing to do, regardless of its ineffectiveness with respect to the unfolding of God's decree. So that "God may be rightly worshipped," one proclaims the divine order.⁹ One must remain faithful to the truth.

Although this argument does not directly address the problem of sinfulness and temporality, at least there is no appeal here to temporal order. There is no confusion or miscomprehension within the argument itself regarding what it might mean for God's plan to unfold. To the extent that this latter argument of Augustine may be correct, it is so by omission.

Perhaps beginning with Anselm and the introduction of original justice, there is an attempt to reconcile predestination with human freedom. All such attempts make the same fundamental mistake. Milton makes explicit the attempted acquittal, an attempt that rests on a distinction between knowledge and cause.

Satan has departed from hell, on his way to earth. The Father speaks to the Son, telling him that man "will hearken to [Satan's] glozing lies," but the failure will rest with man who is "sufficient to have stood, though free to fall."¹⁰ As for the loyal and rebellious angels:

> Freely they stood who stood, and fell who fell.
> Not free, what proof could they have giv'n sincere
> Of true allegiance, constant faith or love,
> Where only what they needs must do, appeared,
> Not what they would? What praise could they receive?
> What pleasure I from such obedience paid,
> When will and reason (reason also is choice)
> Useless and vain, of freedom both despoiled,
> Made passive both, had served necessity,
> Not me. They therefore as to right belonged,
> So were created, nor can justly accuse
> Their Maker, or their making, or their fate.
> As if predestination overruled
> Their will, disposed by absolute decree
> Or high foreknowledge; they themselves decreed
> Their own revolt, not I: if I foreknew,
> Foreknowledge had no influence on their fault,
> Which had no less proved certain unforeknown.¹¹

There are really two important points argued by Milton. One concerns the distinction between knowledge and cause, and the other the necessity

---

9. Augustine, *Gift of Perseverance* XX.51.
10. Milton, *Paradise Lost* III.93, 99.
11. Milton, *Paradise Lost* III.102–19.

for freedom in order that God's creatures may choose goodness. I shall defer my comments on the second of these points until the end of the chapter, although it is worth pointing out here that Milton has God commit to the testing evaluation of prediction, "Where only what they needs must do, appeared, / Not what they would?"

Knowledge is not identical with cause, neither conceptually nor in the world of practice. One practical distinction can be made with regard to a heavy object let go above the surface of the earth. An individual, a human being, may foreknow with a high degree of certainty the path (or apparent path) to be taken by the object. It will move in a straight line perpendicular to a tangent to the surface of the earth. And yet the one who conducts this experiment readily acknowledges that he is not the ultimate cause of the object's movement, despite his participation in the experiment by lifting up the object and then releasing it.

Under normal circumstances, however, we would not attribute will or freedom to the object, and so we might be more concerned when the future of the object seems to be more uncertain, when a human being may not foreknow with a high degree of certainty the future action of the object. In other words, things might be more complicated if we consider an animate object, in fact another human being, as part of the experiment. In this case we consider two human beings, one the observer and the other the observed. The first is not only a student of human nature but, in this particular case, a specialist on the behavior of the other person. He predicts the future action of our test subject, perhaps that the second person will depart from his house in the morning. Let us assume that the prediction comes true. Our observer foreknew the action of the test subject without causing his morning departure. This knowledge could be subjected to testing, all in the context of time. We could insist on the prediction to be made temporally before the test subject departs. Therefore, presumably, knowledge and cause are shown to be separate in both thought and in practice. Apropos the fallen angels:

> Their will, disposed by absolute decree
> Or high foreknowledge; they themselves decreed
> Their own revolt, not I: if I foreknew,
> Foreknowledge had no influence on their fault.

Of course, many concerns and objections come to mind. For example, was the foreknowledge of the observer certain? If so, then we are inclined to say that the result or effect was predetermined, it was forced upon the test subject irrespective of his will. Pharaoh's heart will be hardened. The results could not have come out any other way. Calvin has some strong words for this argument. "Moreover when I say that the will, deprived of liberty, is led or dragged by necessity to evil, it is strange that any should deem the expression harsh, seeing there is no absurdity in it, and it is not at variance with pious use. It does, however, offend those who know not how to distinguish between necessity and compulsion [*necessité et contrainte*]."[12] Back to our concerns, what if the test subject did not depart on that morning? And so forth. The weight of the argument rests on our ability to separate the concepts of knowledge and cause. This distinction appeared briefly above, regarding the fallen angels.[13] There I noted a treatment by Peter King of Augustine's arguments concerning the fallen angels. According to King, Augustine is distinguishing between reasons and cause. "Now Augustine's denial that there are determining causes of the will does not entail that the will's actions are inexplicable or somehow not tied to the agent. Augustine clearly allows that there were *reasons* for action that help us to understand it, although they do not determine the action."[14] In Augustine's thinking, according to King, there is no cause for the devil's sin. There is no other devil that made the devil disobey. There is, however, an explanation for the devil's disobedience, and that is his pride. The devil chose to take delight in himself rather than in God, and he chose so freely. Pride is the reason for the devil's disobedience, not the cause of it.

In this account, "reasons" takes the place of knowledge or foreknowledge in the argument provided by Milton and others. "If I foreknew, / Foreknowledge had no influence on their fault." No reason, no explanation could be any better than divine foreknowledge, that which might be considered to be the ultimate accounting. Augustine's attribution of pride to the devil is, according to King, the reason for the devil's fall. Is this any more than a name applied to an event? Is this any more than looking backward historically? The devil chooses himself over God. We treat the choice historically, as an event, and accordingly say that the devil chose himself. We, along with Augustine, burn to know why things are the way they are, and a way that we commence our investigations is to start talking and naming. We are historians with perfect hindsight.

---

12. Calvin, *Institutes* II.iii.5, 181.
13. Ch. 6, section F.
14. King, "Angelic Sin," 9–10.

Augustine objects to this strictly temporal line of thinking, but for reasons other than those that I propose. We saw in his account of the passage from the First Letter of John (3:8), that the devil must not be thought to have existed for a time without sinning. Augustine's reasoning is based on the everlasting reward or punishment accorded the angels who remained faithful or betrayed, respectively. The unfaithful angels must not be thought to have had any experience other than that of just condemnation. "And from this passage, 'The devil sins from the beginning,' it is not to be supposed that he sinned from the beginning of his created existence, but from the beginning of his sin, when by his pride he had once commenced to sin."[15] In other words, no time is allowed to intervene between the creation of the devil and his sin.

This argument, although ultimately still subject to the temporal fallacy, is better than Milton's in that it recognizes the problem of existence and sin. Augustine's piety and adherence to other Christian tenets regarding the "lives" of the angels and the goodness of all God's creation may keep him from attributing to the devil a moment *during* which the devil might have chosen to remain faithful. All of these arguments, except perhaps for that of Augustine and how it is eventually developed by Calvin, attempt to acquit God from abridging the freedom of the human being. I have postponed consideration of the argument in behalf of meritorious action, the choice to do the right thing. But in all the acquittals, the one who foreknows and therefore predestines is subjected to time in his knowledge and decree. The *fore-* and the *pre-* are given a temporal context. In so doing, each of these arguments subjects God to time. Each binds the hands of the creator with time. And thus, in so doing, each of these arguments renders God a sinner because each makes God into a being that says "I" disruptively. To "justify the ways of God to men,"[16] it has become necessary to turn God into a man.

Given the inadequacy of these accounts of divine foreknowledge and predestination, are we left in the unpleasant position of necessarily acknowledging the limitation of God's decree? Must we once again buckle under the weight of human fallibility and assume that to the best of our ability we cannot know? Must we be reduced to acatalepsy with regard to anything divine? If so, it seems that we can then divide ourselves into two groups. One group will simply reject the reality of God. God is

---

15. Augustine, *City of God* XI.15.
16. Milton, *Paradise Lost* I.26.

a concept, but no more. No beneficence, no power, no omniscience. The other group will consist of sufferers. At best they will become a community of sufferers, babbling to one another, poetizing our mean state (Cadmus and Agave at the end of *The Bacchae*). For neither group will there be any need or desire for theology.

Predestination, as commonly understood, is an unpleasant notion. It strikes right at the heart of each of us, and we instinctively respond, "Unfair!" And I suppose that it is unfair, but unfair in the same way that everything is unfair. Life is unfair. One person gets this and another person gets something else. In one case the *this* includes good looks, keen mind, genial disposition, material wealth, loving friends and family, spiritedness, honor, respect, and a long life. In the other case *something else* comes with an ugly body, dull mind, splenetic disposition, poverty, haters all around, laziness, dishonor, disrespect, and an early but painful death. This is simply the way things are. It is what it is.

As I have shown, the problem, to put it succinctly, is one of perspective. More accurately, the problem arises when we move seamlessly and indistinguishably among perspectives. This movement or seeming motion is one of confusion, and hence a problem. But this movement is not real movement of a sort, but rather the indiscriminate adoption of views or images of cause and effect, time, eschatology, and the Judeo-Christian stories that reveal the truth of the matter. And the truth of the matter is unbearable, or so it seems, from the perspective, our perspective of sin.

What is our perspective when we bristle at the notion that God hardened Pharaoh's heart? Surely we are not dwelling on the fact that the object of our concern, Pharaoh, was an ingrate and a slave owner who lived several thousand years ago and had forgotten about all the good rendered to Egypt by Joseph. No, rather than this, we think it unfair that Pharaoh never had a chance to do the right thing, or at least he did not have infinitely many chances, or if he had infinitely many chances, he did not have a chance when it came to negotiations with Moses and Aaron.

Furthermore, even if Pharaoh did have a chance to do the right thing and hardened his own heart, as we saw above in at least one case, we still sense, if not injustice, something like malicious bullying on the part of God for picking on Pharaoh. Is Pharaoh going to be punished for his poor decisions regarding the Israelites, perhaps even punished with eternal damnation and hellfire? Will not he change his mind at some point while being tortured? We know that he changed his mind, albeit temporarily, when "the Lord smote all the first-born in the land of Egypt" (Exod 12:29). Will not Pharaoh acknowledge his mistake and agree retroactively to let Israel depart for the promised land? Nobody likes to be informed that he has been consigned to burn in hell for all eternity. And if not you yourself, perhaps a dear loved one, and if not a dear loved one, then perhaps poor old Pharaoh.

I present three possibilities that face us, each objectionable in one way or more. First, there is the position intimated by Augustine and embraced fully by Calvin that predestination, while properly understood in ordinary temporal fashion, is simply the revealed truth. The authorities here, among others, are the book of Exodus and the letters of Paul. Second, there is the defense of a good God that rests on distinguishing between knowledge and cause, this defense too being entirely temporal in its understanding. Third, we might explicitly abandon the notion of an all-powerful and omniscient God while clinging to some shred of beneficence. This third possibility attempts to combine the two groups that I just described, the one that walks away and the other that sings songs of suffering to one another.

This third possibility is one that has not been considered in this work. This is the possibility that binds the hand of God with time, and often with much more, and in so doing violates the first axiom. Arguments in favor of this third option are common and vary widely in their character, from the painfully moving to the profoundly philosophical to the contentiously argumentative. According to Hans Jonas, who is writing about the God who is witness to Auschwitz, if God is to be caring, then he must participate in time. "Thus if God is in any relation to the world—which is the cardinal assumption of religion—then by that token alone the Eternal has 'temporalized' himself and progressively becomes different through the actualizations of the world process."[17] Here we have a creator who can do only so much, who cares for us deeply, and accordingly who suffers alongside of us in the face of our cruelty to one another. Here we have our loving parents who do all they can to protect us, to fortify us, to encourage us. Here we have the author, perhaps Cervantes, who has produced a character who subsequently gets out of hand. We may even have here the supreme being, provided that we have in mind the greatest of all the beings: Zeus.

This third possibility is at bottom the Hegelian God, the one who has emptied himself out into the world, and in so doing has become fully

---

17. Jonas, "Concept of God," 7.

temporalized. This is the God of Thomas Altizer, i.e., the God who died on the cross. This is the God who is man's best man, and a very good man is he. Even when exponents of this third possibility do not explicitly acknowledge the temporal context for their thinking, it is undoubtedly there and understandably so. We *are* temporal beings. We have loving parents. But we are more than simply temporal. We have souls.

Before commenting on human freedom, I shall summarize the argument here by recalling a claim from the introductory chapter. There it was asserted that our repeated errors in trying to understand divine foreknowledge and predestination were a result of our attempts to comprehend all that is, to comprehend God and his creation. In particular, the errors arise when we confuse understanding with comprehension.

My argument, especially of the past two chapters, is understandable and based on reason. We *understand* ourselves to be sinners. We understand how our sin comes about, specifically how we originate sin by disruptively saying "I," even if in so doing we simultaneously refuse to use the term "sin." And we further understand that this disruption results in the establishment of dual-faceted time, both phase time and succession time. We understand that we, *by being*, compound our inner organization with the alien who assaults us. This chain of reasoning is admittedly complex, but I believe it to be reasonable, to be understandable.

We err, however, when we ascend to the position of comprehension, when we think that by understanding the many steps involved in our sinfulness we have understood all sin. We present to ourselves evidence of our failure to comprehend every time we attempt to include God into our understanding. Every time we make God play by our rules we make God sin. Every time we bristle at the injustice perpetrated by God on Pharaoh, every time we pray for the repose of the soul of Judas Iscariot, every time we suffer outrage at the thought that our beneficent, all-powerful, omniscient creator *permits* parts of his creation, souls, to reject him and consequently to suffer for all eternity, we make the same mistake. We bind the hands of God with time. We make ourselves into the cause that foresees all of its effects.

At this point, a comment on freedom will serve merely as addendum to the argument regarding divine foreknowledge and predestination. The case has been made that assertions regarding freedom, at least with respect to predestination, are ultimately meaningless. Nonetheless, the plight of Pharaoh remains disconcerting, in particular his apparent destiny to play a pawn-like role in the divine drama, so that "the Egyptians shall know that I am the LORD, when I stretch forth my hand upon Egypt and bring out the people of Israel from among them" (Exod 7:5). "I have made sport of the Egyptians and what signs I have done among them; that you may know that I am the LORD" (Exod 10:2).

All along, I have insisted that freedom was not one of my axioms, and now I believe that it is clear why I have not made that request. From the point of view of sinfulness, blame, and culpability, freedom seems to be a necessary presupposition. How else are we to understand Kierkegaard's *possibility*, Kant's *ought*, and Augustine's and Calvin's *perseverance*? How else can we possibly be moral beings for whom things might have been different? Why are we anxious and desirous of perseverance? Surely it must be that we have within ourselves the capacity to choose this or that, to say yes or no. Surely we can place ourselves in the position of Adam and Eve as construed above, the position that many theologians place the angels at their creation.

We have, for example, the extensive commentary of the theologians on the origin of the devil's sin. Specifically, the theologians argue that the devil himself is the cause. Augustine argues:

> Since the will is the cause of sin, and you are looking for a cause of the will, if I can find this, will you not look for a cause of the cause I have found? What will satisfy these questions, what will put an end to our hesitation and discussion? You ought not to look further than the root. . . . But if you look for the cause of this root, how can it be the root of all evil? Such cause would be the root cause, and if you found it, you will, as I said, look for a further cause, and the inquiry will be endless.[18]

Specifically, the devil spontaneously chooses himself in lieu of God. This is, of course, the temporal view of the sinner. Therefore, my third axiom, that we are fallen, has as a corollary that the devil, and Adam and Eve, and we act spontaneously in our sinful ways. It turns out that we insist upon our culpability, and we do so precisely because we originate our blameworthiness when we say "I" the only way we know how to say "I," disruptively and sinfully. Nonetheless, it is *I* who says "I" and thereby is accountable for what I have said.

One might ask, however, what is the truth of the matter? Irrespective of the bondage of sin, can we say something about the alleged freedom of the individual? In a very limited sense, I defer to Kant's famous

---

18. Augustine, *On the Free Choice* III.17.48.

third antinomy of pure reason, the conflict between the laws of nature according to which everything occurs and freedom.[19] There Kant has his cake and eats it too. Freedom is possible from the perspective of things in themselves, in the noumenal world. Freedom is impossible in the world of appearances, the natural world of law.

I do not for a moment propose that Kant's brilliant treatment of the matter remedies our problem. Kant presumably would emphatically disagree with my understanding of time as both phase-like and succession-like, for he would consider the latter time to be subsistent and therefore erroneous. The complexity that he is willing to grant to the rational being he is unwilling to extend to time. Time, for him, cannot be one and also be in conflict with itself. After all, Kant is writing about rational beings for whom the only sin is inconsistency. I am writing about sinners.

I conclude this section with a consideration of the possibility of human merit and the further possibility that God might intervene favorably on the part of his creation. God says to the Son regarding the angels:

> Not free, what proof could they have giv'n sincere
> Of true allegiance, constant faith or love,
> Where only what they needs must do, appeared,
> Not what they would?[20]

Milton has God say that he wants his creatures freely to choose him, to choose complete and perfect goodness over some lesser form, specifically a created form. This is the merit argument that Augustine found to be anathema to sacred doctrine, the heresy attributed to Pelagius. It is an argument that has been embraced to varying degrees by many Christian theologians, but notably excluding Calvin and some of his most strict followers. God, according to Milton, wants his creation to take the test. "What pleasure I from such obedience paid" if the creatures have no choice? But Milton's God knows the test results beforehand. Nevertheless, he apparently takes pleasure when some angels choose him.

Paul Tillich advanced the notion of finite freedom for the human being. In so doing, he connected the notion directly to sin.

> If one is asked how a loving and almighty God can permit evil, one cannot answer in the terms of the question as it was asked. One must first insist on an answer to the question How could he permit sin?—a question which is answered the moment it

---

19. Kant, *Critique of Pure Reason* B473–79.
20. Milton, *Paradise Lost* III.103–6.

is asked. Not permitting sin would mean not permitting freedom; this would deny the very nature of man, his finite freedom. Only after this answer can one describe evil as the structure of self-destruction which is implicit in the nature of universal estrangement.[21]

Sin, according to Tillich, is manifest as well as being a revealed truth. Therefore the culpability attendant upon the notion of sin necessitates freedom. The freedom is finite in so far as it is limited by the material conditions, the very existence of the human being. "Finite freedom is the turning point from being to existence."[22] It is the freedom of living in this world, and it is characterized by man's use of language. "All the potentialities which constitute his freedom are limited by the opposite pole, his destiny. . . . In man freedom and destiny limit each other, for he has finite freedom."[23] The finitude is no different from Pharaoh's plight. His heart was the sort that would harden in the face of appeals from Moses and Aaron. Pharaoh even seems to forget the horror of the Passover. "What is this we have done, that we have let Israel go from serving us?" (Exod 14:5).

With finite freedom we have the creature that is able to some extent to make itself pleasing to God. Thus far I have not rendered an opinion on this proposition, and I shall not here for the simple reason that it is not a proposal that can be entertained in the true context of time as sin. Tillich comes very close to asserting a connection between time and sin when he claims that the meaning of the fall of mankind is that essence passed into existence. "Mythologically speaking, Adam before the fall was in an essential, though untested and undecided, unity with God. But this is not man's situation, nor is it the situation of anything that exists."[24] Existence, however, is a temporal phenomenon, and explicitly and directly a sinful phenomenon because of that very reason.

Finally, we might ask what relationship the creator has to his temporal creation, and in particular, might not there be a way for the creator to intervene in the existence, the temporality of the creature, in order to mitigate the sinfulness that comes with apperception? This is the question asked by Hans Jonas, above, and Jonas asserts that any relation of the eternal to the world requires a "temporalizing" of God. Indeed, why does not the creator prevent sin? To put the proposal in very simple terms,

21. Tillich, *Systematic Theology*, 2:61.
22. Tillich, *Systematic Theology*, 1:165.
23. Tillich, *Systematic Theology*, 2:31–32.
24. Tillich, *Systematic Theology*, 1:206.

could the creator have made a temporal world just like ours, peopled with human beings just like us, human beings who truly had the capacity to act spontaneously? And in the temporal unfolding of this creation, could God have acted providentially and perfectly, stepping in at each and every occurrence of sin and preventing it before its occurrence? God would serve as the ultimate guardian, never letting sin befall his creatures. A slight variation of this position, assumed by most who pray, is that God will step in if we request assistance, but even then only on his own terms. The apparent negotiations between the Lord and Abraham regarding the proposed destruction of Sodom and Gomorrah ends thus: "And the Lord went his way when he had finished speaking to Abraham; and Abraham returned to this place" (Gen 18:33). Who was negotiating with whom?

This is the conception of God and sin that is portrayed to some extent by the Lord to Cain when he warns him to beware of sin lurking at his door and desiring him (Gen 4:7). A providential guardian will protect us from the predator. Why is not this world and our God like that? Surely God does not *want* his creatures to betray him, to fail. Surely God *wants* his creatures to obey him, and to do so freely.

An alternative to this intrusive creator is one who cleans up after the fact. Such is proposed, only to be rejected, by David Bentley Hart in his argument for universal salvation, or complete restoration, *apokatastasis*. The cleansing would occur apparently by God's annihilation of the sinful soul. The wayward being would thereby be spared never-ending hellfire. The good would go to heaven and the bad would be annihilated. In rejecting this proposal, Hart writes: "there would always be a fixed number of finite histories that ended in a divine absence, and so of inner rational wills where God was present only ever in a relative and partly negative degree. There would exist eternally the residual reality of souls that never surrendered to him."[25]

The annihilation that Hart envisions might rightly be thought of as "annihilation lite." The immortal soul would be rendered as not being, having been reduced to nothing, but the history of the soul would linger. God would in fact be eternally shamed by the "residual reality" of the obstinate souls, the fact that God was wrong at least once, *in the past*. Although I cannot help but to want universal salvation, I acknowledge that I do so only from a sinful point of view. (This matter is taken up in detail in the next chapter.) The argument offered by Hart, even though directed against

---

25. Hart, *That All Shall Be Saved*, 194.

the prospect that there is a Judas Iscariot present in the history of mankind, acquits God by tying him down with time. The residue is a shameful history. A stronger form or annihilation would at least do away not only with the sinful soul but also with the sinful soul's existence. To lapse into sloppy and ultimately incorrect terminology, the sinful soul never was. This, of course, is no better since this conception is also entirely temporal. Here the solution, in certain cases, is to run time backward.

Freedom is not an axiom. It is in a way a presupposition of sin, of fallen man. But freedom is not presupposed at all temporally. There is no place in my argument for prelapsarian man. There is no concern for what the devil might have been doing before he rebelled against God. There is no lapse of time because there is no time. Freedom, if there is such a thing, is metaphysically coincident with sin, which is metaphysically coincident with time. And two-faced time is coincident with apperception, with the *I* that says "I." In a strangely deductive sense, freedom then becomes a corollary of the axiom regarding the fallen state of man, less a presupposition for the commission of sin than a necessary consequence.

All of the treatments of divine foreknowledge and predestination have been shown to be temporal in their essence. These treatments are applicable to this world, our world only because they are the explanations given by sinners for their sins. We are Augustine's devil who sins not from the beginning of his existence but from the beginning of his sin. Our sin is our defense. Because of the way we say "I," whenever we provide an account of providence we must do so by making God sin. "For our sake, he made him to be sin who knew no sin, so that in him we might become the righteousness of God" (2 Cor 5:21).

9

Universalism

THE ARGUMENT FOR THE relationship of sin to time is complete. Put more strongly, time has been shown to be the origin of sin, and one who denies time with expressions such as "Time does not exist" also denies sin. Certainly the converse is not empirically true. Many people deny the existence of sin without denying time, and it is vain folly on my part to think that were those people to read this study they would acknowledge the relationship of sin and time and further acknowledge their common origin. The very word "sin" proves to be an insurmountable obstacle for many, who in effect deny a fact.

In the previous chapter we saw the consequences of this fundamental relationship, time and sin, with regard to foreknowledge, predestination (as traditionally understood), and freedom. The reader might expect at this point a discussion of the goal toward which this entire inquiry has been directed. In a narrowly logical sense, this is the place where we should encounter an argument for reintegration, the argument for being made one not only with Jesus Christ but also by Jesus Christ. "I in them and thou in me, that they may become perfectly one" (John 17:23).

Here I interrupt the flow of this argument, stopping short of its completion, which is postponed to the following chapter. I do so, first, to remind the reader of a working hypothesis. This entire study has been presented backward, doubly so, and this presentation is evidence of the sinful orientation of our thought as well our need for grace. The argument is graceless because it strives to build up to that from which it only can start. The center of this investigation as well as the starting point is Jesus Christ, the revelation of God as he is, at least to the extent that we humans can receive the revelation. We as rational sentient beings can receive the Logos. All that has been written here presupposes the incarnation, which, in the terms of Karl Barth, is the meaning of predestination. The creator loves his creation, he chooses to become a part of his creation, and he reveals his love and choice to his creation. This is the destiny, our destiny that precedes all that is. Quite simply, we are destined to be saved by the Son of God.

More narrowly, all that has been written here presupposes grace, for there is neither sin nor time without grace. I have not written a treatise on grace, but the results of my inquiry would be truly unbearable if grace were not presupposed, if we lived in a world without grace. This presupposition runs exactly counter to our experience. We commit sins and then await merciful forgiveness. Because time is sin, we sin first, and as always, we wait. We stand in the need of prayer. But our sinful experience corresponds to the unfolding of my entire inquiry and argument. In a way, we live life backward. Jesus Christ is, of course, the omega of all Christian thought, but necessarily he is also the alpha. Having been exhorted to put on Jesus Christ, to become the new man, the old man plods on. Secularists, of course, will try to retain both the notion of time and of grace without the notion of sin. This position is not entirely meaningless provided that by grace is meant something like privilege, allowance, ornament, or good luck.

This reminder regarding the working hypothesis, however, would hardly merit a separate chapter. I have interrupted the sequence of argument for a second reason, and that is to apply this newly developed understanding of sin to a perennial topic of all theology and especially of Christian theology. The subject is universalism. The understanding of the relationship of time to sin will clarify aspects of the controversy surrounding the idea of universal salvation. Indeed, the controversial problem has been ill conceived. The problem, if there is indeed a problem, has been deceptively articulated. That universalism is a problem, however, discloses the temporal instinct that motivates our concern.[1]

---

1. The subject of universalism has attracted much interest of late. A small sample of the commentary, from a single publisher, includes the following: Ansell, *Annihilation of Hell*; Artman, *Grace Saves All*; De Young, *Exposing Universalism*; Krieger, *New Universalism*; MacDonald [Parry], *Evangelical Universalist*; Wild, *Catholic Reading Guide*

The question of universalism arises quite naturally, i.e., quite humanly, in any discussion of grace and merit. Who receives what? Are grace and merit inherently contradictory? The reception of one narrowly excludes the achievement of the other, and vice versa. If there is unlimited bounty, does each one of us receive a share, our share? In other words, the question of universalism includes the question of individualism along with common good or general welfare. We, each and every one of us, identify with poor old Pharaoh and his hardened heart, and we wonder: Where is his redemption? Where is my redemption? Why am I anxious?

The simplest, most natural, and not surprisingly most controversial way in which the question of universalism arises in Christian theology concerns salvation. In some ways the arguments for and against, which have a way of being acerbic, seem ludicrous in that they consist of two sides arguing over something that both sides acknowledge they do not understand: salvation. Usually the best we can do in trying to describe our redemption is to poetize our condemnation on one hand, everlasting hellfire, and on the other hand salvation, the New Jerusalem of Revelation (21:2). We have the Sabbath rest of Hebrews (4:9-11) and Augustine,[2] and the satisfaction of all desires for beauty, wisdom, power, security, at the end of Anselm's *Proslogium*.[3] And even if salvation is understood—I dare not say comprehended—by a disputant, that understanding is obscured by the internecine arguments put forth. Thus the controversy surrounding universalism signifies both the merit and the disgrace of all theological discussion. We human beings engage in subtle, logical disputation about the ineffable.

The question simply is: Who is saved? Is each and every human being a recipient of salvation? Is there at least one soul who is damned eternally? Judas Iscariot? These all are common questions that have been asked since the beginning of the articulation of Christianity, and, as we shall see, they have been asked wrongly.

It is not my intent to provide even a survey or summary of this controversy, although a few examples may clarify and exemplify the matter.[4]

---

to Universalism; see also Mickel, "Universalism Booth" podcast series, from Wipf & Stock, 2024.

2. Augustine, *Confessions* XIII.xxxvi–xxxvii.51–52.

3. Anselm, *Proslogium* XXV.

4. See for example Michael J. McClymond's *Devil's Redemption* and David Bentley Hart's *That All Shall be Saved*. The former is a compendium of historical arguments in favor of universalism, although McClymond argues for the unsoundness of them all, an argument epitomized by the title of his last chapter, "The Eclipse of Grace: An

As mentioned in the previous chapter, an early term for the question was *apokatastasis* (ἀποκατάστασις from ἀποκαταλλάσσω—to reconcile again). The expression referred to the restoration of souls, all souls, to a state of righteousness. Historians of the subject cite the teachings of Origen of Alexandria, a third-century Christian scholar and writer, as an early source for universalism. It is evident that the subject of universal salvation was discussed in the early church, and this particular version may have been condemned at the Second Ecumenical Council of Constantinople in 553. These historical details, although perhaps interesting in themselves, are not especially germane to this discussion. I shall provide, presently, a few scriptural quotations as evidence for uncertainty in the matter. It is safe to say, however, that even official church proclamations have not been adequate to extinguish interest in and desire for universal salvation. Christian universalism can be found in seventeenth-century England, eighteenth-century Europe and colonial America, and in the present day in the form of the Unitarian Universalist Church. The latter religion professes no creed, although it does affirm seven principles, none of which mentions Jesus or God. If there is an obvious theological objection to universalism, it must be that the center of discussion has shifted from God to man.

Within the Christian community, recent discussion of the matter has concerned itself with patristic writings in an attempt to ascertain church doctrine, both historical and living. The *all-many-some* question, however, is merely an expansion of the persistent question about ignorance, free will, and salvation. In the previous chapter we took up the matter of free will with respect to the hardening of Pharaoh's heart. The question of ignorance is addressed explicitly in Dante's *Comedia*. In the Paradiso, the pilgrim Dante poses the following question to the eagle of justice: "A man is born on the bank of the Indus, and none is there to speak, or read, or write, of Christ, and all his wishes and acts are good, so far as human reason sees, without sin in life or in speech. He dies unbaptized, and without faith. Where is this justice which condemns him? Where is his sin if he does not believe?"[5] Admittedly this is not the *all-or-many* question. Dante makes the apparent denial of salvation more problematic

---

Appraisal of Christian Universalism." Hart's book is a polemical defense of universalism. McClymond reviewed Hart's book in *The Gospel Coalition*, "David Bentley Hart's Lonely, Last Stand." Hart reviewed McClymond's book in *Eclectic Orthodoxy*, "'Gnosticism' and Universalism."

5. Dante, *Divine Comedy*, "Paradiso" XIX.70–78.

for us by presenting an individual who gives evidence "so far as human reason sees" of being charitable: all his wishes and acts are good. But the man dies "without faith" explicitly in the Savior Jesus Christ.

The eagle of justice immediately responds to Dante. "Now who are you who would sit upon the seat to judge at a thousand miles away with the short sight that carries but a span? Assuredly, for him who subtilizes with me, if the Scriptures were not set over you, there would be marvelous occasion for questioning. O earthly animals! O gross minds!"[6] In short: Shut up! Your question is impertinent.

A few lines later, however, Dante receives an elaboration from the eagle. "To this realm [paradise] none ever rose who believed not in Christ, either before or after he was nailed to the tree. But behold, many cry Christ, Christ, who, at the Judgment, shall be far less near to Him than he who knows not Christ; and the Ethiop will condemn such Christians when the two companies shall be separated, the one forever rich and the other poor."[7] The two companies refer to the separation foretold in the Gospel of Matthew "when the Son of man comes in his glory," like a shepherd with the sheep at his right but the goats at his left (25:31–33).

The elaboration admits of at least two interpretations. The first is that the Ethiop or our man on the Indus is condemned along with many Christians, but his separation from Christ is lesser than the separation of those who have received revelation but have not conformed their will and actions to it. It is less shameful: mild condemnation. A second interpretation places the Ethiop in the company that is forever rich whence he will condemn the wayward Christians.

Under either interpretation, some souls are condemned. After all, we have here the pilgrim who earlier had passed through the Inferno filled with souls who had abandoned hope. But our hypothetical soul is apparently blameless, at least by human standards. And here, Dante adds the important qualification regarding the good acts and wishes of the man born on the Indus, "so far as human reason sees." But regarding David, the LORD said to Samuel, "for the LORD sees not as man sees; man looks on the outward appearance, but the LORD looks on the heart" (1 Sam 16:7). We go further, seeing here tacit acknowledgment that not only the intention of others but even our own intent remains hidden to us ultimately. We assume for ourselves a position of judge regarding

---

6. Dante, *Divine Comedy*, "Paradiso" XIX.79–85; "*Oh terreni animali! oh menti grosse!*"

7. Dante, *Divine Comedy*, "Paradiso" XIX.103–11.

the man on the Indus that we may not be qualified to hold. In this very particular, fabricated case, we cannot say for certain regarding the good intent of our man. And even if we could determine his merit and do so favorably, would that place him among the elect? Paul exclaims that God "will render to every man according to his works." But Karl Barth notes, "Yes, it is [God] who selects; it is [God] who will assign to them their value."[8] Can ignorance be the cause of eternal damnation? Can ignorance be the barrier to salvation? Who are we to try to understand another person's ignorance of Christ, when, perhaps, we do not understand our own ignorance? Presumably the wayward Christians are ignorant of Christ in a sense, even if they know his name.

We have considered these cases, Pharaoh and the man on the Indus, as a way to ease into the more difficult general claim of universalism that all are saved. I shall try to specify the problem before addressing it from the perspective of our inquiry into time and sin, and to do so I shall refer to a particular dispute that took place in the Catholic Church.

Among the many changes within the church instituted by the Second Vatican Council was translation of the Latin Mass into the vernacular. In a form commonly used from 1970 until the new millennium, at the consecration of the wine, which transforms it into the blood of Jesus Christ, the priest recited the following words from the English version of the Mass.

> Take this, all of you, and drink from it: this is the cup of my blood, the blood of the new and everlasting covenant. It will be shed for you and for all so that sins may be forgiven. Do this in memory of me.

This translation replaced the Latin text, for which a more literal translation is:

> For this is the chalice of my blood, of the new and eternal testament: the mystery of faith, which shall be shed for you and for many unto the remission of sins. Do this in memory of me.

This text for the Mass is drawn primarily from the Gospel of Matthew (26:27–28). Jesus instructs his disciples at the Last Supper: "Drink of it, all of you; for this is my blood of the covenant, which is poured out for many [πολλῶν] for the forgiveness of sins." The parallel passage in Luke

---

8. Barth, *Epistle to the Romans*, 43.

(22:20) reads: "This cup which is poured out for you is the new covenant in my blood."

"Shed," "poured out" for many or for all? The controversy centered primarily on the substitution of *all* for *many*, with those favoring the older version asserting that the use of "all" may be heretical and may have the effect of undoing the miracle of transubstantiation. Traditionalists cited a work by Saint Alphonsus de Liguori.

> The words Pro vobis et pro multis ("For you and for many") are used to distinguish the virtue of the blood of Christ from its fruits; for the blood of our Saviour is of sufficient value to save all men, but its fruits are applicable only to a certain number and not to all, and this is their own fault. Or, as the theologians say, this precious blood is (in itself) sufficiently (sufficienter) able to save all men, but (on our part) effectually (efficaciter) it does not save all—it saves only those who co-operate with grace.[9]

Alphonsus then goes on to cite Aquinas and Pope Benedict XIV as authorities. According to Alphonsus, the intent of God's love in giving his only Son is to save all mankind, but the intent is not realized owing to the sinful rejection of grace by some individuals. In so claiming this, Alphonsus attempts to preserve a distinction between justification and works, grace and merit, that would be objectionable to the Reformers.

In 2006, the Catholic Church officially revised this part of the liturgy, reverting to *many*.

> Take this, all of you, and drink from it: for this is the chalice of my Blood, the Blood of the new and eternal covenant, which will be poured out for you and for many for the forgiveness of sins. Do this in memory of me.

This particular controversy, therefore, highlights the issue of universalism. If we turn to Scripture in general, support can be found for both sides. Above in my discussion of the fallen angels, I have cited scriptural passages that describe punishment for some souls, at least of the angelic sort.[10] I add here two more condemnations that expand the scope beyond angels.

> Then Death and Hades were thrown into the lake of fire. This is the second death, the lake of fire; and if any one's name was not

---

9. Alphonsus, *Holy Eucharist*, 44.

10. Ch. 6, section F. Isa 14:12–15; Luke 10:18–19; 2 Pet 2:4–9; Jude 1:6; Rev 12:3–4, 12:9, 20:10.

> found written in the book of life, he was thrown into the lake of fire. (Rev 20:14–15)

> He who conquers shall have this heritage, and I will be his God and he shall be my son. But as for the cowardly, the faithless, the polluted, as for murderers, fornicators, sorcerers, idolaters, and all liars, their lot shall be in the lake that burns with fire and sulphur, which is the second death. (Rev 21:7–8)

The second death, in both Christian and rabbinical writings, refers to the judgment after death, the final judgment.[11] There are, of course, may other assertions similar to the second death in Scripture. Among the best-known condemnation is that issued by Jesus while teaching on the Mount of Olives. There he describes the final judgment by the Son of Man. "Then he will say to those at his left hand, 'Depart from me, you cursed, into the eternal [αἰώνιον] fire prepared for the devil and his angels'" (Matt 25:41). Within the controversy, much seems to ride on the translation of αἰώνιον as "eternal." I shall return to this matter, but at this point I am simply presenting a small amount of scriptural evidence for the contending sides.

Evidence for the other side, that of the universalists, can be found in the letters of Paul.

> Then as one man's trespass led to condemnation for all men, so one man's act of righteousness leads to acquittal and life for all men. (Rom 5:18)

> For God has consigned all men to disobedience, that he may have mercy upon all. (Rom 11:32)

> For as by a man came death, by a man has come also the resurrection of the dead. For as in Adam all [πάντες] die, so also in Christ shall all [πάντες] be made alive. (1 Cor 15:21–22)

> When all things are subject to him, then the Son himself will also be subjected to him who put all things under him, that God may be everything to every one. (1 Cor 15:28)

---

11. As we saw in our discussion of perseverance, ch. 5, Augustine claims that more souls will be stricken with the second death than those who will die but once. In other words, the damned outnumber the saved. *City of God* XIII.23 and XXI.12.

> Here there cannot be Greek and Jew, circumcised and uncircumcised, barbarian, Scythian, slave, free man, but Christ is all, and in all. (Col 3:11)
>
> We have our hope set on the living God, who is the Savior of all men, especially of those who believe. (1 Tim 4:10)
>
> For the grace of God has appeared for the salvation of all men. (Titus 2:11)[12]

In the Gospel of John, we also read:

> And I, when I am lifted up, will draw all men to myself. (12:32)

These passages, of course, are merely some scriptural evidence, pro and con, regarding the controversy of universalism, *apokatastasis*. In no sense is it my intention to provide an even-handed summary of the various positions on the subject, nor do I intend my remarks to be in any way comprehensive. I shall, however, entertain one aspect of the controversy because it will lead to a placement of the matter in terms of sin and time.

"Depart from me, you cursed, into the eternal [αἰώνιον] fire." What is the status of the fire? Context makes clear that whatever the fire is, it is undesirable, perhaps even tortuous. Is it everlasting fire? Is it a-temporal fire, a state but not one measured by duration? Is it perhaps a fire of purgation, after which purging the condemned soul, having had its sins burned away, will freely chose the will of God?

I come finally to the heart of this chapter, an evaluation of the controversy from both sides, and it turns out, from both sides simultaneously. For this evaluation, the contextualization in terms of time and sin, will show the arguments on both sides to be ill formed, and at best of secondary importance. Admittedly in conducting this evaluation, I venture into what might be considered psychoanalysis, perhaps even historical psychoanalysis. I do so strictly to understand the claims for and against universalism, and I hope by doing so to reveal their shaky foundation. I do not mean to attribute any specific motivation to any particular individual, but in a way, I do attribute all the motivations on both sides of the argument to each and every one of us, for our very concern about all or many reveals the role of sin in our deliberations.

Interpretations of the noun αἰών and its adjective αἰώνιος are critical to the dispute between the two sides of universalism, and indicative

---

12. See also Rom 11:25-26; Eph 1:9-10; Col 1:16-17; and 1 Tim 2:1-6.

of the nature of the dispute. The most common translation of αἰών is "a period of existence, an age." The adjective has the same meaning, but also "ever-lasting, eternal." The problem of interpretation here is similar to the one concerning the word ἀεί. Does it mean always, or forever, or eternal? Does always mean all ways? In turn, what does eternal mean? My understanding is that eternal refers to a non-temporal state or condition. The adjective is one of quality, not quantity, and this understanding forms the basis for the entire discussion above about succession, cause and effect.[13] In treating eternal thus I am following Augustine and others, although even those who think of eternity in non-temporal terms do so only intermittently in their writings. The persistent failure of all writers on the subject to maintain this correct interpretation of the word is evidence for the sinfulness of the temporal. Heidegger in *Being and Time* would concur regarding the temporality of the human being, but without the characterization of sin. Even the insight into and momentary understanding of eternal (*aeternus*) cannot be maintained by the sinner. This is so because sin persists. Sin brings with it time. Time, at least succession time, is quantitative and accordingly a matter of duration, and thus among the sinful, quality is regularly given a quantitative cast.

The disputants on the subject of universalism seem to skip over this latter understanding and go directly to the possible distinctions between "forever" and "for an age," i.e., "for some time." The controversy centers on the duration of condemnation to hell. Salvation seems not to be the subject of discussion as much as not condemnation, not hellfire. Salvation, whatever it is, is apparently good, even though the disputants do not appear to be very much concerned with what this good thing is. The key matter of concern is for how long will the soul be deprived of this good thing? (Immediately above I have referred to the "thing" as a state, but in so doing one runs the risk of introducing, at least tacitly, a temporal understanding.)

"Depart from me, you cursed, into the αἰώνιον fire." Join the devil and the disloyal angels in torment, and do so for the following amount of time. One side says forever, by which it means everlasting. Everlasting fire is temporal without end. It burns and burns. The other side says for an age, presumably indicating a purgative punishment, a sentence or project that can be brought to completion, an ordeal that may require perseverance. It is critical to see here that both sides of the controversy

---

13. Ch. 2.

are in agreement that the issue is one of duration. The conditions of the argument have presupposed time. These are the conditions of sin, and thus the argument itself, as is the case with all theological arguments, is one about sin and is one between sinners. It behooves us, therefore, before dispensing with the controversy entirely, to inquire into what sort of presuppositions accompany the critical and ultimately misguided supposition that salvation and damnation are temporal matters.

Both sides no doubt will claim that above all they seek the truth, a high road that one readily grants at least regarding their expressed intentions. But what else can motivate those who favor forever or everlasting for the condemnation of those some souls who have failed to align their will with that of God? Why is Alphonsus of Liguori apparently eager "to distinguish the virtue of the blood of Christ from its fruits"? Why has Augustine consigned the majority of souls to the second death? Has there been a war taking place on earth between the forces of good and evil, and is the final judgment with its everlasting condemnation to hell of those favoring evil a triumph of good? How Manichaean! God has forces that are superior to those of the devil. (Insert here a prayer to Saint Michael the archangel.) Praise the Lord! And in this earthly, temporal struggle, the forces of good will win out. Someone should make a movie about this subject. The wicked, by their very wickedness, deserve punishment. In their refusal to repent, they receive what they deserve. This, of course, is in a way a tautology in that the persistently wicked "receive" their wickedness.[14] They persist or persevere in it. Their punishment, which is wickedness, is drawn out because they extend it.

In this outcome, the righteous, if there be any, may rejoice in the ultimate establishment of justice. Both Augustine and Luther attribute to the elect, to those saved, a kind of pleasure in their election and God's triumph.[15] This sense of triumph is also evident in the writings of Calvin. And this pleasure, if not exclusively and solely directed at the torment of the damned, at least is based on the everlasting continuance of justice in the face of injustice along with full recognition of those who suffer torment because of their persistence in evil. This is a pleasure that ensues from a high-minded respect for justice. In reviewing the harsh treatment that she has received from her father, Princess Mary Bolkonskaya asks

---

14. In a similar vein, Augustine claims that retribution for the first sin of disobedience is disobedience itself. *City of God* XIV.15.

15. Augustine notes that the saints, those who are saved, will be aware of their own past suffering as well as the misery of the damned. *City of God* XXII.30.

herself if her father could be unjust. "And what is justice? The princess never thought of that proud word 'justice.'"[16]

My objection to the argument of this side has nothing to do with triumph, which is entirely extraneous to my concern. And surely one must endorse justice, both temporal and eternal, although presumably without committing the sin of pride. My reply to this side of the argument is simply that the entire dispute along with God's victory has been given a temporal cast. The argument has been conceived temporally, which of course is sinfully. That the condemned are sinners goes without question. Furthermore, their sinfulness is evident not only in their evil actions but also and most importantly in their temporally indefinite extension of the evil actions. This much of the anti-universalist argument is entirely in accord with my study of time and original sin. But here in this version of the argument the elect and saved also reveal themselves to be sinners, and most certainly to be unrepentant sinners. The elect exhibit a kind of schadenfreude that renders them un-elect. They decline the election and do so by clinging to their temporal understanding, i.e., their sinful understanding of redemption. There is a way, however, in which I find accord with this side of the argument, although it does not seem to be the intent of the anti-universalists. In giving a temporal cast to condemnation, they underscore the connection of sin with time, assuming sin is not so much a judgment but rather a state. The condemned are sinners because sinners condemn themselves, and in particular they condemn themselves to the temporal. They wait, and they do so forever.

As disturbing and repulsive as my characterization may be, a characterization admittedly that I have attributed to the proponents of the *many*, i.e., of *not all*, it may not be as misleading and subversive as the motivations of the other side, of the universalists favoring *all*. For here we shall find, couched among the good intentions and seemingly merciful motivations of forgiveness, the same failing that exists among the opponents of universalism.

Who in his right mind would desire that someone, any other soul, suffer endless torment? Although we read about sadists and probably all have our own sadistic tendencies, we do not endorse these tendencies, at least not when we are in our right mind, not in others and especially not in ourselves. Those who favor universalism are making a statement on behalf of the fundamental equality of all mankind. Each human being,

---

16. Tolstoy, *War and Peace*, 529.

each soul, is an irreducible one, created and loved by God. This is the second axiom of the introduction. If we sinners can find a way to forgive, or at least to mete out a temporally delimited punishment, then surely the all-merciful creator can do the same. Surely God in his infinite mercy does not insist upon never-ending torment of souls who, in their finitude, have rejected his love. There must be a way to persuade those souls, among whom we include ourselves, that the love of God is meant for them and that all they need to do is harden not their hearts. Receive the grace of God and let in his eternal love.

The argument here is quite clear. It has been put forth by many, in many ways. Many of the expressions are far more eloquent and elaborate than what I have offered. This is the argument that forms the basis, historically and theoretically, for the Unitarian Universalist Church. And it is an argument that, in its fundamental human decency, has appealed even to those who feel scripturally bound to acknowledge the fiery pit, the *locus perditorum*. A hopeful universalism has been attributed to Karl Barth, and it is expressed explicitly by Hans Urs von Balthasar.[17] Regarding the one who has received God's love, he "will want to save himself only in conjunction with those who have been created with him . . . He will do so in Christian hope, the hope for the salvation of all men, which is permitted to Christians alone."[18] No soul is to be left behind. Yes, Lot's wife looked back and became a pillar of salt (Gen 19:26). And yes, Lord, you have warned that "no one who puts his hand to the plow and looks back is fit for the kingdom of God" (Luke 9:32). These are fair warnings, but surely in the extent of perdition, the soul will re-turn toward the love.

Of course, in expressing concern for the damned, for the unrepentant, we reflect upon ourselves as well as upon others. We question whether our hearts, like Pharaoh's, have been hardened. No one can know for certain his or her intent. We are noumenal to ourselves. By placing ourselves in the position of the condemned one, we ask ourselves: What will it take for you to change your mind? In expressing our concern, we say "I" for the condemned, at which point we are scandalized. We acknowledge the soul of the persistent sinner as a soul just like our own soul. We know that even the venerable Elder Zosima prays for the suicides, church doctrine notwithstanding.[19] Surely sooner or later the unrepentant will repent. No one can refuse God's love forever. God's love is infinitely great, and our

---

17. Balthasar, *Dare We Hope*.
18. Balthasar, *Love Alone Is Credible*, 97.
19. Dostoevsky, *Brothers Karamazov*, 323.

stiff neck can remain that way only for so long. It will bend in the course of time. And what about the man born on the Indus, all of whose "wishes and acts are good, so far as human reason sees, without sin in life or in speech"? Must he too suffer everlasting torment?

All of these good intentions, all of these good questions, all of this moral indignation and outrage contribute to making the argument for universalism more insidious, in an entirely human way, than the argument against universalism. The reason for this is quite simply that the argument on behalf of universalism makes the identical presumption as that made by the *many-but-not-all* proponents. Both sides speak as sinners in a particularly unified way, for both sides, in words attributed to Karl Barth, attempt to "lay hands on God."[20] The arguments from both sides bind the hands of God with time. The universalists are no less triumphant in their faith in reason than are the anti-universalists who serve as God's ministers on earth waging war against the devil.

We, temporal beings to our temporal end despite our eternal essence, aptly characterized in part by Heidegger, cannot understand nontemporal cause and effect when applied to the will of a rational being. We insist upon underpinning all succession in the realm of act with time. This insistence, as has been argued throughout this study, is the hallmark of the sinner. This insistence is the "I" who is unable to say "I" without disruption, exclusion, and ultimately and fundamentally sin. We originate sin.

This inability, this ignorance does not preclude a knowledge and feeling of despair. We understand why Judas, upon being rebuffed by the chief priests and elders, threw down the thirty pieces of silver in the temple and went out and hanged himself (Matt 27:3–5). He despaired of forgiveness. Judas underestimated, as does each and every one of us, God's love and mercy. He abandoned hope. Judas gave up on life, and this surrender is one that we can understand. My deeds, this life, this "I" I reject. I repudiate this gift that looks so sordid to me. Kierkegaard rightly identifies the position of the one who says "I will never forgive myself" as engaging in "the kind of talk [that] is exactly the opposite of the brokenhearted contrition that prays God to forgive."[21] In understanding Judas, in sympathizing and even empathizing with the traitor, we make a double move that confirms our fallen state, our original sin.

---

20. Balthasar, *Theology of Karl Barth*, 51.
21. Kierkegaard, *Sickness unto Death*, 111.

The first move is to take matters into our own hands. Judas tried to undo his betrayal. Failing that, in the throes of despair he tried to save himself by ending himself. He took it upon himself to commit suicide. This life, his circumstance, indeed was nearly or entirely unbearable. But in his refusal, in his despair, in his sin he never abandoned the "I." "*I* will not live any longer!" proclaims the suicide. This *I* is the *I* that cannot be abandoned, that cannot be got rid of. This is the qualifying *I* of apperception, and it is this apperception that signals the second move of our fallen state.

This second move has been developed above (chapter 7) and here I need only remind the reader of the central argument. In apperception, in becoming aware of my soul, I produce the dual manifestation of time as inner organization and as succession time. In "producing" time—one might say, in "undergoing" time—I recognize myself as the originator of sin, my sin. This "act" of mine (or of Judas) is both absolutely necessary for "I" to be "I" and absolutely my will. It cannot be otherwise. In deed I am my own worst enemy.

As universalists, we grant the one who despairs, the condemned, the Judas more time.[22] We extend his existence, and in so doing we condemn him to his own, everlasting existence. It is as if we have become instrumental in the condemning judgment, ministers of the judge carrying out the sentence. With the extension, we harbor hope: hope for his repentance, which is in fact hope for our own repentance; hope for reconciliation; hope for the capacity to forgive; hope for the supremely merciful God to pardon the sinner or commute the sentence to time served. In our hope, we equate eternal damnation with endless damnation, eternal torture with endless torture. Of course, we could do better, but only better. We understand non-temporal cause and effect, as argued above. But when we try to align this knowledge with our temporal existence, when we attempt to bring this knowing into accord with our being, our apperception, we invariably fail. Morality is concerned exclusively with failure. There are moments of clarity, moments of understanding, mathematical or logical in nature, where we focus exclusively on those things that are: God, our soul. But these truly are moments in the context of our being. They are tiny islands in our temporal sea of sin, but before long, i.e., because there

---

22. Balthasar quotes Rudolf Schnackenburg as writing regarding Judas, it "is not certain that he is damned for all eternity." *Dare We Hope*, 19. In this connection, see also Barth's extended discourse of the election and rejection of Judas: *Church Dogmatics*, 2/2:458–506.

is duration in our being, we move away from the island. We refuse to "close the door" on him who has despaired. In one regard, this refusal is a natural development of our being, because the one who despairs is no different from each of us. The one who despairs is overwhelmed by his sin, i.e., by his time. This we recognize, and out of basic human kindness, owing to a divine spark of love within our souls, we withhold final, irrevocable judgment upon the sinner, the condemned.

It would of course be ludicrously presumptuous for us to make this judgment. We have neither the knowledge and qualification to complete our deliberations nor that authority and power to execute them. We are not the judge in the *many-all* dispute. We are the judged. The "question" of *many-all* is a question of sinners and, alas, for sinners. The question itself in the way we ask it is sin itself. And when we address the question to God, the creator and judge, then we attempt to make God into a sinner along with ourselves. We entrap God in the snares of time and insist that he speak to us exclusively in our terms. We lay hands on God and try to reason with him, to make him play by our rules.

The reader might plausibly object at this point to the entire enterprise, indeed to all theology. If we are not "to lay hands on God," then what are we doing when we engage in theological thinking and argument? Who are we to attempt to give an account of God? The short answer is: sinners. There is, however, more to be said here, although I do so very briefly.

Theology itself is evidence of original sin. Theology is a discussion about God among sinners, conducted in a way that sinners can attempt to understand. What we attempt to understand is the discussion. We are bold to do so, but not out of bounds. Not only can we reason our way to some first cause, at least according to many philosophers and theologians, but also we have revelation. Through Jesus Christ, God as he is has been revealed to us to an extent and in a way that we can apprehend. Through Jesus Christ, the Mosaic Law has been elucidated. Through Jesus Christ, creation has been presented to us, first, foremost, as revelation.

For those for whom this apology is overly sectarian, I suggest, although only temporally, i.e., sinfully, to omit the previous remarks about Christ. Perhaps a few more of us can agree that we have the word of God as transmitted by Moses. Perhaps even more can agree that we have the revelation of the natural light of reason. This much agreement, and it is enough, encourages us to embark upon theology, to attempt to fathom the logos of the deity. This logos must always be just that: logos, a reckoning among human beings, for human beings.

This is what we do when we talk about God. We do not in fact lay hands on God, although our sinful predilection is to do so at every point in the conversation. God has revealed himself to his creation, and a portion of this creation has the logos. We are this portion, but we also are creatures of apperception. I have shown that this very apperception is, as we are or do it, our original qualifying sin, our temporalization. Quite easily we turn our attention to the matter of universalism. We seek the truth. But also quite easily do we frame the question as has been indicated in this chapter.

Sinners keep score.

10

Integrity

"You are my eternal Father, but I am scattered in times whose order I do not understand. The storms of incoherent events tear to pieces my thoughts, the inmost entrails of my soul, until that day when, purified and molten by the fire of your love, I flow together to merge into you."

"Lord my God, how deep is your profound mystery, and how far away from it have I been thrust by the consequences of my sins."[1]

I ARRIVE, FINALLY, AT the beginning. I shall take up the matter of salvation, redemption, eternity, and reintegration, for they are a single subject, in the form and fact of Jesus Christ. But Christ is the beginning "only" from the point of view of salvation. This entire study has proceeded along quite different lines. I have presented my argument for understanding original sin and time as the same thing. Time and sin differ only according to perspective. I have attempted to show some of the consequences of this equation, especially regarding divine foreknowledge, traditional predestination, human freedom, and the question of universal salvation or universalism. A consequence of this presentation and these developments

---

1. Augustine, *Confessions* XI.xxix.39 and XI.xxxi.41. Wetzel describes the end of chapter 11 of *Confessions* thus: "Augustine's failure to master time reflects his lack of self-mastery, the breach in his self-encompassment." *Augustine and the Limits*, 37.

is that we are left in a position that is not only difficult or uncomfortable but in fact hopeless in any traditional understanding of hope. The "I" that sins by saying "I" can be absolved of its sin reasonably only by being annihilated as an I, a suggestion that arises in the discussion about universalism. This I must be dissolved, or in Epicurean fashion, absorbed into the all in a way that renders one I indistinguishable from another I, but absorbed in a way to annihilate the I's history, to annihilate its time. In short, the I must become not I. This is the only way that reason affords us if we are to accept the argument as set forth, especially in chapter 7.

It might be better, more graceful, to acknowledge the insurmountable problem, acknowledge that the sinful I cannot be reconciled with the Truth if it is to be preserved. It might be better here to point to the Word of God, identify it as revelation, the article of faith, and be done with it. Surely this is the less foolish course of action. Piety may count for something even if piety accounts for nothing. I shall not, however, proceed this way. The rational but sinful argument that has brought us thus far demands an equally rational reply to the various consequences that we have encountered. In each case the systematic replies will entail the same leap of faith, and each reply will carry with it the graceless equational thinking that has riddled the presentation from the beginning. Each argument, too, sporting its fancy clothes of reason, will rely on the absurd.

Paul's new man begins with Christ. We end with Christ. The Word of God predestines all creation by selecting it, by loving it, by becoming it. We speak of a fix to the problem. Regardless of the title of the chapter, I think and write about re-integration. (*Integrity* is from the Latin *integer*, meaning "complete, whole, entire." The Latin word is composed of *in* and *tangere*, "to touch." Thus the root of the English word is "untouched." But the sinner is anything but untouched, buffeted as he is along with Augustine by all time.) In this way we arrive at the beginning only here at the end. Therefore I shall speak of absolution, reintegration, redemption, salvation. But I shall take up these matters only as they narrowly pertain to the identification of original sin as time, and happily defer in all other respects to the many eloquent and profound treatments of Jesus Christ, the Word of God.

Let us begin with some passages from the Greek Bible that signify Jesus Christ as he who makes the sinner whole, who renders the sinner capable of saying "I" without sinning. These passages come from the letters of Paul and from the Gospel of John.

For if we have been united with him in a death like his, we shall certainly be united with him in a resurrection like his. We know that our old self was crucified with him so that the sinful body might be destroyed, and we might no longer be enslaved to sin. For he who has died is freed from sin. But if we have died with Christ, we believe that we shall also live with him. (Rom 6:5–8)

For he is our peace, who has made us both one, and has broken down the dividing wall of hostility, by abolishing in the flesh the law of commandments and ordinances, that he might create in himself one new man in place of the two, so making peace, and might reconcile us both to God in one body through the cross, thereby bringing the hostility to an end. (Eph 2:14–16)

He is the image of the invisible God, the first-born of all creation; for in him all things were created, in heaven and on earth, visible and invisible, whether thrones or dominions or principalities or authorities—all things were created through him and for him. He is before all things, and in him all things hold together. (Col 1:15–17)[2]

The glory which thou hast given men I have given to them, that they may be one even as we are one, I in them and thou in me; that they may become perfectly one, so that the world may know that thou hast sent me and hast loved them even as thou hast loved me. Father, I desire that they also, whom thou hast given me, may be with me where I am, to behold my glory which thou hast given me in thy love for me before the foundation of the world. O righteous Father, the world has not known thee, but I have known thee; and these know that thou hast sent me. I made known to them thy name, and I will make it known, that the love with which thou hast loved me may be in them, and I in them. (John 17:22–26)[3]

These passages attest to the following. The entire history of salvation, the concupiscent I that sins by saying "I" while attempting to persevere, and sin itself all presuppose the love and grace of the creator as revealed to mankind in Jesus Christ, the Truth who is one with the Father. He is the "first-born" (πρωτότοκος, Col 1:15) of all creation, and all creation comes about through him and for him. The incarnation, crucifixion, and resurrection constitute the destruction of sin and its consequence

---

2. See also Gal 2:20 and Col 3:9–11.
3. See also John 8:19 and 10:30.

death, both of which are transformed, undone in the new man. The one new man, both gentile and Jew, lives on in Christ. This new man is in Christ and Christ is in him, perfectly one, re-integrated. This soul says "I" without disruption, without division, with praise and glory to God. This constitutes the predestination of mankind, the creature of integrity who has been absolved from the sin of apperception.

This terse summary of salvation, according to some, amounts to the Hellenization of the story of Jesus Christ, the "version" of the life of Jesus of Nazareth as interpreted by the Evangelist John and the apostle Paul.[4] But to consider this summary a version of anything is to give it a historical interpretation, and accordingly to locate salvation in the history of thought. In a sense, we cannot help but notice certain elements in our salvation that are reflective of ourselves. We cannot help but see the metaphysics of ancient Greece mingled with the account of a religious reformer who lived two thousand years ago, who lived at a time of turmoil in the history of Israel, as preserved in the Tanakh. In so doing, in noticing, in seeing, we are scandalized. "For Jews demand signs and Greeks seek wisdom, but we preach Christ crucified, a stumbling block to Jews and folly to Gentiles" (1 Cor 1:22–23). No sinner can hold together the story of Jesus of Nazareth with the grace and love of the creator. "It takes a singularly high degree of spiritlessness . . . not to be offended by someone's claim to forgive sins."[5] No sinner undoes his own sin, because sin presupposes God. Sin is sin before God.[6] Those who undo their sins undo something else, perhaps failings or shortcomings or bad habits or mistakes, but definitely not sins. They help themselves.

So far, so good, perhaps. What we have here looks like a truncated version of one of the widely established Christian creeds, a version tailored to meet the questions raised by this inquiry. Are we not still left with many questions? How is one made one with God while remaining an individual? How does one say "I" without sinning? In there any sense at all to the notion of an integrated individual, perfectly united, perfectly one, but undissolved? Who is God and what is eternity?

To address these particulars I know how to proceed only negatively. Specifically, I shall review the consequences of saying "I" sinfully, and then pray that each is dispelled. First, however, let me state the conclusion,

---

4. Some claim further that Augustine advances the Hellenization with his reliance on the Neoplatonists.

5. Kierkegaard, *Sickness unto Death*, 116.

6. Kierkegaard, *Sickness unto Death*, 87.

and then I shall attempt to investigate the relation between the "answer" and the questions.[7]

Phase time and succession time are dissolved as two aspects of time and enfolded into the fullness of time (τὸ πλήρωμα τοῦ χρόνου, Gal 4:4) by the Son of God become man. The contradiction between phase time and succession time is resolved. Succession is no longer the alien. No waiting. No suffering. No holding together.

The fall, the descent from integrity, is beautifully presented by the Neoplatonic teachings of Plotinus. The One (God) did not remain so, but audaciously (τόλμα) wanting to possess everything, it produced the Intellect, which in turn produced the Soul, the counting soul which is identical with time. This amounts to a very simple account of our fallen state, a state that perhaps may be overcome, but it is not exactly clear how to do so. In other words, it is unclear if and how an individual soul could re-ascend to the one, and it is equally unclear how the process of ascension might take place irrespective of the will of the soul. Apparently Augustine and his mother, Monica, achieved ecstasy jointly. While at Ostia, in prayerful conversation about the eternal life of the saints, their minds were lifted up. "That is how it was when at that moment we extended our reach and in a flash of mental energy attained the eternal wisdom which abides beyond all things. If only it could last . . . So too eternal life is of the quality of that moment of understanding after which we sighed."[8] The "life" of eternal life haunts this entire study, and I shall add a comment about this life at the very end. But the "moment" achieved by Monica and Augustine was a moment in this life of succession time, a moment that could not stand up to sin because as a moment it was of sin.

The Neoplatonic doctrine fails, not in accounting for the fall, but in guaranteeing re-ascent.[9] Must one rely on achieving a mystical and trance-like state to return to the one, to reestablish integrity? Are we to recommend to the self-help community that they are in the need of prayer? For the Christian, the "re-ascent" comes from the summit. God loves his creation and reaches down in the form of Jesus Christ, who is

---

7. At the beginning of this study and especially at the beginning of chapter 3, "Sin and Culpability," I explained why my approach to the problem at hand would be synthetic, an explanation that is pedagogically and rhetorically defensible. Here at the end, synthesis has been abandoned for analysis.

8. Augustine, *Confessions* IX.x.25.

9. The Neoplatonic account even of the fall, in my opinion, is rhetorically deficient. Why is the One audacious rather than loving? Why is it fecund?

truly human, who lives a life and dies a death as do each one of us. "He made him to be sin who knew no sin" (2 Cor 5:21). Through revelation, the Christian believes that the One reaches down before the fall to lift the fallen creature. The disintegration, characterized as audacity and greed by Plotinus, is made explicit to us in death, the wage of sin. The wrath of God is an expression of his love. This is the death that has been overcome from the beginning by the crucified Christ, from the begotten Son of God. "It is no longer I who live, but Christ who lives in me" (Gal 2:20).

This is a beautiful story indeed, but surely the skeptical among us, by which I mean everyone, would like to know how this Christian belief leads to integrity of the individual. Furthermore, those of us who find the story "beautiful" have already poetized it because we find it so offensive.[10] The doctrinaire Christian replies that belief itself does not unify the individual. The love of God in the form of Jesus Christ unifies the individual. The skeptic surely asks the further question: How is the Christian's belief related to the re-integration? What is the mechanism by which an individual Christian is made whole? And how is one to know, and what is one to do, especially given the certainty that no one knows whether or not he believes? One can at best believe that he believes.[11]

I shall not repeat here the arguments from *On Faith, Works, Eternity and the Creatures We Are* regarding what is known and what is believed. Neither I nor anyone else can demonstrate the relationship of belief to integrity. One can only say that the condition, as revealed by the Word of God, is integrity. Furthermore, I am in no position to say who does or who does not believe. I can speak neither for the man born on the Indus nor for myself. Additionally, I am unable to give an account for the *many-all* question of universalism. My inability to make any of these relationships clear rests entirely on my position, a position of sin. I do not know. I can do no more than report what has been revealed to all, and to attempt to explain the significance of revelation. (It is a mark of vain theology that one reports what is revealed to all.) We can know no more. We can, however, see how the love of God anticipates the consequences of sin and undoes them from the beginning, i.e., before the sin. We can

---

10. Kierkegaard develops the notion of the "poet-existence" or "poetizing" as sin. The Christian who has accommodated himself to the offense of the incarnation-crucifixion-resurrection by understanding its beauty has missed the point, has turned his back to the offense. He has *dealt* with it. Kierkegaard, *Sickness unto Death*, 77.

11. Barbera, *On Faith, Works, Eternity*.

see how the fullness of time undoes time by dissolving the distinction between phase and succession, inner organization and suffering.

There is a venerable tradition in the Catholic Church of offering prayers for the dead. Throughout the trip undertaken by the pilgrim Dante through the *Purgatorio*, the souls there request prayers from the living so that these imperfect beings may be purged of their sins and thereby ascend the mountain. They need to have the burden of sin lifted. The imagined process of perfection refers directly to the re-integration that takes place in the sinful creature through God's love. Paul Tillich comments, "The Catholic doctrine which recommends prayer and sacrifice for the deceased is a powerful expression of belief in the unity of individual and universal destiny in Eternal Life."[12] This is the process by which the individual, who according to Kierkegaard "is a synthesis of the temporal and the eternal," is rendered wholly eternal.[13] His sin is expiated. He is forgiven but not extinguished. Kierkegaard describes man's inwardness or introspection as "the constituent of the eternal in man."[14] This is his "earnestness." It may not be correct to attribute to Kierkegaard my association of phase time with man's inwardness, but there can be no doubt that man's outward view, his looking around, his desire, his anxiety, his dissatisfaction is evidence of succession time assaulting him. This is man's sin, and he knows it as sin because succession time is but an aspect, a perspective on phase time, his inner organization. This is man's very own, proper alien.

Waiting is clear evidence of the suffering that we undergo by succession time. Further evidence can be found in our attempts to retain not only our own integrity but also the integrity of others. "I am scattered in times whose order I do not understand. The storms of incoherent events tear to pieces my thoughts."[15] This disintegration becomes especially clear in the case of a loved one who is away, perhaps far away, and most especially when the loved one has died. By means of the divine spark of love, we too love, and we love others in their other-ness, in their individuality, in their integrity. In their temporal and spatial absence, we strive to maintain the other individual, the loved one, as wholly, concretely, and completely as possible. We surround ourselves with reminders: letters, photographs, material objects identified with the lost loved one. The

12. Tillich, *Systematic Theology*, 3:418.
13. Kierkegaard, *Concept of Anxiety*, 85.
14. Kierkegaard, *Concept of Anxiety*, 151.
15. Augustine, *Confessions* XI.xxix.39.

objects are intended to aid our memory in constructing, reconstructing, and maintaining the individual. In this regard, in Eva Brann's words, "the memory is more like a workshop than a freezer."[16] It is the place where we go to combat sin in the form of time. It is where we work, inspired by love, which is our instrument of resistance, of perseverance. And it is where ultimately we fail as our loved one begins to disintegrate. The expression "Time heals all wounds" is ironic to be sure, since what it expresses is "sin kills love."

As the quotation from Augustine indicates, however, the love of God revealed in his Word rectifies this condition. The Word makes us righteous. We have seen, above, that sins are decidedly not mistakes, but in fact mistakes are a consequence of original sin. The revelation, therefore, must entail not only the absolution of sin, but also consequently the elimination of mistakes, bad luck, natural disasters. The guilt that has been imputed to the person who fails to pick the winning number in the lottery is absolved. In a sense, it is incorrect to say that the guilt has been absolved, since the absolution comes from the very beginning. Jesus Christ is the alpha.

We have read about the nature of the human being having been compromised by our original sin. Some would prefer the word "corrupted" in lieu of "compromised." From the apostle Paul, through Augustine, the Reformers, and to the present the nature of the human being has been described as having the affliction of fleshly concupiscence. Anselm transforms this application into a debit, the lack of original justice that has been withdrawn owing to our original sin. I have expanded the sinful aspect of fleshly concupiscence to include all desire whatsoever, even "the spirit against the flesh" (Gal 5:17). Thus we must see the righteousness of Jesus Christ as an end to these failures, to this lacking, to this corruption: an omega that is presupposed by the alpha. Of course.

In the glorified state, what is the individual's relationship to desire and satisfaction? What sense can there be to satisfaction without desire, joy without sorrow? What is rewarding about the reward of the beatific vision? These and many related questions point to the problem of making a positive statement about the divinity. Perhaps love alone is credible (Balthasar). I shall address this issue with my concluding remarks about eternal life.

---

16. Brann, *What, Then, Is Time?*, 202.

Along with concupiscence, of course, perseverance is abolished. In the absence of suffering, i.e., in the absence of time, there is no meaning to perseverance. The *per* is annihilated. There is action, but it is eternal action, a kind of action that we know something about, i.e., we contemplate it, although we are unable to imagine it. This much was established at the beginning of this study, in the treatment of the eternal and the temporal. Presently I shall address eternity per se, but before that there are some other consequences of original sin that require comment.

A close inquiry into apperception revealed the *I* to be disruptive. The *I* individualizes, i.e., it divides and separates. In so doing, it chooses itself over and against the other. It falls as do Adam and Eve. The *I* disobeys the creator and does so, in Calvin's terms, both willingly and necessarily. The apperceiving *I* finds itself only by means of inference or deduction. In other words, this *I* finds itself on the condition of the others. Only by stripping away all else is one left with the *I* that in its self-realization chooses itself, separately, in a titanic effort to become god-like. The "move" is one of ill-conceived comprehension. The epistemological origin of this *I* is synthetic, and yet it has the hubris to choose itself. This is the *I*'s originating sin, its foundational pride and ingratitude, its gateway to envy and all other sins. By recognizing the others as others and inferring the self as self, the *I* becomes aware of its sin, called time, by seeing that its very capacity to think, its inner organization, is merely one side of the two-sided thing called time. The other side is the alien, the time to be suffered. The Hegelian dialectic in fact runs backward. The sublation of thesis and antithesis is sin: nothing. This is the condition that must be overcome through the Word of God.

This original sin, as depicted in Genesis, is the disobedience of Adam and Eve, who break God's only command to them. One might wonder, in this understanding of this sin as the two-fold manifestation of time brought about by the apperceiving *I*, who issues the command? Of course it is God who forbids Adam and Eve from eating from the tree of the knowledge of good and evil. This tree, along with all the other trees, is a part of creation. It is creation. There is a world, and it has been chosen by God its creator. For the individual creature who says "I," this fact is in a way unbelievable. Writers of all sorts are always attempting to tell us why there is a world. It is incredible, at least to the created one, who is forced into becoming a phenomenologist. Creation itself is the command, and the apperceiving creature in its very apperception doubts the certainty of creation. This doubt is expressed by the why that is entangled with the *I*'s sinful utterance of "I."

Only by revelation, as pointed to in the biblical passages quoted above from Paul and John, can we look toward an integral being for ourselves, one where we say "I" without sinning. Revelation, in turn, requires not only faith and love but also the virtue of hope, i.e., expectation of the impossible. This is exactly what the Christian foresees, an individuality: that is not disruptive; that is organized so as to be able to praise God the creator of all individuals without suffering the attack of the alien; that in its being participates fully in the act of love. This is the *I* that is predestined by the Word of God, but to speak positively about this *I* from our sinful perspective is impossible. This is why one can do no better than to talk about Christianity, since there is no explanation for it. We can do little more than point, perhaps slightly in jest, to an insensate logician praising God.

This logician, however, will be "equal to angels" (Luke 20:36). This is the individual who, like the loyal angels, knows from the beginning his own loyalty. This is Paul's new man, who has put on Jesus Christ. This is the individual who is free from trial because this person is free from sin. In other words, the one made righteous is obedient in the fullness of time. There is no concupiscence, there is no perseverance, because there is no sinful time. This person knows that his sins have been forgiven, knows that God loves him, and does not worry.

The glorified *I* does not infer itself from appearances. It is not the repository of its thoughts, always dependent upon others for its self. This *I* sees itself glorified by God as it praises God. This *I* does not deduce its soul negatively, as that which must be as the collection of thoughts and appearances. This *I* is neither synthetic nor analytic. This *I* sees its soul directly as created by God, and in so doing it is able to rejoice with all other *I*s in full collectivity (κοινωνία) and absolute independence among God's creation.

The redeemed *I* "lives" in the state of eternity. Writers have characterized this state variously. It is Augustine's Sabbath rest, Aquinas's beatific vision. One need not hide behind the adjective *eternal* in thinking about the blessed state provided that the terms of discourse avoid all quantity, a nearly impossible provision. Even "state" connotes fixity amid change, and the mind quickly relocates change on top of time. But this state, this rest, this vision is in the fullness of time. In Christian writing it is fully eschatological, the last things. It is the state or condition after the last judgment, a judgment that is fully attested to in Scripture (Matt 25:31–46; John 5:28–29). Eternity is the quality by which the temporal in its sinfulness is strongly annihilated. As eternity is the opposite of condemnation, so is it the opposite of annihilation.

The scholastic notion of *nunc stans*, now staying or ever now, is an attempt to refer to this state, this quality. But even this expression, with its *nunc*, must be found to be inadequate. The now that we know is the sinful now, the now that has succeeded other nows and will be succeeded by yet other nows. It is both historical and anticipatory, the counting now. This is a now that remains disintegrated in its connotation. It is archly divisive and yet of a piece with that which it divides. It stands at the intersection of phase time with succession time, the intersection of inner organization with suffering at the hands of the alien. Phenomenologists call it consciousness. In other words, this now stands at the nexus of sin. This is where we stand.

The redeemed soul, the re-integrated individual is in the eternal state. This soul, staring directly at its creator, says "I" with no sin or separation whatsoever, but also with no loss of individuality. The redeemed soul does not disappear into the all. "Christ is all, and in all." "He is before all things," but "in him all things hold together." Although the second all is neuter (τὰ πάντα), we can take this all to include all souls. These souls are not dissolved. They are not dis-individuated, Epicurean atoms. These souls retain the *I* collectively as one and align their individuals with the will of all.

◆ ◆ ◆

I have attempted to show that original sin and time are the same, and here at the end I have attempted to point to the quality of blessed eternity as the supposition and resolution of sin. Of course, many problems and issues remain either unresolved or even untouched at this point. I bring up two that are related indirectly to one another. The first concerns the negative cast of this entire inquiry, focusing on sin and perdition. There must be another side to the story, a fuller treatment of grace, love, and salvation. There must be a positive and uplifting version of what has been written in these pages, something more than a few pages in this final chapter that are structured by the seeming negative account that has preceded them for many chapters. The second concerns eschatology in general, and in particular the final judgment and life hereafter. This is the life of the resurrected body that is boldly proclaimed in Scripture.[17]

The first of these concerns may be the more easily addressed. This inquiry is in a way a treatise on grace, love, and redemption, but it is so indirectly or negatively. The sin into which we have probed, the origin of both our inner organization and outer suffering, presupposes grace and redemption, which must come from love. An alternative to this presentation would be to follow that of Plotinus. Although there are significant differences between his descent of the soul and our *I* that sins by saying "I," no difference is so great as the nomenclature. Plotinus writes of audacity. I write of sin. But as we have seen in the early chapters on sin, culpability, and concupiscence, sin is sin before God. Sin presupposes not only forgiveness but also forgiveness from God the creator. Any product may be in a disordered state relative to its producer, irrespective of whether the producer be creator or poet. A blemish here, an accident there owing to misfortune, and the cup breaks. In its disorder, however, the cup does not sin before or against the potter. It is the individual human being who sins, who lives in disorder, in disruption, in denial of its creaturely state. The human being is proud. The human being is unfaithful. The human being lies and betrays. The human being does all of these things and more, and principally he does them to and against God, his source, and then he is offended and scandalized to learn that God has forgiven him.

Were we to recharacterize all that has been written here about time, perseverance, and our fallen-ness in such a way to avoid terms like sin and culpability, then this would no longer be a treatise on grace in any sense. This then would be an inquiry, a lame one at that, into human fallibility and plasticity. It would be a self-help manual attempting to explain our limitations, our temporal condition, all done with irony. Gallows humor would be our "saving grace," by which we would not mean divine grace at all. We would place ourselves, as we so often do, in a position of coping, of inventing in the face of necessity. We would be Kierkegaardian poets, gracious only in the sense of granting ourselves an allowance.

Therefore, I maintain that I have produced a work, irrespective of its merit, that attempts to limn out the love of God by investigating the originally sinful state of our apperception. There is danger here too, of course, of misunderstanding the wrath of God as God's love. We define pleasure in term of pain, and more generally, presence in terms of

---

17. Augustine wonders and is uncertain about the bodies of saints in eternal life. *City of God* X.20. Perhaps the bodies of saints, if they are extended, are spheres.

absence. "For God has consigned all men to disobedience, that he may have mercy upon all" (Rom 11:32). God's wrath, our death, the wage of sin, is truly a revelation of our election, our salvation by a loving God, but danger lurks in treating our lives as individual battles in the war of all being. God's love, our sin, and preordained redemption do not form the constituent themes of a drama to be played out in our lives. If there is anything beautiful or dramatic about our lives, it is so only secondarily, only in a human, fallen sense. We are not foot soldiers in the war of good against evil. We are the recipients of our creator's gracious love, and this entire work has been an attempt to express that much.

I have just opined that there must be a better, or at least a positive way of presenting grace, love, and salvation. Perhaps that better way is prayer. My efforts here then amount to praying backward. Sin is the promise of salvation.

The second concern to be considered here is the corporeal expression of scriptural eschatology. What about the New Jerusalem? I present some scriptural indications of the final state, again from the writings of John and Paul.

> So Jesus said to them, "Truly, truly, I say to you, unless you eat the flesh of the Son of man and drink his blood, you have no life in you; he who eats my flesh and drinks my blood has eternal life, I will raise him up at the last day." (John 6:53–54)

> Martha said to him, "I know that [Lazarus] will rise again in the resurrection at the last day." Jesus said to her, "I am the resurrection (and the life); he who believes in me, though he die, yet shall he live, and whoever lives and believes in me shall never die. Do you believe this?" She said to him, "Yes, Lord; I believe that you are the Christ, the son of God, he who is coming into the world." (John 11:24–27)

> But if Christ is in you, although your bodies are dead because of sin, your spirits are alive because of righteousness. If the Spirit of him who raised Jesus from the dead dwells in you, he who raised Christ Jesus from the dead will give life to your mortal bodies also through his Spirit which dwells in you. (Rom 8:10–11)

> But some one will ask, "How are the dead raised? With what kind of body do they come?" You foolish man! What you sow does not come to life unless it dies. And what you sow is not the

> body which is to be, but a bare kernel, perhaps of wheat or of some other grain. (1 Cor 15:35–36)
>
> So it is with the resurrection of the dead. What is sown is perishable, what is raised imperishable. It is sown in dishonor, it is raised in glory. It is sown in weakness, it is raised in power. It is sown a physical body, it is raised a spiritual body. If there is a physical body, there is also a spiritual body. (1 Cor 15:42–44)
>
> For the trumpet will sound, and the dead will be raised imperishable, and we shall be changed. For this perishable nature must put on the imperishable, and this mortal nature must put on immortality. (1 Cor 15:52–54)

At the end of the book of Revelation (21), we read about the earthly location of this imperishable, spiritual body. After the passing away of the first heaven and the first earth, "a new heaven and a new earth" will appear. In the holy city, the New Jerusalem, more than 2,000,000 square miles in size, God will dwell with men, "and death shall be no more, neither shall there be mourning nor crying or pain any more, for the former things have passed away" (Rev 21:4). There will be no temple in the city because God is *there*. "And the city has no need of sun or moon to shine upon it, for the glory of God is its light, and its lamp is the Lamb" (21:23).

What is the meaning of the resurrected body, imperishable, living its eternal life in the new city on earth? Of course, I am unable to answer these questions, but I bring them up in the context of this study because it would seem that I am also unwilling to ask these questions. The sin-originating, temporal individual that has been described, when saved from his sin, seems to be someone or something antithetical to living bodies, to life itself. Our redeemed soul does not look like a subject or citizen of the New Jerusalem, an everlasting spirit with its body. Our redeemed soul has overcome time. Can there be any meaning to "living" in the state of eternity? I offer a few remarks here, but must defer such a monumental undertaking to another work, almost certainly to be carried out by another author.

We are closely associated with our bodies. We think of them not only as ours but also as us. A complete renewal of the self, a re-creation would seem to need to concern our bodies as well as every other part of our being: our mind, our soul, our spirit, our history. We do not think of ourselves without our bodies, Descartes's claims about the separation of body and mind notwithstanding. Almost certainly we would like to make improvements in our bodies, perhaps exchanging them entirely for bodies more youthful and beautiful. But equally certain is our desire for our new body to be truly ours, to be the beautiful new residence of our soul. This new body, raised up, is the body associated with the apperceiver who says "I." It is my body.

Thus scriptural references to the new man point to the entire man: body, psyche, spirit, soul. The spiritual body raised up in glory lives, imperishable, immortal. It would seem that this glorified body, this spiritual body is not in a state of eternal blessedness as described in this work. Are we to think of resurrected man as having desires, to be subject to succession time, the very alien who has attacked him throughout his earthly life? Would not such a condition extend original sin into the heavenly state?

Toward the end of the *Proslogium*, Anselm seems to give in entirely to our temporal state of desire. Regarding the blessed state of salvation, Anselm asks: "Who shall enjoy this good? And what shall belong to him, and what shall not belong to him? At any rate, whatever he shall wish shall be his, and whatever he shall not wish shall not be his. For these goods of body and soul will be such as eye hath not seen nor ear heard, neither has the heart of man conceived."[18] Anselm then proceeds to list many desirable things of this life, assuring the reader that in his glorified state these things shall be his if he so desires. He shall have beauty, swiftness, endurance, freedom of body, a long and sound life, satisfaction of hunger, quenching of thirst, melody, wisdom, friendship, concord, power, honor, riches, and true security.

What, then, is the renewed body weighed down by time? The temporal being is incapable of imagining eternity. We can know and understand the quality of eternity as well as eternal action. This understanding was explored above in the chapter on the eternal. What the individual cannot do is to string together images, for by doing so one organizes the images not only successively but also temporally. All matters that concern our will, when they also include the imagination, turn out to be temporal. We cannot and do not imagine satisfaction without desire, although we may have an understanding of satisfaction pure and simple. Therefore, it is not especially surprising that Scripture is filled with expressions such as "imperishable" and "immortal." Paul Tillich gives a different meaning to immortality in these circumstances. He refers to it as "a quality which

---

18. Anselm, *Proslogium*, XXV, 30–31.

transcends temporality."[19] I agree entirely with Tillich in this regard and note that there is no appeal here to the imagination. In fact, this is a description of immortality that reveals what it is not.

Our problems with bringing our faith, understanding, and imagination together with respect to eternal life reflect a necessary consequence of Christian theology, at least since Augustine, and really since the writings of John and Paul. In so commenting, I run the risk of providing historical context, a kind of human and rational understanding for the Word of God. The Word, as revealed, is given to all, which includes us rational human beings. In other words, Jesus of Nazareth is proclaimed to be the Christ, the Messiah to a group of metaphysicists. The metaphysicists, in their faith, accept the history of Israel as expressed in the Tanakh. And of course, they believe the revealed Truth of the Greek Bible. The faithful Christian theologian holds on to two contrasting accounts, never abandoning either. Of course he is torn by one account away from the other. Of course he is unfaithful, repeatedly, to one and then to the other. Of course he is a hypocrite. What else could a Christian theologian be? This is, after all, someone who purports to make sense of sin and grace, of damnation and redemption. That Scripture is filled with physical images, mundane desires, bodily appetites is not intrinsically nonsensical if one "understands" these writings and locates them in their historical context. The revealed Word of God, although most definitely factual and historical regarding the incarnation, crucifixion, and resurrection of Jesus of Nazareth, the Christ, is trans-historical at best, i.e., it comprehends history. And in its appeal to us who can think and reason the Word of God is principally ahistorical. The Christian theologian, in his insistence on bringing his own human faculties of logic and reason to bear on the story of Jesus, makes explicit to himself and to all who will listen to him that he is laboring under the burden of original sin.

When we understand Christianity as a combination of the metaphysics of ancient Greece and the recorded history of Israel, then we have located ourselves in a position to comprehend our subject, a subject that is both beautiful and endlessly interesting. When we accuse John and Paul of hijacking the story of Jesus of Nazareth and Hellenizing it, we locate ourselves in a position of knowing. Our knowledge exudes a clear, cool vision, one that is both rational and experienced. And most certainly such a vision is experienced because it betrays in all ways its temporal

---

19. Tillich, *Systematic Theology*, 3:410.

wisdom. In this wisdom we locate ourselves in community with our brothers and sisters by dissolving the transcendence of the Word of God. In our wisdom we tell charming stories to one another that are largely devoid of words such as sin, soul, and God, because these are the very words that we find so discomforting. It seems better, or at least easier, to understand sin than to confront it.

Bibliography

Alphonsus de Liguori. *The Holy Eucharist: The Ascetical Works*. Edited and translated by Eugene Grimm. The Complete Works of Saint Alphonsus de Liguori 6. New York: Benziger, 1887.

Altizer, Thomas J. J. *The New Gospel of Christian Atheism*. Aurora, CO: Davies Group, 2002.

Ansell, Nicholas. *The Annihilation of Hell: Universal Salvation and the Redemption of Time in the Eschatology of Jürgen Moltmann*. Eugene, OR: Cascade, 2013.

Anselm. *On the Fall of the Devil*. In *Basic Writings*, edited and translated by Thomas Williams, 167–212. Indianapolis: Hackett, 2007.

———. *On the Virginal Conception, and on Original Sin*. In *Basic Writings*, edited and translated by Thomas Williams, 327–59. Indianapolis: Hackett, 2007.

———. *Opera omnia ad fidem codicum*. Edited by Franciscus Salesius Schmitt. Edinburgh: Thomas Nelson, 1946–51.

———. *Proslogium*. Translated by S. N. Deane. In *Saint Anselm: Basic Writings*, 1–34. 2nd ed. La Salle, IL: Open Court, 1962.

Aquinas, Thomas. *Summa theologica*. Translated by Fathers of the English Dominican Province. Christian Classics Ethereal Library. New York: Benzinger, 1947. http://www.ccel.org/ccel/aquinas/summa.html.

———. *Summa theologiae*. *Corpus Thomasticum*. *Opera omnia*. Fundacíon Tomás de Aquino, 2019. http://www.corpusthomisticum.org/iopera.html.

Aristotle. *Aristotelis*. *Physica*. Edited by W. D. Ross. London: Oxford University Press, 1950.

———. *Nicomachean Ethics*. Translated by R. P. Hardie and R. K. Gaye. The Complete Works of Aristotle 2. Princeton: Princeton University Press, 1984.

———. *Physics*. Translated by R. P. Hardie and R. K. Gaye. The Complete Works of Aristotle 1. Princeton: Princeton University Press, 1984.

Artman, David. *Grace Saves All: The Necessity of Christian Universalism*. Eugene, OR: Wipf & Stock, 2020.

Attwater, Donald, ed. *Catholic Encyclopædic Dictionary*. New York: MacMillan, 1931.

Augsburg Confession. Book of Concord. 1530. https://bookofconcord.org/augsburg-confession/.

Augustine. *The City of God against the Pagans*. Edited and translated by R. W. Dyson. Cambridge: Cambridge University Press, 1998.

———. *Confessions*. Translated and annotated by Henry Chadwick. Oxford: Oxford University Press, 1991.

———. *Confessions*. Edited and commentary by James J. O'Donnell. 3 vols. Oxford: Clarendon, 1992.

———. *The Confessions of Augustine*. Edited by John Gibb and William Montgomery. Cambridge: Cambridge University Press, 1927.

———. *Contra Faustum*. Translated by Richard Stothert. Nicene and Post-Nicene Fathers, First Series 4. Edited by Philip Schaff. Buffalo, NY: Christian Literature, 1887. Revised and edited by Kevin Knight. https://www.newadvent.org/fathers/1406.htm.

———. *De Trinitate a S. Augustino Hipponensis Episcopi*. Edited by Ryan Grant. Mediatrix, 2015.

———. *Enarrationes in psalmos*. https://www.augustinus.it/latino/esposizioni_salmi/index2.htm.

———. "Homilies on the Gospel of John." Translated by John Gibb. Nicene and Post-Nicene Fathers, First Series 7. Edited by Philip Schaff. Buffalo, NY: Christian Literature, 1887. Revised and edited by Kevin Knight. http://www.newadvent.org/fathers/15061.htmhttp://www.newadvent.org/fathers/1701029.htm.

———. *The Literal Meaning of Genesis*. Translated and annotated by Edmund Hill. In *On Genesis*, edited by John E. Rotelle, 157–581. Hyde Park, NY: New City, 1999.

———. *On Christian Doctrine* [*De doctrina Christiana*]. Translated by James Shaw. Nicene and Post-Nicene Fathers, First Series 2. Edited by Philip Schaff. Buffalo, NY: Christian Literature, 1887. Revised and edited by Kevin Knight. http://www.newadvent.org/fathers/12022.htm.

———. *On Marriage and Concupiscence*. Translated by Peter Holmes and Robert Ernest Wallis. Revised by Benjamin B. Warfield. Nicene and Post-Nicene Fathers, First Series 5. Edited by Philip Schaff. Buffalo, NY: Christian Literature, 1887. Revised and edited by Kevin Knight. http://www.newadvent.org/fathers/1507.htm.

———. *On Rebuke and Grace* [*De correptione et gratia*]. Translated by Peter Holmes and Robert Ernest Wallis. Revised by Benjamin B. Warfield. Nicene and Post-Nicene Fathers, First Series 5. Edited by Philip Schaff. Buffalo, NY: Christian Literature, 1887. Revised and edited by Kevin Knight. http://www.newadvent.org/fathers/1513.htm.

———. *On the Free Choice of the Will, On Grace and Free Choice, and Other Writings* [*De libero arbitrio*]. Translated by Peter King. Cambridge: Cambridge University Press, 2010.

———. *On the Gift of Perseverance* [*De dono perseverantiae*]. Translated by Peter Holmes and Robert Ernest Wallis. Revised by Benjamin B. Warfield. Nicene and Post-Nicene Fathers, First Series 5. Edited by Philip Schaff. Buffalo, NY: Christian Literature, 1887. Revised and edited by Kevin Knight. http://www.newadvent.org/fathers/1512.htm.

———. *On the Grace of Christ, and On Original Sin* [*De gratia Christi, et de peccato originali*]. Translated by Peter Holmes and Robert Ernest Wallis. Revised by Benjamin B. Warfield. Nicene and Post-Nicene Fathers, First Series 5. Edited by Philip Schaff. Buffalo, NY: Christian Literature, 1887. Revised and edited by Kevin Knight. http://www.newadvent.org/fathers/15061.htm.

———. *On the Predestination of the Saints* [*De praedestinatione sanctorum*]. Translated by Peter Holmes and Robert Ernest Wallis. Revised by Benjamin B. Warfield. Nicene and Post-Nicene Fathers, First Series 5. Edited by Philip Schaff. Buffalo, NY: Christian Literature, 1887. Revised and edited by Kevin Knight. http://www.newadvent.org/fathers/1512.htm.

———. *On the Trinity* [*De trinitate*]. Translated and annotated by Edmund Hill. 2nd ed. The Works of Saint Augustine: A Translation for the 21st Century. Hyde Park, NY: New City, 1991.

Balthasar, Hans Urs von. *Dare We Hope "That All Men Be Saved."* Translated by David Kipp and Lothar Krauth. San Francisco: Ignatius, 1988.

———. *Love Alone Is Credible*. Translated by D. C. Schindler. San Francisco: Ignatius, 2004.

———. *The Theology of Karl Barth*. Translated by Edward T. Oakes. San Francisco: Ignatius, 1992.

Barbera, André. *On Faith, Works, Eternity and the Creatures We Are* [*Anxious Faith*]. Reading Augustine. London: Bloomsbury Academic, 2020.

Barth, Karl. *Church Dogmatics*. 2/1: *The Doctrine of God*. Edited by G. W. Bromiley and T. F. Torrance. Translated by G. W. Bromiley et al. Edinburgh: T. & T. Clark, 1957.

———. *Church Dogmatics*. 4/1: *The Doctrine of Reconciliation*. Edited by G. W. Bromiley and T. F. Torrance. Translated by G. W. Bromiley. Edinburgh: T. & T. Clark, 1956.

———. *The Epistle to the Romans*. 6th ed. Translated by Edwyn C. Hoskyns. London: Oxford University Press, 1933.

Beauvoir, Simone de. *The Second Sex*. Translated by Constance Borde and Sheila Malovany-Chevalier. New York: Vintage, 2011.

Beckett, Samuel. *Waiting for Godot: Tragicomedy in 2 Acts*. New York: Grove, 1954.

Biblia Hebraica Stuttgartensia. 5th ed. Stuttgart: Deutsche Bibelgesellschaft, 1997.

Brann, Eva. *What, Then, Is Time?* Oxford: Rowan & Littlefield, 1999.

———. "WHERE, Then, Is Time?" *St. John's Review* 57.2 (Spring 2016) 12–24.

———. "World without Time." *St. John's Review* 56.1 (Fall 2015) 1–15.

Brown, Francis, et al. *The Brown-Driver-Briggs Hebrew and English Lexicon*. Peabody, MA: Hendrickson, 2018.

Buber, Martin. *Two Types of Faith*. Translated by Norman P. Goldhawk. London: Routledge & Kegan Paul, 2003.

———. *Zwei Glaubensweisen*. Zürich: Manesse, 1950.

Buckley, Theodore Alois, trans. *Canons and Decrees of the Council of Trent*. London: Routledge, 1851. https://en.wikisource.org/wiki/Canons_and_Decrees_of_the_Council_of_Trent.

Calvin, John. *Institutes of the Christian Religion*. Translated by Henry Beveridge. Peabody, MA: Hendrickson, 2008.

———. *Ioannia Calvini opera quae supersunt omnia*. Edited by Edouard Cunitz et al. Braunschweig: C. A. Schwetschke et Filium, 1864.

Catechism of the Catholic Church. Vatican City: Liberia Editrice Vaticana, 1993. https://www.vatican.va/archive/ENG0015/_INDEX.HTM.

Cervantes Saavedra, Miguel de. *El ingenioso hidalgo don Quijote de la Mancha*. Edited and annotated by Tom Lathrop. Newark, DE: Juan de la Cuesta, 1997.

Cicero. *De inventione*. Translated by H. M. Hubbell. Cambridge, MA: Harvard University Press, 1949.

Dante Alighieri. *The Divine Comedy*. Translated and annotated by Charles S. Singleton. 3 vols. Princeton: Princeton University Press, 1970–75.

Dedekind, Richard. "The Nature and Meaning of Numbers [1893]." In *Essays on the Theory of Numbers*, translated by Wooster Woodruff Beman, 29–115. New York: Dover, 1963.

Descartes, René. *Discourse on the Method*. Translated by John Cottingham et al. The Philosophical Writings of Descartes 1. Cambridge: Cambridge University Press, 1985.

———. *Meditations on First Philosophy*. Translated by John Cottingham et al. The Philosophical Writings of Descartes 2. Cambridge: Cambridge University Press, 1984.

De Young, James B. *Exposing Universalism: A Comprehensive Guide to the Faulty Appeals Made by Universalists Paul Young, Brian McLaren, Rob Bell, and Others Past and Present to Promote a New Kind of Christianity*. Eugene, OR: Resource, 2018.

Dostoevsky, Fyodor. *The Brothers Karamazov*. Translated by Richard Pevear and Larissa Volokhonsky. New York: Random House, 1990.

Dusen, David van. *The Space of Time: A Sensualist Interpretation of Time in Augustine, Confessions X to XII*. Leiden: Brill, 2014.

Epictetus. *Enchiridion*. In *Discourses, Fragments, Handbook*, translated by Robin Hard, 287–304. Oxford: Oxford University Press, 2014.

Euclid. *The Thirteen Books of Euclid's Elements*. 3 vols. Translated and annotated by Thomas L. Heath. New York: Dover, 1956.

Euripides. *The Bacchae*. Translated by William Arrowsmith. Euripides V. Chicago: University of Chicago Press, 1959.

The Greek New Testament. 3rd ed. New York: American Bible Society, 1962.

Halfwassen, Jens. *Plotinus, Neoplatonism and the Transcendence of the One*. Edited and translated by Carl Séan O'Brien. Steubenville, OH: Franciscan University Press, 2021.

Hart, David Bentley. "'Gnosticism' and Universalism: A Review of 'The Devil's Redemption.'" *Eclectic Orthodoxy*, Oct. 2, 2019. https://afkimel.wordpress.com/2019/10/02/gnosticism-and-universalism-a-review-of-the-devils-redemption/.

———. *That All Shall Be Saved: Heaven, Hell and Universal Salvation*. New Haven, CT: Yale University Press, 2019.

Hegel, Georg Wilhelm Friedrich. *The Encyclopaedia Logic (with the Zusätzes)*. Translated by T. F. Geraets, W. A. Suchting, and H. S. Harris. Indianapolis: Hackett, 1991.

———. *Phenomenologie des Geistes*. 1807. https://www.gutenberg.org/cache/epub/6698/pg6698.html.

———. *Phenomenology of Spirit*. Translated by A. V. Miller. Annotated by J. N. Findlay. Oxford: Oxford University Press, 1977.

Heidegger, Martin. *Being and Time*. Translated by John MacQuarrie and Edward Robinson. New York: Harper & Row, 1962.

———. *Introduction to Metaphysics*. Translated by Gregory Fried and Richard Polt. New Haven, CT: Yale University Press, 2000.

———. *Sein und Zeit*. Frankfurt: Vittorio Klostermann, 1977.

Hobbes, Thomas. *Leviathan*. Edited by C. B. MacPherson. London: Penguin, 1968.

Hochschild, Paige E. *Memory in Augustine's Theological Anthropology*. Oxford: Oxford University Press, 2012.

Hume, David. *A Treatise of Human Nature*. Edited by L. A. Selby-Bigge. 2nd ed. Oxford: Clarendon, 1978.
Husserl, Edmund. *The Phenomenology of Internal Time-Consciousness*. Edited by Martin Heidegger. Translated by James S. Churchill. Bloomington: Indiana University Press, 1964.
———. *Zur Phanomenologie des inneren Zeitbewusstseins*. Edited by Rudolf Boehm. Haag: M. Nijhoff, 1969.
Jonas, Hans. "The Concept of God after Auschwitz: A Jewish Voice." *Journal of Religion* 67.1 (Jan. 1987) 1–13.
Kant, Immanuel. *Critique of Pure Reason*. Translated by Werner S. Pluhar. Indianapolis: Hackett, 1996.
———. *Grounding for the Metaphysics of Morals*. Translated by James W. Ellington. Indianapolis: Hackett, 1981.
Kierkegaard, Søren. *The Concept of Anxiety: A Simple Psychologically Orienting Deliberation on the Dogmatic Issue of Hereditary Sin*. Edited and translated by Reidar Thomte and Albert B. Anderson. Princeton: Princeton University Press, 1980.
———. *Concluding Unscientific Postscript to the Philosophical Crumbs*. Edited and translated by Alastair Hannay. Cambridge: Cambridge University Press, 2009.
———. *Fear and Trembling*. Edited and translated by Howard V. Hong and Edna H. Hong. Princeton: Princeton University Press, 1983.
———. *Philosophical Fragments*. Edited and translated by Howard V. Hong and Edna H. Hong. Princeton: Princeton University Press, 1985.
———. *Practice in Christianity*. Edited and translated by Howard V. Hong and Edna H. Hong. Princeton: Princeton University Press, 1991.
———. *The Sickness unto Death*. Edited and translated by Howard V. Hong and Edna H. Hong. Princeton: Princeton University Press, 1980.
King, Peter. "Angelic Sin in Augustine and Anselm." In *A Companion to Angels in Medieval Philosophy*, edited by Tobias Hoffman, 261–81. Brill's Companions to the Christian Tradition 35. Leiden: Brill, 2012.
Knibb, Michael A., trans. *The Ethiopic Book of Enoch*. Oxford: Clarendon, 1978.
Krieger, David J. *The New Universalism: Foundations for a Global Theology*. Eugene, OR: Wipf & Stock, 2006.
Leibniz, Gottfried Wilhelm. *Discourse on Metaphysics*. Edited and translated by Roger Ariew and Daniel Garber. Philosophical Essays. Indianapolis: Hackett, 1989.
Liddell, Henry George, and Robert Scott, eds. *Greek-English Lexicon, Intermediate*. 7th ed. Oxford: Clarendon, 1994.
Loehnen, Elise. *On Our Best Behavior: The Seven Deadly Sins and the Price Women Pay to Be Good*. New York: Dial, 2023.
Lucretius. *The Nature of Things*. Translated by Frank O. Copley. New York: Norton, 1977.
Luther, Martin. *Disputation against Scholastic Theology*. Translated by H. J. Grimm. https://www.checkluther.com/wp-content/uploads/1517-Disputation-against-Scholastic-Theology.pdf.
———. *Martin Luther: Selections from His Writings*. Edited by John Dillenberger. New York: Doubleday, 1961.
MacDonald, Gregory [Robin Parry]. *The Evangelical Universalist*. 2nd ed. Eugene, OR: Cascade, 2012.

McCall, Thomas H. *Against God and Nature: The Doctrine of Sin*. Wheaton, IL: Crossway, 2019.

McClymond, Michael J. "David Bentley Hart's Lonely, Last Stand for Christian Universalism: A Review of 'That All Shall Be Saved.'" *The Gospel Coalition*, Oct. 2, 2019. https://www.thegospelcoalition.org/reviews/shall-saved-universal-christian-universalism-david-bentley-hart/.

———. *The Devil's Redemption: A New History and Interpretation of Christian Universalism*. 2 vols. Grand Rapids, MI: Baker Academic, 2018.

McCracken, Andy, trans. *The Book of Enoch*. 2003. http://www.bookofenoch.org.

Mickel, Zechariah. "Universalism Booth Pt. 1, Robin A. Parry, Evangelical Universalism." *The Theology Mill* podcast, Mar. 19, 2024. https://wipfandstock.com/blog/2024/03/19/universalism-booth-pt-1-robin-a-parry-evangelical-universalism/.

———. "Universalism Booth, Pt. 2, David W. Congdon, Existential Universalism." *The Theology Mill* podcast, Apr. 2, 2024. https://wipfandstock.com/blog/2024/04/02/universalism-booth-pt-2-david-w-congdon-existential-universalism/.

———. "Universalism Booth, Pt. 3, Jordan Daniel Wood, Catholic Universalism." *The Theology Mill* podcast, Apr. 16, 2024. https://wipfandstock.com/blog/2024/04/16/universalism-booth-pt-3-jordan-daniel-wood-catholic-universalism/.

Milton, John. *Paradise Lost*. Edited by Scott Elledge. New York: Norton, 1975.

Minkowski, Hermann. "Space and Time." In *The Principle of Relativity*, translated by W. Perrett and G. B. Jeffrey; annotated by A. Sommerfeld, 73–91. New York: Dover, 1952.

The New Oxford Annotated Bible with the Apocrypha [RSV]. Oxford: Oxford University Press, 1962.

Nietzsche, Friedrich. *Beyond Good and Evil*. Translated by Walther Kaufmann. New York: Random House, 1966.

Nightingale, Andrea. *Once out of Nature: Augustine on Time and the Body*. Chicago: University of Chicago Press, 2011.

O'Neill, Taylor Patrick. *Grace, Predestination, and the Permission of Sin: A Thomistic Analysis*. Washington, DC: The Catholic University of America Press, 2019.

Pelikan, Jaroslav. *The Mystery of Continuity: Time and History, Memory and Eternity in the Thought of Saint Augustine*. Charlottesville: The University Press of Virginia, 1986.

Plato. *Phaedrus*. Translated by Reginald Hackforth. The Collected Dialogues of Plato. Princeton: Princeton University Press, 1961.

Plotinus. *Enneads*. Translated by A. H. Armstrong. Loeb Classical Library. Cambridge, MA: Harvard University Press, 1969–88.

Ricoeur, Paul. *Time and Narrative*. Translated by Kathleen McLaughlin and David Pellauer. 3 vols. Chicago: University of Chicago Press, 1984-1988.

Robinson, Marilynne. "Psalm Eight." In *The Death of Adam: Essays on Modern Thought*, 227–44. New York: Picador, 1998.

Sorabji, Richard. *Time, Creation, and the Continuum: Theories in Antiquity and the Early Middle Ages*. London: Duckworth, 1983.

Strong, James. *Strong's Exhaustive Concordance of the Bible*. Cincinnati: Jennings & Graham, 1890. https://biblehub.com/strongs.htm.

Thirty-Nine Articles. Anglicans Online. http://anglicansonline.org/basics/thirty-nine_articles.html.

Tillich, Paul. *The Courage to Be*. 3rd ed. New Haven, CT: Yale University Press, 2014.
———. *Dynamics of Faith*. New York: Harper, 1957.
———. *Systematic Theology*. Vol. 1. Chicago: University of Chicago Press, 1951.
———. *Systematic Theology*. Vol. 2, *Existence and the Christ*. Chicago: University of Chicago Press, 1957.
———. *Systematic Theology*. Vol. 3, *Life and the Spirit: History and the Kingdom of God*. Chicago: University of Chicago Press, 1963.
Tolstoy, Leo. *War and Peace*. Translated by Aylmer Maude and Louise Maude. New York: Simon and Schuster, 1942.
Wetzel, James. *Augustine and the Limits of Virtue*. Cambridge: Cambridge University Press, 1992.
Wild, Robert. *A Catholic Reading Guide to Universalism*. Eugene, OR: Resource, 2015.

Subject Index

Abraham, 18, 81, 82, 152, 201, 205, 218
action (eternal, non-temporal), 9, 26–31, 34, 36, 41, 42, 119, 175, 183, 245, 251
Adam and Eve, 15, 17, 23, 75, 83–84, 89–92, 98, 113, 114, 121–55, 158, 162, 174, 177, 180–81, 185, 191, 215, 217, 227, 245
age (αἰών), 26, 227–29
alien, 20, 46, 49, 50, 92, 97, 98, 117–18, 126, 147–49, 151–52, 168–69, 184–85, 187–88, 193, 199, 214, 241, 243, 245–47, 251
alpha and omega, 221, 244
Alphonsus de Ligouri, 227
    Holy Eucharist, 226
Altizer, Thomas, 214
always (all-ways, ἀεί), 33, 116, 180, 183, 229
angels, 10, 56, 57, 71, 141, 188, 211, 215–16, 220, 230, 246
angels, fallen, 10, 14, 18, 56, 71, 112–15, 141, 153–65, 182–83, 208–11, 226, 227, 229
Anglican Church, 89
Ansell, Nicholas, *The Annihilation of Hell*, 221
Anselm of Canterbury, 10, 13, 14, 18, 23, 65, 69, 73, 75, 82, 86, 88, 91, 92, 97, 152, 153, 157, 162, 172, 173, 174, 182, 208, 244
    Fall of the Devil, 100, 112–18, 161
    Proslogium, 222, 251
    Virginal Conception, 83–84
Anxious Faith. See Barbera, André.
aorist, 103, 110, 200
Apocrypha, 59, 79, 101, 140, 155
apokatastasis, 218, 223, 228
apperceiver, apperception, 4, 9, 11, 12, 23, 60, 147, 168, 178, 179, 184–85, 189–93, 195, 217, 219, 234, 236, 240, 245, 248, 251
Aquinas, Thomas, ix, 7, 10, 18, 29, 55, 59, 61, 64, 69, 73, 75, 79, 82, 84, 86, 97, 99, 101, 116, 117, 118, 157, 161, 170, 180, 182, 185, 187–88, 190, 226, 246
    Summa theologica, 56–57, 62, 78, 85, 100, 110–13, 162–64, 172, 181
Aristotle, 7, 30, 46–47, 54, 55, 56, 111, 117, 147, 188
    Nicomachean Ethics, 100–102
    Physics, 33, 185
Artman, David, *Grace Saves All*, 221
Attwater, David, *Catholic Encyclopædic Dictionary*, 100
audacity (τόλμα), 177, 241–42, 248
Augsburg Confession, 89

SUBJECT INDEX

Augustine, viii, ix, 7, 9–11, 14, 16, 18, 23, 29, 40, 44, 48–50, 57, 59, 61, 64–65, 69–72, 73–74, 75, 79, 84–88, 90–93, 97, 100, 102, 110–12, 115, 117–18, 121, 130, 136, 143, 145–46, 149, 152, 154, 157, 161, 162, 164, 167, 169, 170, 171, 172, 173, 179, 182, 183, 191, 206–8, 210–211, 213, 216, 219, 229, 238, 240, 244, 246, 252
  Christian Doctrine, 80
  City of God, 105, 107, 147, 160, 179, 211, 227, 230, 248
  Confessions, 50, 53, 186–88, 222, 237, 241, 243
  Enarrationes, 121
  Faustus, 55–56
  Free Choice, 158–59, 178, 215
  Genesis, 35, 78, 81, 107, 133, 158, 160
  Marriage, 76–78, 82
  Perseverance, 103–5, 108–11, 208
  Predestination, 108
  Rebuke, 113–14
  Trinity, 35, 61, 72

Balthazar, Han Urs von, 54, 244
  Dare We Hope, 232, 234
  Love Alone is Credible, 232
  Theology of Karl Barth, 233
baptism, 88, 89, 90, 92, 98, 104, 107
Barbera, André, *On Faith, Works, Eternity and the Creatures We Are [Anxious Faith]*, vii, 2, 3, 10, 31, 33, 242
Barbera, Mary, vii
Barth, Karl, 6, 14, 50, 52–54, 65, 74, 92, 167, 221, 232, 233
  Church Dogmatics, 6–7, 40, 51, 52, 53, 59, 134, 143, 146, 148, 149, 174, 197
  Epistle to the Romans, 225
beatific vision, 22, 29, 55, 96, 182, 244, 246
Beauvoir, Simone de, *The Second Sex*, 74
Beckett, Samuel, *Waiting for Godot*, 173, 174, 186, 193
Big Bang, 126, 143, 144

blameworthy, vii, 5, 15, 23, 60, 63, 64, 68, 98, 149, 151, 193, 195, 198, 216
Brann, Eva, ix, 12, 23, 49, 168–69
  What, Then, Is Time?, 44, 46–48, 50, 244

Caesar, 20
Calvin, John, ix, 7, 66, 70, 75, 82, 86, 91, 97, 98, 104, 138, 139, 146, 149, 152, 173, 179, 187, 211, 213, 215, 216, 230, 245
  Institutes of the Christian Religion, 87–88, 210
Cain and Abel, 58, 59, 70, 71, 183, 186, 218
Canaan, 201
Catechism of the Catholic Church, 90–91
Catholic Church, 88, 90, 91, 104, 225, 226, 243
cause and effect, 9, 17, 21, 22, 23, 28–43, 49, 59, 64, 124, 131, 139, 143, 144, 151, 157, 169, 170, 198, 203, 212, 229, 233, 234
Cervantes, 213
chastity, 77, 99, 102, 167
Chorazin and Bethsaida, 106, 108, 207
Cicero, 111, 117
  De inventione, 100
Confiteor, 16
Council, Second Vatican, 225
Council of Constantinople, 223
Council of Orange, 90
Council of Trent, 75, 88, 90, 91, 104, 140
culpability, culpable, vii, 5, 7–9, 11, 13, 19, 33, 50, 58, 64, 68, 69, 73, 92, 97, 98, 107, 108, 120, 136, 137, 140, 149, 151–53, 157, 170, 193, 196, 207, 215, 217, 248
Cupid, 79
Cyprian, St., 82, 103

Dante, 18, 243
  The Divine Comedy, 129, 223–24
Dasein, 18, 37, 43, 47, 149, 169, 175, 183
David, 224
Day Star (Venus), 155

SUBJECT INDEX

Dedekind, Richard, ix
  "The Nature and Meaning of Numbers," 47
Delphic oracle, 179
Descartes, 9, 14, 26, 27, 37
determinate negation (*bestimmte Negation*), 16
devil, 10, 16, 23, 71, 112–17, 140–41, 153–65, 170, 178–79, 182, 191, 210–211, 215, 219, 227, 229, 230, 233
De Young, James B., *Exposing Universalism*, 221
disaster, natural, vii, 8, 14, 98, 140, 189, 194, 244
distension of the mind (*distentio animi*), 10, 48, 169, 171, 188, 198
dogs, 188, 190
Don Quixote, viii
Dostoevsky, Fyodor, *The Brothers Karamazov*, 66–67, 189, 232
Dusen, David van, *The Space of Time*, 48

earnestness, 31, 243
Egypt, Egyptians, 201–3, 212–15
Einstein, Albert, 44, 46, 48
Enoch, The Book of, 155
envy, 8, 80, 87, 140, 161–62, 180–81, 185, 194, 245
Epictetus, *Enchiridion*, 60
Epicurean, Epicurus, 36, 190, 238, 247
Eros, 79
Euclid, 31–35, 41, 49, 203–4
  Elements, 31, 93–95
Euripides, *The Bacchae*, 212
evil inclination, 23, 75, 136, 152. *See also* yetzer hara.
ex nihilo, 17, 60, 84

fall of the devil, 100, 112, 114–15, 178, 182, 210
Fifth Postulate, 31, 32, 34, 36, 41, 204
final perseverance, 100, 102, 104, 106, 110, 111, 117
foreknowledge, viii, 1, 7, 11, 18–21, 34–36, 61, 105–7, 112, 118, 149, 154, 158, 164, 195, 196–219, 220, 237

fortitude, 100, 110, 111
futural, 8, 18

Gödel, Kurt, 35, 36, 178, 204
Goldbach conjecture, 95
Greek Bible, 3, 59, 101, 238, 252
Greeks, 27, 228, 240
Griffiths, Paul, ix

Halfwassen, Jens, *Plotinus*, 177, 179
Hart, David Bentley
  "Gnosticism and Universalism," 222–23
  That All Shall Be Saved, 218, 227
Hebrew Bible, 3, 136. *See also* Tanakh.
Hegel, Georg Wilhelm Friedrich, viii, 11, 15, 46, 144, 158, 178, 184, 192, 213, 245
  Encyclopedia Logic, viii
  Phenomenology of Spirit, 16, 26
Heidegger, Martin, 18, 27, 42, 47, 49, 97, 169, 183, 233
  Being and Time, 8, 36–38, 149, 184, 229
  Introduction to Metaphysics, 60
Heisenberg, Werner, 45
hell, hellish, 11, 17–18, 42, 66, 156, 186–87, 208, 213, 229, 230
Hellenize, 240, 252
hellfire, 212, 218, 222, 229
Heraclitus, 27, 40, 175
Hobbes, Thomas, 26, 30, 36, 37, 96, 144, 172, 183, 199
Hochschild, Paige E., *Memory in Augustine's Theological Anthropology*, 48
Hume, David, 4, 9, 36, 38, 189, 191, 192
  A Treatise on Human Nature, 192
Husserl, Edmund, 175
  The Phenomenology of Internal Time-Consciousness, 40, 44, 48
hypostases, three primary, 168

intuitionist, 31, 45

Jerome, St., 74, 75
Jesus of Nazareth, 35, 50, 152, 240, 252

Jew, Jewish, 3, 70, 75, 92, 108, 138, 142, 152, 228, 240
Jonas, Hans, 217
   "The Concept of God," 213
Judas Iscariot, 19, 35, 197, 214, 219, 222, 233–34

Kant, Immanuel, ix, 7, 14, 29, 31, 42, 47, 64, 69, 86, 87, 95, 120, 150, 169, 175–76, 179, 180, 183, 184, 188, 189, 192, 215
   Critique of Pure Reason, 38–41, 43, 48–49, 63, 154, 175, 191, 215–16
   Grounding for the Metaphysics of Morals, 30, 154
kenosis, 41, 184
Kierkegaard, Søren, ix, 7, 8, 20, 31, 74, 87, 97, 157, 161, 175, 179, 190, 215, 248
   The Concept of Anxiety, 30, 59, 68, 75, 243
   Practice in Christianity, 50, 65
   The Sickness unto Death, 13, 29, 50, 51, 53, 62, 65, 68, 101, 167, 169, 182, 233, 240, 242
King, Peter, "Angelic Sin," 158, 210
Krieger, David J., *The New Universalism*, 221

Latin Bible, 55
lawlessness (ἀνομία), 11, 13, 55, 170
lay hands on God, 233, 235, 236
Leibniz, Gottfried Wilhelm, 48
   Discourse on Metaphysics, 4
liar paradox, 178
Lobachevsky, Nikolai, 31, 33
locus perditorum, 232
Loehnen, Elsie, *On Our Best Behavior*, 127
logos, 221, 236
Lord's Prayer, 103, 105
Lucifer, 153, 155, 157, 180–81
Lucretius, 36, 184, 192
lust, 8, 76–81, 86, 87, 89, 90, 97, 149, 173
   flesh against the spirit, 78, 86, 87, 89, 149
   spirit against the flesh, 78, 90

Luther, Martin, 66, 70, 75, 82, 88, 91, 97, 104, 152, 173, 190, 230
   Commentary on Galatians, 86
   Disputations against Scholastic Theology, 87
Lutheran Church, 16, 89

MacDonald, Gregory (Robin Parry), *The Evangelical Universalism*, 221
Manichee, 17, 71, 72, 82, 230
Markel, 66–68, 98, 189
Mass, 225
McCall, Thomas H., *Against God and Nature*, 55, 58
McClymond, Michael J.
   "David Bentley Hart's Lonely Last Stand," 223
   The Devil's Redemption, 222
Michel, Zechariah, "Universalism Booth," 221–22
Milton, John, 14, 113, 146, 182, 191
   Paradise Lost, 126, 150, 157, 208–11, 216
Minkowski, Hermann, ix, 44, 45, 48
mortal sin, 112, 162
Mosaic Law, 236
Moses, 3, 137, 142, 201–2, 213, 217, 235
muth, 130

naked, nakedness, 127–28, 145–46, 174
Neoplatonism, 22, 53, 240–241
New Jerusalem, 222, 249, 250
Newton, Isaac, 48
Nietzsche, Friedrich, 74, 75
Nightingale, Andrea, *Once out of Nature*, 48, 50, 121
Noah, 70, 138–39
noumenal, noumenon, 86, 176, 178, 190, 192, 195, 216, 232
nunc stans, 199, 247

offense, the, 1, 242, 248
One, the, 47, 53, 65, 168, 169, 177, 178, 197, 241, 242
O'Neill, Taylor Patrick, *Grace, Predestination*, 55, 164
Origen, 223

original justice, 13, 16, 23, 65, 75, 83–85, 87–88, 91, 92, 97, 98, 120, 152, 153, 172, 173, 174, 208, 244
Orthodox Church, 75, 92, 152, 223

paradox, 1, 11, 42, 66, 96, 119, 178, 190
Parmenides, 27
Parry, Robin. *See* MacDonald, Gregory.
Pascal, Blaise, 12, 52
Passover, 202, 217
Paul, 23, 64, 65, 67, 70, 73, 76–81, 84–87, 89–91, 93, 97, 102, 105–6, 114, 130, 136–38, 142, 152, 153, 156, 162, 172, 173, 187, 199–201, 203, 205–8, 213, 225, 227, 238–40, 244, 246, 249, 252
Pelagius (Pelagian), 81–82, 89–90, 102, 104, 105, 108–10, 118, 206, 207, 216
Pelikan, Jaroslav, *The Mystery of Continuity*, 49–50, 72, 188
perfect number, 93–96, 203, 204
permanence, permanent, 9, 13, 18, 37–43, 49, 61, 62, 65, 71, 101, 102, 120, 168, 169, 170, 175–76, 181, 183, 186, 192, 196
perseverance, 7, 8, 20, 23, 50, 65, 99–118, 120, 123, 130, 145–48, 150, 161, 179, 182, 183, 187–89, 206, 207, 215, 227, 229, 230, 239, 244, 245, 246, 248. *See also* final perseverance.
phallus, 127
Pharaoh, 19, 201–3, 210, 212–14, 217, 222, 223, 225, 232
phase time, 15, 16, 20, 23, 44, 46, 48, 49, 92, 98, 117, 169, 185, 188–89, 193, 195, 199, 214, 216, 241, 243, 247
phusis, 27
piety, vii, 2, 7, 10, 11, 23, 104, 109, 110, 158, 160, 164, 167, 207, 210, 211, 238
Plato, 22, 46, 68
Phaedrus, 117
Platonism, Platonists, 22, 53
Playfair's Axiom, 31, 36

Plotinus, 35, 47, 53, 65, 169, 178, 241, 242, 248
Enneads, 13, 25, 26, 116, 168, 177, 179
predestination, viii, 1, 7, 18, 24, 34, 35, 36, 61, 105–6, 108–9, 112, 118, 196–219, 220, 221, 237, 238, 240, 246
pride, viii, 8, 86–87, 90, 97, 148–49, 157–62, 170, 173, 179–81, 194, 210, 211, 231, 245
prime numbers, 93–96
Protestant, 13, 75, 89, 90–92, 140, 149
Pythagorean Theorem, 31–32, 34, 36, 41, 204

quantum mechanics, 38, 45

redeem, redemption, 17–19, 52, 54, 68, 74, 92, 138, 145, 149, 152, 176, 190, 222, 231, 237, 238, 246–50, 252
Reformation, Reformers, 6, 66, 75, 86, 88–91, 105, 173, 226, 244
reifying (*Verdinglichung*), 37, 184
relativity, 38, 43–45, 48
Revelation, revelation, 1, 6–7, 14, 21, 25, 30, 36, 52, 54, 64, 65, 69, 90, 120, 152, 166, 181, 189, 198, 221, 224, 235, 238, 242, 244, 246, 249
Revised Standard Version, 134, 200
Ricoeur, Paul, 175
Time and Narrative, 39–40, 44, 46–49, 143
Robinson, Marilynne, "Psalm Eight," 42

Sabbath Rest, 29, 187, 222, 246
Samaritan woman, 183
Satan, 141, 153, 156–57, 208
Scripture, 7, 17, 53, 87, 113, 199, 224, 226, 227, 247, 248, 251, 252
second death, 60, 105, 226–27, 230
self-reference, vii, 10, 11, 23, 36, 42, 171, 178, 189, 195, 245
serpent, snake, 15, 127–29, 133–34, 141, 143, 145, 148, 150, 151, 154, 156–58, 174, 177, 185
Socrates, Socratic, 167

Sodom and Gomorrah, 218
Sorabji, Richard, *Time, Creation*, 42, 46
St. John's College, ix
St. Michael, 230
St. Vincent de Paul, Society of, ix
substrate (Kantian), 38, 40, 42, 43, 130, 168, 175–76, 180
succession time, 15, 20, 44, 46, 49, 92, 98, 105, 110, 111, 117, 168–69, 185, 187–90, 193, 199, 214, 229, 234, 241, 243, 247, 251

Temporal Garden, 15, 112, 121–25, 126, 128, 129, 133, 174
Thirty-Nine Articles, 89
Tillich, Paul, 12, 92, 151
    Systematic Theology, 28, 29, 30, 57, 61, 75, 151, 179–80, 216–17, 243, 251–52
Tolstoy, Leo, *War and Peace*, 231
Truth, the, 113, 190, 238, 239, 252
Tyre and Sidon, 106–8, 207

Unitarian Universalist Church, 223, 232
universalism, universal salvation, viii, 1, 218, 220–236, 237, 238, 242

venial sin, 112
Venus (Day Star), 156
Vetus latina, 74
Vulgate, 74, 79, 80, 81, 82, 101, 102, 106, 130, 135, 173

wage(s) of sin, 138, 149, 152, 242, 249
waiting, vii, 1–2, 11, 18, 23, 50, 66, 77, 82, 114, 125, 126, 134, 169, 171, 172–74, 181–83, 186–88, 194, 221, 231, 241
Wetzel, James, *Augustine and the Limits of Virtue*, 48, 237
Wild, Robert, *A Catholic Reading Guide*, 221
Williams, Thomas, 115, 116
Word, the, 6–7, 21–22, 53–54, 238, 242, 244–46, 252–53
wrath of God, 3, 57, 62, 87, 89, 138, 142, 242, 248–49

Xerxes, 170

yetzer hara, 70, 91, 92, 138, 173. *See also* evil inclination.

Zeus, 213
Zosima, 66–67, 98, 189, 232

Scripture Index

HEBREW BIBLE

Genesis

	126–27, 132–33, 141–42, 145, 146, 150, 245
1:11–12	132
2:15–17	128, 131, 134
2:9	131
3	11, 148, 156
3:3	131
3:6	150
3:22	129
4:6–7	58, 70, 186, 218
6–8	134, 142
6:1–4	155
6:5–6	23, 70, 75, 91, 92, 138, 152, 173
6:7	139
6:8	139
8:21	23, 70, 75, 91, 138, 139, 152, 173
18:33	218
19:26	232
22:14	205

Exodus

	201, 213
1:8	201
4:21	202
7:5	202, 215
7:22	202
8:15	202
10:2	202, 215
12:29	213
14:5	217
32:9	3
33:11	3

1 Samuel

16:7	224

Job

	72
38:2	205

Psalms

4	186
14:1–3	139, 146
51:5	12, 139
84:2	78

Isaiah

14:12–15	155

Jeremiah

17:6	194

Malachai

6:3	3

SCRIPTURE INDEX

APOCRYPHA

Wisdom

	141
2:23–24	140
6:20–21	82

Sirach

1:26	78
10:13	158
25:24	140–41

2 Esdras

	140
3:19–22	141–42
3:7	141
4:30	142
7:48	142

GREEK BIBLE

Matthew

10:20–22	102
11:20–22	106, 207
12:30	6
16:17	108
20:1–16	106, 117
22:30	113
24:13	102
25:31–46	224, 247
25:41	155, 227
26:27–28	225
27:3–5	233

Mark

13:13	102

Luke

9:32	232
9:50	6
10:13–14	106, 207
10:18–19	141, 156, 226
16:24	18
20:36	246

22:20	226

John

	10
1	53
4:7–15	183
5:28–29	247
6:53–54	249
8:19	239
8:44	160
10:30	239
11:24–27	249
12:32	228
17:22–26	220, 239

Acts

4:28	200

Romans

	79, 91, 142
1:19–20	56, 57, 69
1:24–25	79
5:15–21	137, 227
6	76
6:5–8	239
6:12–14	80, 85
6:23	152
7	76
7:15–20	65, 77, 85–86, 154
7:7–8	80
7:23	76
8	86
8:6–8	90
8:20–22	140
8:28–30	199, 205
8:10–11	249
8:22–23	68
8:24	171, 188
11:25–26	228
11:20	200
11:32	227, 249

1 Corinthians

2:7	200
6:2–3	156

15:21–23	137, 227, 240
15:42–44	250
15:52–54	250
15:35–36	200
15.28	227

2 Corinthians

5:7	114
5:21	52, 219, 242

Galatians

	91
2:20	239, 242
4:4	199, 241
5:19–21	86–87
5:17	77–78, 80, 81, 82, 86, 244

Ephesians

	105
1:9–10	228
1:11–12	106, 201, 206–7
1:5	200
2:1–3	137–38
2:14–16	239
4:22–24	81

Philippians

2:12	206

Colossians

1:15–17	228, 239
3:9–11	239
3:11	228

1 Timothy

2:1–6	228
2:4	199
4:10	228

2 Timothy

2:12	102

Titus

2:11	228

Hebrews

4:9–11	222

James

1:13–15	81
1:14–15	172–73
1:12	102

1 Peter

1:20	200

2 Peter

	81
1:3–4	81
2:4–9	156, 226

1 John

2:16	149
3:4	11, 55
3:8	160, 179, 211

Jude

1:6	156, 226

Revelation

9:1	141
12:3–9	156–57, 226
20:14–15	227
20:10	157
21	250
21:7–8	60, 227
21:2	222
21:4	250
21:23	250

www.ingramcontent.com/pod-product-compliance
Lightning Source LLC
Chambersburg PA
CBHW071244230426
43668CB00011B/1578